احياء علوم الدين

IMAM GHAZZALI'S
IHYA ULUM-DIN
(The Book of Religious Learnings)

THE BOOK OF WORSHIP

AL-HAJ MAULANA FAZLUL KARIM

VOL. I

Islamic Book Service

ISBN: 81-7231-101-X

Revised Edition: 2004

Published by *Abdul Naeem* for
Islamic Book Service
2241, Kucha Chelan, Darya Ganj, New Delhi-110 002
Tel.: 23253514, 23265380, 23286551, Fax: 23277913
E-mail: ibsdelhi@del2.vsnl.net.in & islamic@eth.net
website: www.islamic-india.com

Printed at: *Noida Printing Press,* C-31, Sector-7, Noida (Ghaziabad) U.P.

CONTENTS

Preface   5-16

CHAPTER–I

   Acquisition of Knowledge 17-104
   Excellence of Learning
   Praiseworthy and blameworthy branches......... Learning
   Blameworthy Sciences
   Harms of the science of polemics......... disputations
   Manners to be observed......... duties
   Evils of knowledge and signs......... hereafter
   Intellect and its Noble Nature

CHAPTER–II

   Foundation of Belief 105-129
   Belief in God
   Proof of belief
   Rules of Articles of Belief

CHAPTER–III

   Mysteries of Cleanliness 130-141
   Purification from Impurities
   Purification of Body from Excrements
   Cleansing the external bodily.........

CHAPTER–1V

   Prayer 142-173
   Excellence of Prayer
   Open Actions in Prayer
   Internal Conditions
   Imamate
   Merits of Juma Prayer
   Prayers other than Obligatory Prayers

CHAPTER–V

Zakat.. 174-192
Different Kinds of Zakat
Payment of Zakat and its Conditions
Fitness for Receiving Zakat
Optional Charity and its Excellence

CHAPTER–VI

Fasting 193-200
Six Compulsory Duties of Fast
Secrets of Fast
Optional Fast and its Rules

CHAPTER–VII

Secrets of Pilgrimage 201-223
Excellence of Pilgrimage
Eight Duties of Haj from First to Last
Ten Secret Things of Haj

CHAPTER–VIII

Recitation of the Quran 224-245
Excellence of the Quran
External Rules Reciting the Quran
Internal Rules of the Quran-reading
To Interpret the Quran According.......... Opinion

CHAPTER–IX

Zikr and Invocations 246-268
Excellence of Zikr
Tasbih, Tahmid and Other Zikrs
Selected Invocations

CHAPTER–X

Division of Time for Action.................................... 269-288
Divine Service
Excellence of Night Worship

PREFACE

Through the unbounded grace of the Almighty God and blessings of the greatest Apostle of God, the English version of the Book of Worship of the world-renowned Ihyaul Ulum (Revival of Religious Learnings) of Imam Ghazali, the greatest thinker of the world of Islam, the Proof of Islam, the famous Sufi, has now been published in full. This book Ihya is a sea of knowledge full of reason and arguments, full of Quranic verses, traditions of the Holy Prophet and of the companions and the famous saints of early ages. Each subject is supported by the Quran, traditions and sayings of the learned sages and wise men and established by reason and arguments.

As the great Imam belonged originally to the Shafeyi Sunni sect, some of the religious doctrines will be found in line with that sect, but nevertheless its importance is very great. In his advanced age, Imam Ghazali was not a blind follower of sects but followed his independent thinking and as such indirectly created a sect of his own. As the world is advancing with ever new ideas and scientific discoveries, so also this work is full of novelty and great ideas and scientific discoveries. The Imam revived truly the religious sciences and gave them an impetus never given by his predecessors in such a manner. He saved Islam from the currents and cross currents of devilish thoughts and pagan ideas that imperceptibly entered into Islam and clearly showed their fallacies and misconceptions. For this reason, he was given the title of Hujjatul Islam or the Proof of Islam. His thoughts prevailed upon those savants who came after him. Had not the Almighty blessed him with the necklace of reason and intellect, the true belief of Islam would have been carried away by the strong current of irreligious and misguided thoughts.

Truly there are many weak traditions in this book, but at the same time it should be remembered that the authors of six authentic traditional books specially Bukhari and Muslim selected some few thousand traditions and most of them were not proved to have been founded by trustworthy narrators from the Holy Prophet down to the narrator or did not meet with all the rules laid down for an authentic tradition. For want of proof, many guilty persons are acquitted. For that, it cannot be said that all acquitted persons are innocent. So in this perspective the traditions in the Ihya should be regarded. Had Imam Ghazzali not found them trustworthy, he would not have incorporated them in his book. There is no complete English translation of Ihya at present. Ashraf Publications of Lahore published some chapters of the first book of Ihya. The present translation is an attempt to bring out a complete translation of Ihya in English in four books. The first book deals with worship and divine service, the second book with worldly usages, the third book with destructive evils and the fourth book with constructive virtues. Ihya in original is a book in Arabic comprising four parts and its abridged addition in Persian was termed by the author himself as 'Kimiyae Sa'adat' or the Touchstone of fortune. Unnecessary arguments of different sects prevalent nearly one thousand years ago, some matters not heeded at the present time and some sayings of some sages of less reputation have been omitted in the present English version. The book has been, however translated into Bengali in full by the author himself without omission.

Short Life of Imam Ghazzali

Imam Ghazzali was born in 450 A.H. (1058 A.D.) in the village Taberan in the district of Tus in Persia and his name is Abu Hamid Muhammad. His title is Hujjatul Islam or Proof of Islam and his dynastic title is Ghazali. His father was a famous person but his grandfather was one of the leading men of that age. His father died while he was young leaving him under the care of his mother and grandfather. Ghazali is said to be the name of a village in the district of Tus in the province of Khorasan in Persia. According to Maulana Shibli Nomani, his ancestors had the business of weaving

(Ghazzal) and therefore he retained his family title Ghazali (weaver).

His education: At the time of the death of Ghazzali's father, he entrusted the education of his two sons, Muhammad and Ahmad, to one of his trusted friends. The latter imparted to them primary education and then sent them to a private Maktab. The boys within a short time committed the whole Quran to memory and after that began to learn Arabic.

They were then admitted in a free Madrasah. After sometime, Imam Ghazzali left his native village for higher education for Zarzan and began to study under a great learned man Imam Abu Nasr Ismail. He used to take notes of his lectures but in a certain journey he was robbed of these notes by some dacoits along with his other belongings. He took courage, went to the chief of the robbers and begged for the notes only to be returned to him. It was returned to him at his earnest entreaties.

Then he joined Nizamia Madrasah at Nishapur which was a reputed seat of learning and a great educationist named Imamul Haramain was its principal. He had 400 students of whom three were most noted-Harrasi, Ahmad.b. Muhammad and Imam Ghazzali. The latter became so much grieved at his death that he left Nishapur and went to Baghdad, the capital of the Caliphs. He was then a young man of 28 years of age.

At Baghdad, he was appointed principal of Nizamiyah Madrasah by Nizamul Mulk, the chief vizier of Turkish ruler Malek Shah. Being thus appointed at an early age to such a high post, his popularity as a great learned man spread far and wide and the rulers and the chieftains used to consult him in state affairs and theological matters.

Lectures of Imam Ghazzali: In the lectures of the Imam, hundreds of learned men and dignitaries of the state and even the ruling princes attended. His lectures were full of arguments and reason and they were mostly recorded by Sayeed.b. Fares and Ibn Lobban. They recorded nearly 183 of his lectures which were compiled in a book named Majalesse-Ghazzalia.

The great Imam then turned his mind to gain spiritual heights and the circumstances leading to it were recorded by him in his book Munkezum Minad dalal (Deliverance from error). He was a follower of Imam Shafeyi in his early age but in Baghdad he mixed freely with the peoples of all sects and thoughts and ideas. There were then the Shias, the Sunnis, Zindiqs, Magicians, Scholastic theologians, Christians, Jews, Atheists, fire worshippers and idol-worshippers. There were also the Deists, the Materialists, the Naturalists, the philosophers. They used to meet in mutual wars of argumentations and debates. This had such an effect on the mind of the Imam that his whole life changed and he began to search for truth with a free mind. His old ideas disappeared and he began to live in doubts. He then became inclined to Sufism but here practical actions were more required than mere belief. Being imbued with such an idea, he gave up his lucrative post at Baghdad, wore Sufi dress and left Baghdad suddenly one night in 488 A.H.

He then went to Damascus and closeted himself in a room of its mosque and began attentively the divine services, meditations and Zikr. Thus he spent here two years in solitude. At the age of 27 years, he was initiated by Pir Abu Ali Farnedi who was the spiritual guide of also the vizier Nizamul Mulk. After two years he went to Jerusalem and visited the birth place of Jesus Christ and in 499 A.H. he visited the holy shrine of Hazrat Abraham and made there three promises- (1) he will not go to the Darbar of any ruler, (2) he will never accept their presents, (3) he will not join any religious debates. He fulfilled these promises up to his death. Then he went to Mecca for pilgrimage and visited also Medina and stayed there for a long time. When he returned home, he was requested by the then ruler to accept the post of the principal of Nizamia Madrasah and he accepted it. When the ruler was assassinated by an assassin, he gave up the post and went to Tus and closeted himself in a khankah. The new ruler requested the Imam to join his post of the principal but he declined the offer.

He died at his native village Taberan on 14th Jamadis-Sani in 505 A.H. corresponding to 19th December 1111 A.D. Ibne Jauzi narrated a story about his death. He said: On Monday early in the morning he got up from his bed, performed his morning prayer and then sent a man to bring his coffin cloth. When it was brought, he lifted it up to his eyes and said: Lord's command is to be obeyed. Saying this, he stretched his legs and immediately breathed his last. The Imam left no son, but only daughters.

His books: The Imam lived nearly 55 years and he began to write books from his early age when he was 20 years old. He travelled for nearly 10 to 11 years and spent his time in reading, writing and teaching. Besides this, he had to reply two thousand letters which came from far and near for his decision and opinion. He wrote nearly 400 books of which the following are famous.

Theology: Wasit (Shafeyi jurisprudence), Basit, Wajiz (Canon Law, compendium), Bayanul Qaolaine li Shafeyi, Khulasatul Rasail (Quintessence of jurisprudence), Ekhtesarul Mukhtesar, Gayatul Gaur, Mazmatul Fatwah (collection of legal decisions), Risalatul Qudsiyya (canon laws of Prophet).

Principles of Theology. Tahsinul Muakhej, Shefaye Alil (cure of diseases), Mankahul, Mustastfa (jurisprudence).

Jurisprudence: Khulasatul Fiqh (quintessence of jurisprudence) Wajiz, Iqtisad-fil-l'tiqad (exposition of faith), Al-Qaestas Mustaqim.

Logic: Mizanul Amal, Mihakhul Nazar fil Mantiq (whetstone of reflection on Logic), Mayatul llm (weighing scale of science), Al-Ma'arif (Discourse on Logic), Mayarul Ilm fi Fannil Mantiq (the weighing scale of the science of Logic).

Philosophy: Maqasidul Falasifah (aim of the Philosophers), Munqezum Minaddalal (Deliverance from error, an autobiographical statement of his spiritual progress), Kitabul Arbayin (abridgement of Ihya), Resalatul Laduniyya (Ilham and Wabi).

Scholastic theology: Tahafatul Falasifah (destruction of the philoscphers), Iqtisad, Mustajhari (guide of novices), lljamtil Awam (vilification of peoples), Faysatul Zindiq (refutation) of atheists),

Fikhrol wal Ibrah (meditation and contemplation), Al Hikmat (Wisdom of God), Haqiqatur Ruh (realities of soul).

Spiritual and Moral: Ihya Ulumiddin (Revival of Religious Learnings), Kimiyae Sa'adat (Touchstone of fortune), Akhlakul Abrar (conduct of the pious), Jawaharul Quran (Jewels of Quran), Minhajul Abedin (path of the devout), Mirajus Salekin (steps for the sojourners), Bidayatul Hidayah (beginning of guidance), Mishkatul Anwar (niche of lights).

Tafsir: Yakutut-Ta'wil (a commentary of the Quran in 40 volumes now lost).

Of the 400 books he compiled, some only have been preserved in many libraries of Europe, while the Muslims did not accept them as they should have been accepted. Besides, they went so far as to burn some of his books which were lost forever to the world.

Ihya Ulumiddin: Revival of Religious Sciences is a masterpiece of Imam Ghazzali, Abul Gafer Farsi was a contemporary of Imam Ghazzali. He said that a book like Ihya was never compiled before. Imam Nudi said: Ihya is near the Quran. Shaikh Abu Muhammad said: If all the lights of knowledge of the world are extinguished, they can be revived from lhya. Shaikh Abdullah Idrees was a great saint. He committed to memory the whole book Ihya. Shaikh Ali read it 25 times from first to last and at the end of each reading gave a feast to the students and the poor. Many students of the Imam committed it to memory. Many saints regarded the book as a result of Ilham or inspiration. The great saint Qutub Shaji one day held the book in his hand and said to the people: Do you know which book is in my hand? Immediately he showed them the signs of lashes on his back and said: I was not a supporter of the book. Last night, Imam Ghazzali took me in presence of the Holy Prophet and inflicted on me these lashes on my back for my disregard of the book. These are the signs of lashes on my back.

Imam Ghazzali and Europe: The books of Imam Ghazzali were so much accepted and honoured in Europe that they preserved them in many libraries. But they did not receive so much attention in Muslim countries. Some Muslim learned men even did not open their eyes to see them, but rather prohibited the people to read them. For this reason, his books are rarely found in the libraries of Muslim countries. Mankul is a book compiled by the Imam at his early age. Therein he wrote with completely free and independent mind and was not a blind follower of Mazhabs or sects. This book fell into disregard in Muslim countries only for this fault. Mankul and Ihya were ordered to be burnt and it was translated into action. Europe accepted them with honour and preserved them from destruction. The book 'Maqasedul Falasefa' is not found in Muslim countries but it is preserved in the libraries of Spain. Europe also accepted his other books.

Ghazzali's influence: It is no exaggeration to say that the modern opinion about religion is much due to the influence of the Imams thoughts. The many books that were written after his death reflect greatly the thoughts of the great Imam. His views on Sufism were accepted by the latter Sufis. After him Maulana Rumi, Ibne Rushd, Shah Waliullah and such other noted learned men -wrote many books which resound with the opinions of Imam Ghazzali. In short, his thoughts reigned supreme in their minds. His influence on Persian literature was also great. He himself wrote Kimiyae Sa'adat in Persian which influenced to a great extent the minds of Maulana Rumi, Shaikh Sadi, Farid Uddin Attar, Shirazi, Hafez and other poets and Sufis. The works of such a learned man held in high esteem by all should be widely read and circulated. Mr. Watt, says: Ghazzali has sometimes been acclaimed in both east and west at the greatest Muslim thinker after Muhammad and he is by no means unworthy of that great dignity.

Preface of Imam Ghazzali

Take whatever the Apostle gave you and keep away from whatever he forbade you—59 : 7 Quran.

Firstly, I begin with the praise of God though our praise is quite insignificant and meagre in relation to His real glory. Secondly, I invoke His blessings on all the prophets and specially on His last and greatest Prophet Muhammad (peace be on them all). Thirdly, I pray for His help and grace that there should remain in me firm will and incentive for writing the book Ihya Ulumiddin or the Revival of Religious Sciences.

Fourthly, O defamer, O heedless, O one denying truth, God has removed from my tongue the tie of silence and put on my neck the necklace of arguments and reason. It is my duty to reply to what you argue. In other words you have closed your eyes from open truths and taken help from whatever is void and untrue and praise ignorance. If a man wants to remove something from the evil practices and habits of men or expresses his wish to translate his learning into action in order that the Almighty may prefer to purify his soul, let him keep himself engaged in divine services and seek to atone for the sins that he committed in his past life and for which he has become despaired. Let him keep aloof from the society of those persons about whom the Holy Prophet said: The greatest punishment on the Resurrection Day will be meted out to that learned man whom God has not given any benefit to his learning.

It is my firm conviction that there is no reason for your refusal to accept the truth except what has been stated below. In other words, the disease which entered into the minds of the majority of people has also entered your mind. The meaning is that they have given up the rules and regulations for acquiring ranks in the hereafter. They do not know that this affair is very serious and grave, that the hereafter is coming forward and this world is receding backward, that death is near and the journey is long, that provision is scanty, dangers are great but the paths are blocked.

The learnings and actions which have got no connection with God are fit to be entirely rejected by the wise and those who seek wisdom. It is very difficult for a traveller to the next world to tread the paths because there are injurious and destructive elements on the way but there are no passports and means to cross them. The learned are the guides to these paths. They are the heirs of the prophets. Time has slipped out of their hands. Those who are slaves to evil habits are alive. The devil is powerful over the majority among them and various kinds of sins misguide them. Almost every one among them is engrossed in the luxuries of this world and its comforts and enjoyments. For this reason the majority of them consider good as bad and bad as good. Even the religious learnings and sciences have become obsolete. The lights of guidance have almost disappeared from this world. They duped the people to believe that there is no other science than that of Fiqh (jurisprudence). These are the laws of administration which help the judges in the administration of justice and the rulers in the administration of their countries. They say that there is no learning except that of Munazara or debates. The present learned man cherishes hope of victory over his adversary and seeks means to make him silent. Or they informed the people that there is no learning except the science of scholastic theology by help of which a speaker seeks to influence the minds of the public. They see no other science except these three sciences. The sciences of the next world and the learnings of the sages of early times have disappeared from the people and the learning which was described by God in His Holy Book as theology, wisdom, light and guidance has been immerged in the deepest recess of forgetfulness.

When such is the condition of the religion, such downfall and catastrophe, I have thought it prudent to write this book entitled. Ihya Ulumiddin (Revival of Religious Sciences). By this book the path of early Muslim sages has been opened and the impediments that lay in the path of acquiring learnings beneficial to the prophets and sages have been removed.

I have divided this Ihya into four books—(1) the Book of Worship, (2) the Book of Worldly Usages, (3) the Book of Destructive Evils, and (4) the Book of Constructive Virtues. I have discussed the chapter of knowledge at the very beginning as it is of extreme importance. It is necessary to discuss such learning at the outset which is a great help towards divine service according to a saying of the Holy Prophet. He said: To seek learning is compulsory on every Musiim. I began with the chapter on knowledge in order to separate the useful knowledge from the harmful knowledge as the Prophet said: We seek refuge to God from the knowledge which is not useful.

(1) The Book of Worship comprises ten chapters—

(1) Knowledge, (2) Articles of Faith, (3) Secrets of Purity, (4) Secrets of Prayer, (5) Secrets of Alms-giving, (6) Secrets of Fasting, (7) Secrets of Pilgrimage, (8) Rules of Quran-reading, (9) Rules of invocations and supplications, and (10) Observance of daily duties according to fixed times.

(2) **The Book of Worldly Usage** consists of ten chapters- (1) rules of eating and drinking, (2) rules of marriage, (3) rules of earning livelihood, (4) lawful and unlawful things, (5) rules of companionship and brotherhood, (6) rules of habitation in solitude, (7) rules of journey, (8) music and ecstacy, (9) rules of enjoining good and forbidding evil, (10) rules of living as exemplified by the character and conduct of the Prophet.

(3) **The Book of Destructive Evils** comprises ten chapters (1) wonders of soul, (2) discipline of soul, (3) harms of stomach and sexual passion, (4) harms of tongue, (5) harms of anger hatred and envy, (6) evils of the world, (7) evils of wealth and miserliness, (8) evils of show and pomp, (9) evils of self-conceit and pride, and (10) evils of vanity.

(4) **The Book of Constructive** Virtues comprises ten chapters (1) repentance, (2) patience and gratefulness, (3) fear and hope, (4) poverty and asceticism, (5) Tauhid (unity of God) and God-reliance, (6) love and contentment, (7) intention, truthfulness and sincerity, (8) self examination and self-accounting, (9) meditation, and (10) death and ponder over death.

Some people wrote some books on these subjects, but this book has got five special characteristics which are not found in those books. Firstly, I have opened by the grace of God what they closed up and I have written in detail what they kept secret. Secondly, I have arranged what they kept scattered and I have brought together what they kept separate. Thirdly, I have made short what they made long and corrected what they approved. Fourthly, I have deleted what they repeated. Fifthly, I have made this book easy to understand after disclosing the subtle matters. These are the five specialities of this book.

I have placed the foundation of this work on four books for two reasons. The first basic reason is that I have incorporated in this book well-arranged rules and their real nature, so that they may be easily understood, as the knowledge by which the next world is known is of two kinds-knowledge of revelation, inspiration, secret and subtle matters. What I mean by this knowledge is the knowledge for attaining the subnum bonum or the ultimate object of life. What I understand by the science of outward behaviours and usage is the knowledge of practical religion attended with actions in accordance with that knowledge. The object of this work is only to narrate the science of practical religion and usage and not to narrate the science of revelation and inspiration, as there is no permission to put the latter into black and white though the science of revelation is the ultimate object of those who search after truth and the most coveted matter in the eye of the extremely truthful, and the best way of acquiring knowledge of worldly usages. The Holy Prophet did not speak anything about the science of revelation except through signs and symbols, because he knew that the wisdom of men to understand it is very little. There is no means of the learned other than the path of the prophets, as the learned are the heirs of the prophets. The science of practical religion are of two kinds-open science of the actions of the physical senses and the secret science of the functions of the heart The actions which keep connection with the physical senses are the actions of habits or usages of life. The heart which comes from the unseen world and is removed ultimately from the senses is influenced by either the praiseworthy virtues or the blameworthy vices. In short, the science of practical religion is divided into open and secret sciences. The open science belongs to the senses and is subdivided into acts of worship and usages of life. The secret science keeps connection with the condition of heart and its qualities and it is subdivided into praiseworthy virtues and blameworthy vices.

The second basic reason is this. I see a great enthusiasm of student is for study of jurisprudence or Fiqh. To those who do not fear God, jurisprudence has turned into an object of pride and a means for acquiring name and fame. Jurisprudence is of four kinds. As the objects which adorn the dear things are also dear, I think it better that this book should be modelled into the from of

Fiqh or jurisprudence, so that the minds may be inclined to it. For this reason, one who wants to attract the attention of the minds of some men to the science of medicine remodels it after astronomical tests and writes a book after

naming 'Tablets of Health.' So also I have adopted some measures in this work, so that the minds of the people are attracted towards such learning which is beneficial to human life. As the minds of the people are attracted to the science of medicine for preservation of the health of body, so also it is necessary that the minds of the people are attracted to the treatment of the diseases of soul and mind in expectation of a happy and prosperous life in the next world which will last forever and forever. Physical happiness is short and transient as compared to spiritual happiness in the hereafter. Physique is mortal while soul is immortal. So I pray to the Almighty for his help and succour for writing and completing this book lhya Ulumiddin as He is the most Compassionate, the most Merciful.

Chapter 1

ACQUISITION OF KNOWLEDGE

SECTION – I
Excellence of Learning

Proof of the Quran. God says: God, angels ana those learned men who stand on justice bear testimony that there is no deity but He—3 : 18. Now look, O dear readers, how God began attestation first by Himself, then by His angels and then by the learned. It is understood from this verse that the rank of the learned and their honour are much high. God says: Those who are believers among you and the learned, God will increase their rank—58 : 12. Hazrat Ibn Abbas said about them: The rank of the learned is seven hundred times more than that of the believers, and the difference between the two ranks is the distance of the path of five hundred years. God says: Are those who are learned equal to the illiterate—39 : 9? God says: The learned among His servants fear God most—35 : 28. God says: Say, God is sufficient as a witness between me and you and those who have got knowledge of the Quran—13 : 43. God says: But those who had been granted knowledge said: Alas for you the reward of God is best for those who believe and do good—28 : 80. God says: These parables, We set forth for men and none understands them except the learned—29 : 42. God says: If they had only referred it to the Apostle and to those charged with authority among them, those of them who would investigate it would have known it—4 : 93. God thus made knowledge dependent upon their efforts. In the practical religion God's commands have been placed upon the investigation of the learned and their rank with the prophets for propagation of God's commands. God says: O the children of Adam, I have sent down to you raiment to cover your shame and adornment to you but the raiment of piety is best—7 : 25. God says: I have sent to them a book and with knowledge I explained ice in detail, a guide and a mercy to all who believe—7 : 52. God says: I shall recount their story with knowledge—7 : 6. God says: Ice is a clear sign in the hearts of those to whom knowledge has reached—29 : 41. God says : He created man and taught him to speak—55 : 2.

Hadis. The Holy Prophet said: God gives knowledge of religion and guidance to truth to one whose good He intends. He said: The learned are the heirs of the prophets. From these ice is understood that there is no rank above the rank of prophethood and there is no honour higher than ices inheritance. He said: Whatever is in heavens and the earth seeks forgiveness for the learned. So the angels of heaven and earth remain busy in seeking forgiveness for the learned and they remain busy with themselves. What can be greater than this rank? The Prophet said: Wisdom increases the honour of the noble and exalts a servant as high as to raise him to the level of kings. From this tradition ice is understood that even in this world the frights of learning can be enjoyed. This is also true that the Hereafter is better and more lasting than this world.

The Holy Prophet said: Two traits of character are not united in a hypocrite-good guidance and knowledge of theology. The meaning of theology or jurisprudence will be discussed soon. The lowest knowledge of a jurisprudence is that the Hereafter is better than this world. When this knowledge will prevail over him he will be free from hypocrisy and show. The Prophet said: The best of people is a believing learned man who does good when sought for and when the people keep away from him he also keeps away from them. He said: Belief is without dress and ices dress is God-fear, ices ornament is shame and ices fruit is knowledge. He said: The learned and the warriors are nearest to the rank of prophethood. The learned have been sent for which the prophets were sent. They are guides to the people and the warriors wage war in the path of God with their arms like the apostles. He said: The death of a people is easier than the death of one learned man. He said: Men are like the mines of gold and silver. Those who were best in the days of ignorance are the best in Islam provided they have got the knowledge of theology. He also said: I shall intercede on the Day of Resurrection and be a witness for one who commits to memory forty traditions out of my followers and transmits these to them. The Holy Prophet said: The ink of the learned will be weighed against the blood of the martyrs on the Resurrection Day. He said: Whoever of my followers commits to memory forty traditions will meet with God as a learned theologian. He said: God is sufficient for the worries of one who acquires knowledge of God's religion. He gives him provision from a source which he has never conceived. He said: God revealed to Abraham : O Abraham, I am All wise and I love every wise man. He said: A learned man is a trust of God on earth. He said: There will be two groups among my people. When both the groups are good, the people are Good and when they are corrupt, the people become corrupt-the rulers and the theologians. He said: Should the day come wherein my knowledge for nearing God does not increase, let not the sun rise on that day. The superiority of a learned man over a worshipper is like my superiority over the ordinary men. So see how he linked knowledge with prophethood and how he belittled the rank of the learned man without action even though a worshipper is worshipping always and he would not have worshipped had he not possessed knowledge. He said: The superiority of a learned man over a worshipper is like the superiority of moon over the stars. He said: There will intercede on the Resurrection Day the prophets, then the learned and then the martyrs. So the rank of the learned is next to that of the prophets and higher than that of the martyrs.

The Holy Prophet said: God has not given any man more excellence than the knowledge of religion and one theologian is more formidable to the devil than a thousand worshippers.

Everything has its foundation and the foundation of this religion is knowledge of theology. He said: The best part of your religion is its easiest and the best worship is (the acquisition of) religious knowledge. He said: The superiority of a believing learned man over a believing worshipper is seventy degrees. He said: You are living in an age wherein the theologians are many, the Quran-readers and the preachers are few, the beggars are few and the givers are many, wherein deeds are better than knowledge. But soon there will come over you such an age wherein the theologians will be few, the preachers and the Quran-readers many, the givers few, and the beggars many, wherein knowledge will be better than deeds. He said: There is difference of one hundred degrees between a worshipper and a learned man. The distance between two degrees is as the run of a racing horse for seventy years.

The Holy Prophet was once asked: O Prophet of God, which action is best? He said. Knowledge. He was then questioned: Which knowledge do you mean? He said: With your knowledge of God a few actions will suffice and your ignorance about God will not suffice even though actions are numerous. He said: On the Day of Resurrection, God will raise up the worshippers and the learned men. He will say: O the congregation of the learned men I have not imbued you with My knowledge but for My knowledge about you, I have not placed knowledge in you in order to punish you. Go, I have forgiven you.

Sayings of the sages: Hazrat Ali said to Kamil: O Kamil, knowledge is better than wealth. Knowledge guards you but you are guarding wealth. Knowledge dispenses justice while wealth seeks justice. Wealth decreases with expense while knowledge increases with expense. He said: A learned man is better than one who prays and fights in the way of God. When a learned man dies, such a calamity befalls on Islam which cannot be removed except by his successor. Hazrat Ali said in poem

> Glory is due to none other than to the learned;
> Guided are they anti proofs to the seekers of guidance.
> Everybody is honoured proportionate to his knowledge; But the illiterate are disgraced as enemies of the learned.
> Acquire knowledge, you will be immortal; All men are dead, only the learned are alive.

The sage Aswad said: Nothing is more honourable than knowledge. While the kings rule over the people the learned rule over the kings. Hazrat Ibn Mubarak was asked: Who are men? He replied: The learned. He was again asked: Who are kings? He replied: The ascetics. He was again asked: Who are the meanest?

He said: Those who exchange the religion for the world. He did not consider anybody as a man except the learned. Knowledge distinguishes men from the lower animals and it is only for knowledge that men are honoured. This honour is not due to man for his physical strength because a camel is physically stronger than a man. This honour is not for his large body as the body of an elephant is bigger than that of a man. This honour is not on account of his bravery as a ferocious beast is braver than a man. This honour is not for his strength of too much eating as the stomach of an ox is bigger than that of a man. This honour is not for his strength of sexual passion as a sparrow has got more strength for coition than that of a man. This honour of a man is on account of his knowledge and intellect.

The Holy Prophet said: Whoever has been given the Quran and thinks that any one has been given something better, he has degraded what God has exalted. Once the saint Fathul Musolli asked: does not a sick man die for want of food, drink and medicine? The people said: Yes. He said: Such is the condition of heart. When the heart is not given wisdom and knowledge for three consecutive days, it dies. It is a veritable truth that the food of the heart is knowledge and wisdom. As food keeps the body alive these two things similarly keep The heart alive, He who misses knowledge has got his heart diseased and its end is its death but he does not understand it. When he leaves the world and its works, his power of sense goes away just as excessive fear keeps one forgetful for a moment of the pangs of wound. But when death takes away the burden of this world from a man, he repents at the advent of his death but it comes to no use. His condition is just like that of one who does not feel any pain in swoon but as soon as he recovers from his swoon he begins to feel pain. Men are in sleep but they are awake at death.

The sage Hasan Basri said: The ink of the learned will be weighed against the blood of the martyrs and then it will be found that the ink of the learned is heavier than the blood of the martyrs. Hazrat Ibn Mas'ud said: You should acquire knowledge before your death. By One in whose hand there is my life, those who were killed in

the way of God would every time wish that God should resurrect
them as learned men as they will find the honour meted out to the
learned men there. Nobody is born learned. Learning is to be
acquired. Hazrat Ibn Abbas said: To discuss about learning in a
portion of night is dearer to me than to keep up awake throughout
the night in prayer. Hazrat Abu Hurairah and Imam Ahmad held
this view. God advised us to pray thus: O God, give us good in this
world and good in the hereafter 2 : 297. In explaining 'good' in this
verse, Hazrat Hasan Basri said that it means knowledge so far as
this world is concerned and Paradise so far as the hereafter is
concerned. A certain wise man was once asked: Which thing is to
be hoarded? He replied: That thing which remains with you even if
your boat capsizes, that is knowledge.

Excellence of Learning

Quran: God says: If a party from every band of them remained
behind, they could devote themselves to the religion—9 : 123. God
says: If you know not, then ask those who have got knowledge of
the Book—16 : 43.

Hadis: The Holy Prophet said: If a man seeks the path of
acquiring knowledge, God guides him to a path leading to Paradise.
He said: Angels spread their wings out of cheer for the seeker of
knowledge. He said: To rise up at dawn and learn a section of
knowledge is better for you than to pray one hundred rak'ats. He
said: If a man learns a chapter of knowledge, it is better than the
world and its contents. He said: Seek knowledge even if it be in
China. He said: To seek knowledge is compulsory on every
Muslim male and female. He said: Knowledge is a treasure house
and its key is enquiry. So enquire and there are rewards therefor
for four persons-the inquirer, the learned man, the audience and
their lover. He said: The ignorant should not remain silent over
their ignorance, nor the learned over their knowledge. He said: To
be present in an assembly of a learned man is better than visiting
one thousand sick men and attending one thousand funerals. The
Prophet was asked: O Messenger of God, is it better than the
reading of the Quran? He said: What benefit can the Quran do
except through knowledge? He said: He who seeks knowledge to

revive Islam and dies in that condition, there will be the difference of only one step between him and the prophets.

Sayings of Sages

Hazrat Ibn Abbas said: When I sought knowledge, I became degraded but when I was sought for knowledge I became exalted. Ibn Mubarak said: I wonder for one who does not seek knowledge. How can he call himself towards honour? A certain wise man said: I do not feel sympathy for anybody more than two persons—(1) one who seeks knowledge but does not understand it, and (2) one who understands knowledge but does not seek it. Hazrat Abu Darda'a said: To learn one point is better than to pray the whole night. He said: Either be a learned man or a student or an auditor but not anything else. Hazrat Umar said: The death of one thousand persons who pray all the nights and fast all the days is a lesser calamity than the death of one learned man who is versed in lawful and unlawful things of God. Imam Shafeyi said: To seek knowledge is better than optional prayers. Hazrat Abu Darda'a said: He who thinks that to go at dawn in search of knowledge is not jihad is deficient in intellect.

Excellence of Teaching

Quran. God says: When they return to them they warn their people, so that they may guard themselves—9 : 122. It means teaching and guidance. God says: Remember when God took a covenant from the People of the Book-you shall surely make it known to mankind and not conceal it 3:187

It shows that teaching was binding on them. God says: A party from them conceal the truth although they know it—2 : 140. This shows that concealing truth is unlawful. God says: Don't conceal evidence for whoever conceals it is wicked at heart—2 : 283. The Prophet said: God does not give a learned man any knowledge until He takes from him a covenant as He took covenant from the prophets, namely to make it known to the people and not conceal it. God says: Who is better in speech than one who calls towards God and does good—41 : 33? God says: Call towards the way of your Lord with wisdom and good sermon—16 : 125. God says: He teaches them the Book and wisdom—2 :125.

Hadis: The Holy Prophet said to Mu'az when he was about to start for Yemen: If God gives guidance to a man through your help, it is better than the world and its contents. He said: If a man learns a section of knowledge to teach it to the people, he will be given the rewards of seventy Siddiqs (true righteous men). Jesus Christ said: He who acquires knowledge, acts up to it and teaches it to the people will be called great in the kingdom of heavens. The Prophet said: On the Day of Resurrection God will say to the worshippers and the warriors: Enter Paradise. The learned will then say: By virtue of our learning you have worshipped and fought. God will then say: You are like some of my angels Intercede and your intercession will be accepted. So they will intercede and enter Paradise. This rank they will get for that knowledge which reached others and not for the knowledge which did not reach others but remained with them. The Prophet said: God will not take away knowledge from men after He has given it to them, rather He will withdraw it after taking the lives of the learned men. Wherever a learned man will pass away the knowledge with him will also pass away and at last there will be none left except the ignorant leaders. Whenever anything will be asked to them, they will give decision without knowledge for which they will be misguided and will misguide others. The Prophet said: If a man after acquiring knowledge keeps it concealed, God will drag him with the bridle of fire on the Resurrection Day.

The Holy Prophet said: How excellent a gift and how excellent a present is a word of wisdom which you hear and remember and then carry it and teach it to your brother Muslim. It is equal to worship for one year. He said: Accursed is the world and what is therein a except one who remembers the glorious God, one who makes friendship with Him, one who learns and teaches. God, His angels the inmates of heaven and earth even the ant in its hole and the fish in the sea like one who teaches good to the people. He said: A Muslim gives his brother Muslim no greater benefit than a fair tradition which has reached him and which he subsequently transmits to him. He said: If a believer hears a good advice and then translates it into action, it is better than his worship for one year. The Prophet once came out and saw two assemblies, one was calling God and offering their supplications to God. If He wishes, He may grant them and if He wishes He may reject them. Another group was giving good instructions to the people, I have been sent as a teacher. Then he went to them and took his seat among them.

The Prophet said: the simile of guidance and knowledge with which God sent me is like that of profuse rain falling upon a certain locality. One spot becomes full of water and consequently abundant herbs and grass grow therein. The ditches and the canals in another spot reserve water and God gives benefit to mankind therewith. They drink water therefrom, irrigate their lands and grow crops. Then there is a spot which neither hoards water, nor grows any grass and herb. The first simile is that of a man who gets benefit from his know ledge. The second simile is that of a man who does benefit to others. The third simile is that of man who is deprived of both the benefits. The Prophet said: One who guides towards something good is like one who does it.

The Holy Prophet said : When a man dies, all his actions stop except three—(1) a permanent endowment for charity, (2) useful knowledge, and (3) righteous successors. He said: There is no envy except for two persons—(1) one whom God has given knowledge according to which he conducts himself and teaches it to the people, and (2) one whom God has given wealth and power to spend it and he spends it in good deeds. He said: May God's mercy be upon my successors. He was asked: Who are your successors? He said: Those who love my ways and teach them to the people.

Sayings of Sages

Hazrat Umar said: He who learns a Hadis and induces one to act up to it will get the rewards of one who translates it into action. Hazrat Ibn Abbas said: If a man teaches good to the people, everything seeks forgiveness for him, even the fish of the sea. A certain wise man said: A learned man is an intermediary between

God and men. So see how he acts as an intermediary. A learned man said: The learned men are the lights of the ages. Each is a light to the people of his time.

Hazrat Hasan Basri said: But for the learned the people would have been animals. In other words, learning takes a man to the limit of humanity from the limit of animality. The Prophet said as reported by Mu'az-bin-Jabal: Acquire knowledge because its acquisition is fear of God, search for it is worship, its study is praise, search for it is jihad, teaching it to him who does not know is alms-giving, imparting it to those who are worthy is meritorious. It is friend in journey, companion in solitude, guide to religion and light to them in happiness and misfortune, bosom friend to a stranger and become to the path of Paradise. Through it, God exalts a nation, makes them leaders and guides of good. Seeing them, others also become guides to good and the people follow them. The angels urge them to work. Everything dry and fresh seeks forgiveness for them, even the fish in sea, insects and worms in forests, cattle and sheep and even the stars in sky seek forgiveness for them. Knowledge gives life to a dead heart, it is a light of eyes in darkness and gives strength to body after removing weakness. By its help a man reaches the rank of the pious. To think of it is like fasting and its study is like prayer. By its help God is obeyed and worshipped, by its help warning is given, by its help unity of God is understood, tie of blood is maintained and lawful things are known.

Proof of Reason

The proof of reason for the excellence of knowledge is this. If the word excellence is not understood, it is not possible to know the excellence of other things. For instance if one desires to know whether Zaid is a wise man, he should know first the meaning of the word wisdom and then of Zaid or else he will go astray. Excellence is the additional quality of a thing which has got no defect. It is said that a horse is better than an ass. If the quality of carrying loads is taken, both are the same but a horse has got some additional qualities which are not found in an ass-the quality of running fast and physical beauty. An Animal is sought for its quality and not for its body. Now understand why knowledge is better. As a horse is called better than an ass for its quality of running fast, so you will call knowledge better if it is compared to other qualities. Knowledge is good for its own sake and not for its connection with other qualities.

All precious things fall into one of three groups—(1) what is sought for its own intrinsic value, (2) what is sought as a means to an end, and (3) what is sought for both. What is sought for its own intrinsic value, for instance knowledge, is noble. What is sought as a means to an end is gold and silver which are mere pieces of stone having no value of their own. If God had not made them instruments of purchasing things, their value would have been equal to other stones. Knowledge is precious for its own sake, because with its help the happiness of the next world and Divine Vision can be gained. It is not so in case of gold and silver. What is sought for both, that is for its own sake and as a means to an end is physical health. If the body is healthy, all things can be easily done such as eating and drinking and other works. But the object of these things is to gain happiness in the hereafter and nearness to God. If this object is kept in view, you will get pleasure in the acquisition of knowledge. The highest rank of man is the attainment of happiness in the next world and the most excellent things are the ways that lead to it. So knowledge is the root of good fortune in this world and in the next. The result of knowledge is to enjoy nearness of God, to keep company with the angels and the pious divines with are objects of the next world and its result in this world is honour, influence over the rulers and the people. So acquisition of knowledge and its teaching are excellent actions in order to seek good of this world and good of the next and it is most laudable with the above object.

The affairs of this world do not become orderly except through activities, but the human activities are divided into three categories. (1) The first category includes four fundamental activities without which the world can not go on in order Agriculture for raising food stuffs for maintaining lives, weaving for manufacturing clothes, architecture for building houses, and government for regulating human relations for living in peace and harmony. (2) The second category includes such activities as are helpful to the above mentioned activities, such as iron-crafts or ploughs for cultivation, instruments for spinning and weaving clothes and other implements. (3) The third category includes such activities as are supplementary to the principal industries previously mentioned, such as eating, drinking, making dresses and sewing clothes.

These activities are necessary for human habitation just as the various organs of the body are necessary for upkeep of the human body. The organs of body also are divided into three categories- (1) The fundamental organs, such as heart, liver and brain. (2) What is helpful to these principal organs are stomach, veins, and backbone without which they can not function. (3) What is supplementary to the above two categories for perfection are nails, fingers, eye brows etc. Out of these three categories, the most noble are the fundamental things, out of which the most noble is government on account of which peaceful habitation becomes possible. For this reason, experienced and expert men are necessary to run the government.

Administration is divided into four classes. (1) The first class is the highest as it is the government of the prophets and their jurisdiction spread over the public and private matters of the people. (2) Next is that administration of temporal rulers over the public matters of the people and not their private matters. (3) Next is the administration of the learned and the wise over the people in the matter of the religion of God as they are the heirs of the prophets. It involves thoughts of the privileged few. (4) Next is the administration of the preachers which involves the thoughts of the common men. After the administration of the prophet; the most noble is the diffusion of knowledge whereby the people are saved from evils and destructive habits and are led towards fortune and constructive virtues. This is the goal of knowledge and education.

Intellectual activities are more excellent than the other activities, because the excellence of an activity is known by three things- (1) by examining the natural qualities of a man by the help of which an activity is recognised. For instance, acquisition of knowledge is better than learning a language as knowledge can be acquired by intellect, while language can be learnt through the sense of hearing. As intellect is better than the sense of hearing, so knowledge is better than language. (2) By examining the extent of human usefulness, for instance, agriculture is superior to the craft of a goldsmith. (3) By observing the excellence of a business, for instance, the business of a goldsmith is better than that of tanning hides. Knowledge also has got the above three qualities. (1) Firstly, it is widely known that the science of religion is the path of the hereafter. Perfect knowledge and bright intellect can acquire it. This is the most noble attribute of a man, because owing to this attribute, trust of God has been accepted by him and through it, he can enjoy the neighbourhood of God. (2) Secondly, there is no doubt that the people in general get benefit of knowledge as its extent of usefulness is very wide and it contributes to the happiness of this world and the hereafter. (3) Thirdly, knowledge is a thing which heals and governs the hearts and souls of men. Man is the lord of creation and the lord of human organs is his heart. A spiritual teacher purifies the heart, guides it towards God. So teaching is the finest mode of worship. The heart of a learned man is one of the good stewards of God. What rank is therefore higher than that in which a man is an intermediary between his Lord and fellowmen to draw them closer to God and to paradise?

SECTION – II

Praiseworthy and blameworthy branches of knowledge Compulsory Learning (Farze Ayin)

The Holy Prophet said: To seek learning is compulsory on every Muslim. He said: Seek knowledge even though in China. There is difference of opinion among the learned as to which branch of knowledge is obligatory on an individual. There are about twenty different groups in this matter. The scholastic theologians say that it is scholastic theology because it contributes towards understanding of Tauhid and the attributes of God. The Jurists say that it is Fiqh or jurisprudence because with its help worship, worldly affairs, lawful and unlawful things can be understood and known. The traditionists say that it is the knowledge about the Quran and ways of the Holy Prophet. The Sufis say that it is

Sufism. So on and so forth. Abu Taleb Makki said that it is the knowledge about the five pillars of Islam.

Knowledge is of two kinds-knowledge of practical religion and knowledge of spiritual matter. The knowledge which is compulsory appertains to practical religion which deals with three matters– beliefs, actions, and prohibitions. For instance, when a sane man attains puberty, it becomes compulsory on him to learn the words of attestation -There is no deity but God and Muhammad is the servant and apostle of God. To know its inner meaning does not then become compulsory on him. He is to believe it without any doubt and proof. The Prophet first required only mere verbal acceptance of Islam and confession of faith from the Arabs. What was compulsory on them at that time was fulfilled. After that, knowledge of the duties to do became compulsory on them.

These duties deal with actions and prohibitions. As regards actions, if a Muslim reaches the early afternoon prayer, it becomes compulsory on him to know first how to pray it and to put it into action. This is the case with him in case of other prayers also. If he lives up to the month of Ramadan, it becomes compulsory on him to know the rules of fasting and then to fast. This is the case with Pilgrimage, Zakat and other duties ordained by God and binding on all Muslims.

As to prohibitions, it depends upon circumstances and new events. It is not compulsory on the blind man to know which words are unalwful. So to know a thing is not compulsory on Muslim who does not require it. If after the acceptance of Islam there is anybody who wears silk dress or takes property of another man by force or looks to a strange woman with passion, he must know how to restrain himself from these things.

As to beliefs and thoughts of mind, their knowledge is obligatory according to the state of mind. Thus if a man feels any doubt in his mind about the meaning of attestation formulas, it then becomes compulsory on him to know what will remove that doubt. When a duty becomes binding on a man, to acquire knowledge about it becomes binding on him. As a man is not free from hatred, envy and impulses of evils, it becomes compulsory on him to know some of the evils as described in the Book of destructive evils. Why should it not be compulsory when the Prophet said: Three things are destructive-sordid miserliness, vehement passion and self-conceit. Other evils follow these three destructive evils. To remove these evils from mind is compulsory. If a man is converted to Islam, what is compulsory on him is to believe in Paradise, Hell, Resurrection Day, Judgment Day. The Prophet said: To acquire learning is binding on every Muslim. He did not say to learn Alif, Lam or Mim, but he said to learn the science of actions. As actions become gradually compulsory on him, to acquire knowledge abcut these duties becomes gradually compulsory on him.

Fard-e-Kefayah (compulsory duty on community)

Know, O dear readers, that learning, about the duties are divided into two categories-those which are connected with religion and those which are not so connected. The religious learnings are those which came from the Holy Prophet and in which there is no question of intellect, and the learnings that are not connected with the religion are Mathematics Medicine etc. They are of three kinds-Praiseworthy, Blameworthy and Permissible. The sciences which are necessary for progress in the world are praiseworthy, such as Medicine, Mathematics etc. These are Farze Kefayah or binding on the community as a whole. Farze Kefayah is such compulsory duty without which no nation can go on in this world. If a man at least acquires such learning or science in a town or locality, all other people in the town or Locality get absolved from its sin. If, however, nobody learns it, all will be transgressors. The sciences which should be learnt for agriculture, administration, industry, horticulture, weaving etc. are Farze Kefayah. To be expert in such learnings is not Farde Kefayah. The]earnings which are blameworthy are sorcery, talismanic science, juggling, gambling and the like. The learnings which are permissible are poetry, history, geography, biology etc. All learnings connected with the religion are praiseworthy, but when any other learning is mixed with any of them, it becomes sometimes blameworthy. The praiseworthy learnings comprise sources, branches, helpful and supplementary learnings. They are therefore of four kinds.

(1) Sources of religious learnings are four in number -the Book of God, the Sunnah or usages of the Holy Prophet, the unanimous opinions of Muslim jurists (Ijma), and the sayings of companions. Ijma is the third source of Islam as it shows the path towards the usages of the Prophet. The first source is the Quran and the second is the Sunnah. The fourth source is the sayings of the companions because they saw the Prophet, witnessed the coming down of revelations and they saw what others did not see through their association with the Prophet.

(2) Branches of learnings of religion are drawn from the sources not according to the literal meaning but according to the meanings adduced by the mind, thereby writing the understanding as indicated by the following Hadis: A judge shall not sit in judgment when angry. This means that he shall not pass judgment when he is pressed by calls of nature, hunger and disease. The last thing is of two kinds. One kind relates to the activities of the world, such as the books of law and is entrusted to the lawyers and jurisprudents; and the other kind relates to the activities of the hereafter. The latter is the science of the conditions of the heart and of its praiseworthy virtues and blameworthy evils.

(3) The third is the sciences helpful to the praiseworthy sciences such as the science of language and grammar which are necessary to know the Quran and Sunnah. They are not themselves religious education. They were not necessary for the Holy Prophet as he was illiterate.

(4) The fourth kind is the supplementary science and is connected with pronunciation of words and different readings, and meanings, such as tafsir, knowledge of revocation of verses, books on authoritative transmission, biographies of illustrious companions and narrators of traditions.

These are the religious learnings and are praiseworthy and as such Farze Kefayah or binding on the community as a whole.

If you question: Why have you included Fiqh or jurisprudence within the worldly sciences and Faqihs or jurists as worldly scholars, the reply is this. Fiqh contains the laws of the administration of the world and Faqihs are such lawyers. There is of course no doubt that a Faqih also deals with religion, but that is done through the intermediary of this world, as the world is the seed ground of the hereafter. The religion does not become perfect without the world. If you leave the religion with the rulers, you will find that the religion is the foundation and the ruler is its guard. That which has got no foundation is destroyed and that which has got no guard is also destroyed. Rule can not go without a ruler and the instrument of rule is Fiqh or administrative laws. The government does not belong primarily to the religious sciences. It is well-known that pilgrimage does not become perfect unless a companion is taken for protection from the ruffians and robbers in journey, but Haj or pilgrimage is one thing, rule for pilgrimage is another thing, guard is a third thing and the laws are a fourth thing. The object of Fiqh is to give knowledge of administration. This is supported by the following Hadis: Nobody can give legal decision except three, ruler, authorised agent and not so authorised and who gives decision out of his own accord. A ruler or leader is qualified to give legal decision. One who is authorised by him is his deputy. Except these two, the third person is called an intruder who undertakes the responsibility himself. The companions in general refrained from giving legal decision, but when they were asked about the Quran and the learnings of the hereafter, they did not remain silent.

It may be said that the argument does not apply to various acts of worship about which a Faqih gives decision. In reply, it may be said that Fiqh gives decision about the following matters of religion-Islam, Prayer, Zakat, Halal and Haram. About Islam, Faqih pays attention only to outward confession of Kalema Tauhid but the heart or mind is outside his domain. The Prophet kept the rulers and the warriors outside it. He questioned a man who praised another man as a martyr: Have you examined the heart of the killed? He uttered Kalema Tauhid out of fear of being killed and then he was killed. The jurist will give decision that his Islam was good even though he uttered it under the shadow of sword. This is therefore a matter of this world. For this reason, the Holy Prophet said: I have been ordered to fight the people until their lives and properties are safe in my hand, but it will come to no help in the hereafter. What will help him there is the light of heart, its secret thoughts and its sincerity which are outside the domain of Fiqh.

About Prayer: A Faqih will give decision of correctness of prayer if the outside formalities are observed even though one's mind was absent in prayer from first to last. This kind of prayer Will be of no use in the hereafter. As verbal expression of Kalema Shahadat will be of no use in the hereafter, so also the outward formalities of prayer will come of no use there. The actions of mind and God-fear which appertain to the actions of the hereafter and which help the outward actions are outside the domain of a Faqih or jurist.

About Zakat: A Faqih will see whether Zakat has been realised according to the prescribed rules It is related that the judge Abu Yusuf gave decision that if a man makes gift of his wealth to his wife at the end of a year and takes back that wealth to him by gift, it is alright although it is done to avoid payment of Zakat. On this point, Imam Abu Hanifa declared that it is the result of his knowledge of Fiqh and it is correct and the result of worldly wisdom, but it will be of no use in the hereafter and its harms in the hereafter will be greater than its benefits.

About Halal and Haram: To abstain from an unlawful thing is piety and there are four grades of piety- (1) Piety which is required for attestation of truth. If a man gives it up, he is not qualified to act as a judge, administrator or witness. This kind of God-fear is only to save oneself from all unlawful things. (2) The second grade of piety is that of a pious man. He saves himself even from doubt whether a certain thing is lawful or unlawful. The Holy Prophet said: Discard that which is doubtful for that which is not doubtful. He also said: Sin is heart alluring. (3) The third grade of piety is that of the God-fearing man who gives up even a lawful thing for fear of falling into an unlawful thing. The Prophet said: Nobody can be a God-fearing man unless he gives up what causes no harm to him for fear of what causes harm. For instance, such a man does not state all affairs to the people lest he is drawn to backbiting or he fears to eat a delicious food or drink lest it stimulates passion and lust which drive the people to commit unlawful things. (4) The fourth grade is the piety of the Siddiq or extremely religious man who gives up everything except God for fear of spending one single hour of life for nothing.

Out of the above four stages, only the first one is within the domain of a Faqih and not the other three. The Holy Prophet once said to Wabisa: Consult your conscience even though they give you decision (thrice). A Faqih does not express opinion regarding the machinations of the heart but confines his opinion on things which are subject matters of courts. His jurisdiction is limited to the matters of the world.

Science of the road to the hereafter is divided into two parts-the science of revelation and the science of practical religion. The science of revelation is the primary object of the science of practical religion. A certain Sufi said: I fear the bad end of a man who has got no portion of the knowledge of revelation. The least portion is to believe it and place it to those who are worthy of it. A certain sage said: Whoever has got two characteristics-heresy and pride-will never be blessed with this secret science. Another sage said: Whoever is addicted to this world or persists in his low desires will not attain this secret science though he might learn the other sciences. This secret science is the science of the Siddiqs and those who are in the neighbourhood of God. This is a light which illumines the heart, cleansing it of all impurities and blameworthy sins. He understands now what he heard before but did not understand. He comes to learn the eternal and perfect attributes of God, His works and wisdom in the creation of this world, the meanings of prophethood, the devil, the angels, the cause of revelation on Prophets, the meaning of Paradise and many other things.

Some say that these things are mere examples. But God has reserved for the pious what no eye has seen, no ear has heard and no heart has conceived. Some say that man knows nothing of Paradise except its attributes and names. Others hold that some are mere patterns and some are identical with the realities which these names signify. Likewise others hold that limit to the knowledge of God is one's inability to reach it. The object of secret knowledge is to remove the covers of doubt over these things from mind and the appearance of such light therein which clears everything like daylight It is possible owing to the light of heart. It is like a mirror through which one can see clearly everything that falls on it if is cleared of all impurities therein. The science of the heart is that by which these impurities are removed from the heart as these impurities are impediments or obstacles to the knowledge of God's attributes. The mode of clearing them is the abstinence form low desires and passions and following the ways of the prophets. Thus to whatever extent the heart is cleansed and made to face the truth, to that same extent will it reflects its reality. This cannot be attained without discipline and efforts. This secret science cannot be written in books, but it can be gained by experience as a gift of God. About this science, the Holy Prophet said: This is such a knowledge which is like a hidden thing. None can grasp it except those who know God. Don't despise such learned man whom God has given a portion of it, as God does not despise a man to whom He gives a gift.

The second kind of practical religion is the praiseworthy and blameworthy sciences of the states of the heart. Its praise worthy qualities are patience, gratitude fear, hope, contentment, asceticism, God-fear, generosity, recognition of the gift of God under all circumstances, good faith, good conduct, truthfulness and sincerity. To know the limits of these attributes, their real nature and the means whereby they are attained, their results and their signs are included in the Science of the hereafter. The blameworthy evils are the following-fear of poverty, displeasure over pre-decree, envy, hatred, hypocrisy, flattery, hope for living long, pride, show, anger, enmity, greed, miserliness, self-conceit, to honour the rich, to look the poor with contempt, haughtiness, vanity, boasting, loss of fear of God, expression of piety, lukewarm support for truth, secretly fostering enmity with outward show of friendship, revenge, deceit, breach of trust, harsh treatment, contentment with the world, oppression, loss of shame and kindness. These are the faults of the mind, roots of evil deeds and miseries.

The opposing qualities are praiseworthy and the fountain heads of all good deeds. To know their real nature belongs to the Science of the hereafter and to know it is compulsory on the part of a learned man of the hereafter. Whoever turns away from it will be destroyed at the bands of the King of kings just as anybody going against the temporal rulers and the laws of a state would be destroyed. The attention of the jurisprudents with respect to the compulsory sciences is towards the world and the attention of these people is towards the good of the hereafter. If any Faqih is asked about Sincerity, God-reliance etc., he would make delay in reply, but as soon as he is asked about divorce and other matters, he will at once reply and deal with subtle intricacies.

Among the learned men of practical sciences, those who are God-fearing keep attached to the learned men of secret sciences. As a student sits in school, so Imam Shafeyi used to sit near Shaiban Ray and ask him: How shall I do this work? The people asked Imam Shafeyi: Are you asking questions to a Beduin? He said: This man has learnt what we have not learnt. Imam Ahmad-b-Hanbal and Ihya-b-Mayen could not agree on a certain ;matter and they therefore went to Maruf Karkhi who was not equal to them in the science of practical religion. They said to him: The Prophet said: What will you do when you will not find a matter in the Quran and Sunnah? He said: Ask the pious men among you and consult them in this matter. We have come to you for this.

Someone said: The learned men of exoteric knowledge are the ornaments of the world and the state but the learned men of esoteric knowledge are the ornaments of kingdoms and angels. Hazrat Junaid said: My spiritual guide said to me once: With whom do you keep company when you leave my house? I said: I keep company with Mohasabi. He said: Yes, follow his knowledge and manners but avoid the subtleties of his scholastic theology and return it to him. When I left him, I heard him say: May God make you first a Muhaddis (traditionist) and then an ascetic (Sufi), but not first an ascetic and then a traditionist. Its meaning is that he should acquire first the science of tradition and learning and then become an ascetic and he will then get salvation, but he who becomes an ascetic before acquisition of knowledge throws himself into faults.

As to Philosophy, it is not a single branch of science but comprises four subjects. The first subject includes Geometry and Arithmetic, both of which are permissible for those who are firm in faith. The second subject is Logic which is a science of reason, and it states proof, reason and cause. Both these are included within theology. The third subject is the science of Sufism or the science of His being and attributes of God. This is also included within theology. The fourth subject is Physics of which some portions contradict Shariat and true religion and are therefore not right.

I shall describe the character and conduct of the early Faqihs. They had no other object except to gain the pleasure of Lord and the signs of the learned men of the hereafter were known to them from their conditions. They lived not only for the science of Fiqh, but also for the science of heart. The companions did not publish books on Fiqh or read them. So also the Imams did not compile books. Soon we shall narrate the lives of some noted Faqihs not to attack them but to attack those who claim to be their followers, act contrary to their character and conduct. The noted Faqihs are five- Imam Abu Hanifa, Imam Malek, Imam Shafeyi, Imam Ahmad-b-Hanbal, and Imam Sufiyan Saori. Everyone of them was an ascetic, devout, learned in the science of the hereafter, law giver for the people, seeker of God's pleasure through the help of Fiqh. Everyone of them possessed five qualities, but the modern Faqihs accepted only one of these qualities. That is research into the minutest details of Fiqh. The four other qualities relate to the good of the hereafter and only one relate to the good of this world. They are followed only in respect of one quality and not the other four.

Imam Abu Hanifa

He was a great Imam and a great ascetic and God-fearing man. He sought God's pleasure by his knowledge. Ibn Mubarak said that Imam Abu Hanifa had good character and conduct and observed prayer and fasted too much. Hammad-b.Sulaiman said that he was in the habit of praying the whole night, and in another narration half the night. Once Abu Hanifa was walking in a street when the people hinted at him saying: This man spends the whole night in prayer. He said: I am ashamed before God that I am described by something which I don't possess. Regarding his asceticism, Rabia-b-Asem said: Caliph Yezid sent me once to Abu Hanifa and he wanted to appoint him as cashier of the state treasury. On his refusal to accept the post, he was given twenty stripes. Now see how he fled away from a prize post and as a result he received punishment. Hakim-b-Hashim said: I heard about Abu Hanifa at Syria that he was the most trusted man for which the Caliph wanted him to be appointed as a Treasurer of the state treasury and threatened him with punishment if he would not accept it. He preferred King's punishment to that of God.

Ibnul Mubarak narrated about Abu Hanifa: Do you say of that man who was given the treasures of the world but who fled away from them? Muhammad-b-Shuja narrated: Caliph Al Mansur ordered 10,000 dirhams to be given to the Imam but he declined the offer. On the day when the wealth would be delivered to him, he covered his body with a cloth after prayer and did not talk with anybody. The man of the Caliph went to him with Dirhams but the Imam did not talk with him. One of the people present said: This is his habit. Put it in a corner of his room. This was done. Thereafter Abu Hanifa left death instruction with regard to this wealth and said to his son: When I die and you finish my burial, take this purse to the Caliph and tell him: This is your trust which you have deposited with Abu Hanifa. His son said: I did accordingly. The Caliph said: May God have mercy on your father. It is narrated that he was once offered the post of the chief justice of the state, but he said: I am not fit for this post. When he was asked about the reason, he said: If I have told the truth, it is good for the post: and if I have told a lie, I am unfit for that post as I am a liar. Abu Hanifa's knowledge of the things of the hereafter and his concern over the important matters of religion are proved by the following narrations. Ibn Jury said: I was informed that Abu Hanifa was a great God-fearing man. Sharik said: Abu Hanifa used to spend long time in silence and meditation and converse little with the people. These actions prove his exoteric knowledge. He who has been given silence and asceticism has been given all knowledge.

Imam Shafeyi

He was a devout worshipper. He divided the night into three parts-one part for study, one part for prayer and one part for sleep. The narrator said that Imam Shafeyi used to finish the Quran 60 times in the month of Ramadan and every time he finished it in prayer. Hasan Qarabasi reported: I spent many nights with the great Imam. He used to spend one-third of the night in prayer and yet I have not seen him reciting more than fifty to one hundred verses. At the end of each verse, he would beseech God's mercy upon himself and upon all Muslims. The Imam said: I used not to take food with satisfaction for the last 16 years as a full stomach makes the body heavy, makes the heart hard, increases sleep and renders a man lazy for worship. He also said: Never have I taken oath by God whether true or false. He said: He who claims that the love of the world and love of God are united in him, is a liar. Humaidi said: Imam Shafeyi once went to Yemen with some men and returned to Mecca with 10,000 dirhams. A tent was fixed for him in the outskirts of Mecca and people began to come to him. He did not move from that place till he distributed all dirhams among the people. Generosity of the Iman was great and the root of asceticism is generosity. Whoever loves a thing keeps it with him and everything is insignificant to one to whom the world is insignificant. This is asceticism which leads to God-fear. Once Sufiyan-b-Aynabat fell in swoon before the Imam. He was told that he had expired. He said: if he has died, the best man of his time has died. Umar-b-Nabatah said: I have not found more God-fearing man than Imam Shafeyi. 1, he and Haris-b-Labeed went one day to the valley of Safa. Haris had a student with him and he was a Qari or reader of the Quran. He had a sweet voice and began to read: This is a day on which they will not speak and they will not be given permission to make excuses (77 : 35). 1 saw that the colour of the face of the Imam changed and he was trembling vehemently and then fell in swoon. When he recovered, he began to say: O God, I seek refuge to Thee from the place of the liars and the scoffing of the heedless. O God, the hearts of agnostics have submitted and the necks of those who yearn for Thee bowed. O worshipped, bestow Thy bounty upon me and cover me with

Thy mercy. Forgive my faults through the grace of Thy countenance. Then he along with us left the place. When I reached Baghdad, he was then in Iraq. I was making ablution on the bank of the river for prayer. A man then was passing by me and said: O young man, make ablution well, God will then treat good with you both in this world and in the next, I followed him. He looked at me and said: Have you got any necessity? I said: Teach me something of what God has taught you. He said: Know that he who knows God as true Generosity of the Iman was great and the root of asceticism is generosity. Whoever loves a thing keeps it with him and everything is insignificant to one to whom the world is insignificant. This is asceticism which leads to God-fear. Once Sufiyan-b. Aynabat fell in swoon before the Imam. He was told that he had expired. He said: if he has died, the best man of his time has died. Umar-b-Nabatah said: I have not found more God-fearing man than Imam Shafeyi. 1, he and Haris-b-Labeed went one day to the valley of Safa. Haris had a student with him and he was a Qari or reader of the Quran. He had a sweet voice and began to read: This is a day on which they will not speak and they will not be given permission to make excuses (77 : 35). 1 saw that the colour of the face of the Imam changed and he was trembling vehemently and then fell in swoon. When he recovered, he began to say: O God, I seek refuge to Thee from the place of the liars and the scoffing of the heedless. O God, the hearts of agnostics have submitted and the necks of those who yearn for Thee bowed. O worshipped, bestow Thy bounty upon me and cover me with Thy mercy. Forgive my faults through the grace of Thy countenance. Then he along with us left the place. When I reached Baghdad, he was then in Iraq. I was making ablution on the bank of the river for prayer. A man then was passing by me and said: O young man, make ablution well, God will then treat good with you both in this world and in the next, I followed him. He looked at me and said: Have you got any necessity? I said: Teach me something of what God has taught you. He said: Know that he who knows God as true gets salvation and he who fears his religion, remains safe from destruction. He who remains indifferent from the world, will be cool at seeing the rewards which God will give him tomorrow. Shall I give you more advice? I said: Yes. He said: The faith of one who has got three characteristics is perfect—(1) to enjoin good and to act according to it, (2) to prohibit evil and to desist from it, and (3) to guard the limits of God. Shall I give you more advice? I said: Yes. He said: Adopt asceticism in the world, entertain hopes for the next world and believe God in all your affairs, you will then be among those who will get salvation. Then he went away. I asked: Who is he? They said: Imam Shafeyi. Such fear and asceticism are the result of nothing but for his knowledge of God and not for his knowledge of legal questions like advance payment, loan, wages etc. as are embodied in Fiqh.

Imam Shafeyi said: The knowledge of one who does not make himself perfect will come of no use to him. He also said: Whosoever confesses his obedience to God through the help of his knowledge, his heart becomes illumined. He also said: Every one has got some persons who love him and some who hate him. If it be so, be among those who obey God.

Abdul Qader-Abdul Aziz was a God-fearing man. He once asked Imam Shafeyi: Which of these virtues is better-patience, trial, and peace of mind (Tamkin)? The Imam replied: Peace of mind is the rank of the Prophets and it is not attained except by trial, and patience comes after trial. Don't you see that God examined Abraham and then He gave him peace of mind? He examined Solomon and then gave him peace of mind and kingdom. He did the same to Moses, Job, Joseph and others. This reveals the deep knowledge of Imam Shafeyi about the Quran. Sufyan Saori said: I or anybody has not seen like Shafeyi.

Imam Malik

He was adorned with five qualities. Once he was asked: O Malik, what do you say about search or knowledge? He replied: It is fair and beautiful. If anybody does not separate from you morning to evening, don't be separate from him. When the Imam intended to narrate traditions, he used to make ablution, sit in the middle of his bed, comb his beard, apply scent and then become fearful and grave and then narrate traditions. When asked about these formalities, he said: I intend to show honour to the traditions of the Prophet. He said: Knowledge is light. God places it wherever He wishes. Regarding the seeking of pleasure of God by knowledge, he said: There is no benefit in arguments about religion. This is proved by a saying of Imam Shafeyi who said: Once I was near Malik. He was asked about forty-eight legal questions. He replied regarding thirty-two questions: I don't know. When the learned were mentioned, Imam Malik was counted as a bright star. It is said that once the Caliph Manner prohibited him to narrate the particular tradition on the illegality of divorce made under compulsion. The Caliph thereafter instigated some one to question the Imam on the subject. He declared among the people that divorce pronounced under compulsion is not binding. For this, the Caliph had him flogged.

The Caliph Harun Rashid once asked Imam Malik : Have you got any house? He said: No. The Caliph then gave him 3,000 dinars and said: Go and buy with this money a house. The Imam accepted the money but did not spend it for the purpose. When the Caliph intended to return to Baghdad he asked Malik You should come along with us, because we have decided to make the people follow 'Muatta' as Osman made them follow the Quran. Malik said: This is not the way to make the people follow 'Muatta' because the companions of the Prophet after his death dispersed around the different countries and they related the traditions in each place. Further the Prophet said: Difference of opinion among the people is a blessing. As for my going with you, there is no way as the Prophet said: Had they known, they would have known that Medina is best for them. Again he said: Medina removes the corruption just as the furnace removes the dross of iron. Therefore here are your dinars. If you like, take them back and if you like, you may have them. Does this mean that you ask me to leave Medina in return for what you have given me? I prefer nothing more than the city of the Messenger of God, not even the whole world. Such was the asceticism of Malik. When as a result of his diffusion of knowledge and the spreading of his companions, large wealth began to come to him from different corners of the earth, he used to distribute them in charity.

Such an ascetic was Soloman despite his royal glory. Another example of his asceticism is that Imam Shafeyi once said: I noticed a number of Korasani horses at the door of Malik. I have never seen any other horse better than them. I said to Malik : How beautiful are they! He said: These are then present from me to you. I said to him: Keep one of them for yourself for riding. He said: I shall he ashamed before God to tread with the hoof of any beast of burden the soil wherein lies His Prophet. See therefore his benevolence and his veneration for the soil of Medina.

There is yet another report of his asceticism. He said: I once went to the Caliph Harun Rashid. He asked Malik: O Abu Abdullah, you should come frequently to my place, so that I may learn from you 'Muatta'. He said : May God exalt my master, this knowledge has come from you. If you honour it will be exalted; and if you dishonour it, it will be despised. Knowledge is something you shall learn and not something you should receive. Then the Caliph said: You are right. He said to his sons: Go out to the mosque and acquire from him knowledge along with the people.

Imam Ahmed and Sufiyan Saori had many followers. Nevertheless, they arc known for asceticism and God-fear. All books contain their sayings and stories of their asceticism. Now examine the lives of the Imams and scrutinize those who claim to be their followers. Did the Imams rise to such eminence only for their knowledge of Fiqh which now means contracts of the type of salam, hire, rental, lease and other worldly laws?

SECTION – III

Blameworthy Sciences

(1) Knowledge is not held to be blameworthy except for one of three reasons. Firstly, if it leads to the harm of another, it becomes blameworthy, such as magic, talisman, sorcery. These sciences are true no doubt as the Quran testifies. The Sahih Bukhari and Muslim narrate traditions also that the Prophet of God was once victim of sorcery for which he fell ill. Gabriel informed the Prophet of this matter. The enchantment was taken out from underneath a

stone in the bottom of a well. It is a kind of knowledge obtained through the learned men of the precious stones and mathematical calculations of the places and times of the rising of stars.

(2) The second reason is that if a science causes much harm to the acquirer, it is blameworthy, such as the science of Astronomy. It is of two kinds, one deals with Mathematics and is connected with accounts. The Quran says: The sun and the moon have got courses reckoned-55 : 4. It says again: As for the moon, I decreed stations for it till it changes like an old and crooked palm branch-36 : 59. The second kind deals with Astrology, the gist of which is that the future events are indicated by the present causes. Astrology is therefore an attempt to know the course of the laws and ordinances of God in connection with His creations. The Shariat has declared it as blameworthy. The Prophet said: Whenever Taqdir is mentioced, remain silent and whenever my companions are mentioned, remain silent. The Prophet said: I fear three things for my followers after me, the oppression of the leaders, faith in Astrology and disbelief in Taqdir (pre-decree). Hazrat Omar said: Learn Astrology to conduct you in land and not more. There are three causes for this prohibition. Firstly, it is harmful for majority of the people, because thoughts occur in their minds that it is the stars which influence the course of events and so the stars are to be worshipped. The wise man knows that the sun, the moon and the stars are subject to the command of God. The second reason is that Astrology is purely guess work. It has been termed blameworthy because its command is that of only ignorance. Once the Prophet was passing by a man surrounded by the people. He asked: Who is this man? They said: He is a great learned man. The Prophet asked: Of what learning? They said: Of poetry and Arab genealogy. The Prophet said: Such a learning which does not do any benefit and such ignorance which does not do any harm. The Prophet said: Learning is of decisive verses or lasting usages (of Prophet) and just ordinances (based on the Quran and Sunnah). It appears from this that discussion about Astrology and the like sciences are useless undertakings.

(3) The third reason that this science is blameworthy is that it becomes of no use to one who acquires it, for example, learning of

trivial sciences before the important ones, learning of subtleties before fundamentals. Ignorance, however, in some cases is beneficial as is seen from the following story.

A certain person once complained to a physician that his wife was sterile and that she bore no children. The physician felt the pulse of the woman and told her that she would die after 40 days. The woman got extremely frightened and gave away all her wealth and lived these forty days without food and drink. After the period, her husband came to the physician and said that his wife did not die. The physician said: Now cohabit with her and you will get an issue. He asked: How will it be? The physician said: I saw that the woman was too fat and that grease was blocking her uterus and that it could not be removed except by fear of death. Then she became lean and fit for conception. It is gathered from this story that ignorance is sometimes good. Ignorance of some branches of knowledge is good and it will be clear from the following Hadis of the Holy Prophet. He said: I seek refuge to God from useless knowledge.

So don't discuss about those learnings which have been declared by Shariat as useless. There are many things which, if inquired into, will do harm.

Second Matter

Change of the meanings of some words connected with knowledge: The people have changed the original meanings of the words Fiqh, Ilm, Tauhid, Tazkir and Hikmat and have given them the meanings of their own. As a result they have become now blameworthy.

Fiqh (religious learning). It has now the meaning of the science of unusual legal cases, mystery of the minutest details of jurisprudence and excessive debates on them. The man who gives attention to such a science is called now Faqih or juris-prudent. In the first century, it had a different meaning. It was a science of the path of the hereafter and knowledge of the beneficial and harmful matters of soul, knowledge of the meanings of the Quran and the domination of God-fear over the heart. This is proved by the words of God in the following verse: that they may become expert in religion and may warn their people when they come back to them- 9 : 193. Fiqh or juris-prudence is that which gives such a warning and fear rather than the details of divorce, manumission, rental etc. God says: They have got hearts but they do not understand therewith-2: 178. Those who were present before the Prophet did not know the details of laws.

Someone asked Sa'ad-b-Ibrahim: Who is the greatest Faqih in Medina? He said: He who fears God most. This points out to the result of Fiqh. The Prophet once said: Shall I not inform you about a prefect Faqih? The companions said: Yes. He said: A prefect Faqih is one who does not deprive the people of the mercy of God, does not give hope of freedom from punishment, nor makes them lose hope of His mercy, nor discards the Quran in favour of something else. When Anas-b-Malek narrated the following tradition-'To sit with those who remember God from dawn to sun-rise is dearer to me than the manumission of four slaves,' the Prophet said: A man cannot become a perfect Faqih unless he makes the people understand about the existence of God and believes that there are several objects in the Quran. Hazrat Hasan Basri said:

A Faqih is one who renunciates the world, remains stead fast to the hereafter, is wise in his religion, worships his Lord cons-tantly, restrains himself from attacks on the reputation of his fellow Muslims, is indifferent to their wealth and wishes good of the Muslims of the world. He did not say: One who commits to memory the intricacies of law is Faqih. Ilm is the science of religion, the science of the knowledge of God and His verses. When Caliph Omar died, Hazrat Ibn Mas'ud exclaimed: Nine-tenths of the science of religion have passed away. The present people used the term Urn to mean the science of those who can well debate the cases of jurisprudence with their adversar ies and those who cannot do that are termed weak and outside the category of the learned men. But what has been said about the excellence of learning and the merits of the learned men apply to those who are versed according to the former meaning.

Tauhid (unity of God). The present meaning of Tauhid is scholastic theology or Ilm Kalam, the knowledge of the methods of agrumentation, the manner of confronting adversa-ries. Tauhid was then the belief that all things come from God and it ruled out all intermediary causes, the belief that good and evil all come from God and that the result of Tauhid is God-reliance. Such people believed that another fruit of Tauhid is to avoid complaints to the people, not to get angry at them and to remain staisfied with the decree of God. Another fruit of Tauhid is the saying of Hazrat Abu Bakr in his illness. The people said to him: Let us call a physician for you. He said: The Physician Himself has given me this disease. In another narration, he said: The Physician said: I certainly do what I wish-1I : 109, 85 : 16Q.

Tauhid is therefore a precious fruit which is engaged into several husks, the outer husk is distant from the inner. The modern people have taken up the husk and given up the pith. The people have termed it as the science of husk and given up the science of pith. The meaning of the husk of Tauhid is to utter by tongue 'There is no deity but God'. It is opposite to Trinity of the Christians. The hypocrite Muslims also utter it. The pith of Tauhid is confirmation by heart what the tongue confesses. The heart believes it to be true. This is real Tauhid which is to entrust every affair of man to God in such a way that his attention is not diverted to any other matter except to God. Those who follow their passion do not conform to this monotheism.

God says: Have you seen such one who takes his passion as God-25 : 43Q? The Prophet said: The worst deity in the sight of God that is worshipped in the world is the deity of passion. Idol worship is also done according to the wishes of passion. For this reason, the soul of such a man inclines towards the religion of his ancestors. Such a man is like one who rises up in the morning and says facing the Ka'ba. I have turned my face towards One who created the heavens and the earth, but he really does not turn his heart towards God and begins the day with a lie. The direction of the Ka'ba is not the direction of God. He who turns his face towards the Ka,ba can't be called to have turned his face towards God as God is not confined within space and direction. Mind is the mine of Tauhid and its fountainhead. A man of Tauhid turns his mind towards God and not towards any other direction.

Zikr or Tazkir (God's remembrance). This is the science of invocation and admonition , God says: Remind them because Zikr or admonition benefits the believers- 51 : 55. There are many traditions regarding the merits of the assemblies of Zikr. The Prophet said: When you pass by the gradeu of Paradise, enjoy yourselves. He was asked: What are the gardens of Paradise? He said: Assemblies of Zikr (remembrance of God). The Prophet said: Angels of God roam in the horizon except the angels of creation. When they see any assembly of Zikr, they accost themselves and say: Come unto your goals. They then come to the place, surround them and hear them, remember God and take lessons. Now the assembly of Zikr means the assembly of lectures wherein the modem lecturers deliver long speeches, tell stories, recite poems and poetries and sing songs. Such was not the practice at the time of the four rightly guided Caliphs. Story-tellling is an innovation. Ibn Omar once came out of the mosque exclaiming: None has sent me out except a storyteller. Hazrat Ali turned out the story-tellers from the congregational mosque of Basra. He did not turn out Hasan Basri as he used to deal with the hereafter, contemplation of death, defects of soul, machinations of the devil. Such is the assembly about which the Prophet said: To be present at the assembly of Zikr is better than one thousand rak'ats of prayers, visiting one thousand sick men and attending one thousand funerals. Hazrat Ata said: One assembly of Zikr expiates the sins of seventy assemblies of useless talks. The Prophet once heard three talks from Abdullah-b-Rawahah and said: O Abu Rawahah, keep yourself far from ornamental talks. He asked the Prophet one day about the blood money of a child which died in the womb of its mother saying: How shall we pay the blood wit of a child who has taken no food, no drink, nor cried, nor breathed. Such murder is excusable. The Prophet said: Are you like the desert Arabs who indulge in ornamental words?

Poetry. As to poetry, its general use in sermons is bad, God says: As to poets, those who go astray follow them. Don't you find them wandering in every valley and say what they do not do-26 : 225?

God said: I did not teach him (Prophet) poetry, nor it is becoming of him. Furthermore what is narrated of poetries in sermons comprises mostly of love episodes, descriptions of the beauties of the beloved, the joys of union and pangs of separation. This gives rise to lust and sexual passion more than religious enthusiasm. There are however such poetries which contain wisdom. The Prophet also said: There is wisdom in poetry.

Hikmat. The word Hakim derived from the word Hikmat is now used in the case of physicians, astrologers and those who tell the future of the people by examining hands, but God says about the word Hikmat (wisdom): He gives wisdom to whom He whishes. Whoever has been given wisdom has been given a great.good-2 : 272. The Prophet said: If a man learns a word of wisdom, it is better than the world and what it contains. Now think what was Hikmat and what it has come to. Now think also of the meaning of many words which have come down to us. One day a man asked the Prophet: Who is the worst creature in creation? The Prophet said: God, pardon me. On being repeatedly asked, the Prophet replied: They are wicked learned men.Now you have come to know. about praiseworthy and blameworhy sciences and how they intermingled with one another. Now choose either of the two. If you want good, you may follow the path of the ancient sages and saints, and if you want, you may follow the paths of the later generations. All knowledge which the ancient sages loved have vanished. The Prophet said: Islam began with a few and it will soon return to a few as it began. Good news to those few. He was asked: Who are those few? He said: Those who purify my Sunnah after the people polluted them and those who revive my Sunnah after their deatli. In another narration: The few are a few righteous people in the midst of many unrighteous men.

Third Matter

How much is praiseworthy of the praiseworthy sciences?

Knowledge is divided into three parts. One part is blameworthy in whole or in part, one part is praiseworthy, in whole or in part and one part is praiseworthy upto a certain limit and beyond that it is blameworthy. Look to the condition of physique. A little of health and beauty is good, but a little of ugly figure and bad conduct is bad. Moderate expense or wealth is praiseworthy but immoderate expense is blameworthy.

(1) The knowledge of which a little or much is blameworthy has got no benefit either in this world or in the next, because there is such harm in it which is greater than its benefit, for example magic, astrology or talismanics. A valuable life shouldnot be spent uselessly but there are some sciences which have got moderate benefits, but their harms are greater.

(2) The science which is beneficial up to the end is the science of knowing God, His attributes and His works, His laws affecting this world and thereafter. This is the science which is sought for its own attributes and by which the blessings of the hereafter is gained. To exert oneself to the utmost of one's capacity to gain it falls far short of what is required, because it is such a sea of which the depth is unlimited. Those who search it are remaining constantly in its shores and edges. The Prophet, the saints and the learned with faith according to their different ranks, power and strength and according to the decree of God could not even navigate its ends. This is the hidden science which can never be recorded in books. For it, precaution shall have to be taken, efforts shall have to be made and the condi-tion of the learned men of the hereafter shall have to be examined. For this science, a great deal of efforts, purification of mind, renunciation of the world and the following of the Prophet and friends of God are necessary. He who does all these things earns it according to his fate and not to his efforts, but there is no escape from efforts as efforts are the only keys of guidance and there is no other key.

(3) The sciences which are praiseworthy up to a certain limit are those which have been narrated at the time of discussion of Farz Kefayah. Each has got three limits-first limit up to necessity, second up to moderation and third up to excessive quantity and there is no end of it during life. Beware of the two persons. Either be busy with yourself or be busy after finishing your work with others. Be careful of correcting others before you correct

yourself. If you keep busy with yourself, be busy with acquisition of knowledge which is compulsory according to your need, for instance, knowledge of open deeds such as prayer, fast etc. More importance however is the science which everybody neglects. It is the science of heart. Know which of these sciences are bad and which are good as there is nobody who is safe from envy, hatred, pride, self-conceit and such other destructive faults. Performance of these outward deeds is like the external application of ointment to the body when it is stricken with scabies and boils while neglecting to remove the pus by means of surgery. The learned men lay stress upon the outward actions and the learned men of the hereafter remove the impurities of mind.

So you should not engage yourself in Farze Kefayah duties till you are pure in heart and acquire strength to give up open and secret sins. Give attention first to the Holy Quran, then to the Sunnah of the Holy Prophet, then to Tafsirs of the learned men and then to other learnings. Don't engage your life to the learning of only one branch of education as life is short but the learnings are many. The acquisition of these learnings are weapons for the hereafter. There is no learning which has got no limits of necessity, moderation and perfection. This is applicable also to Hadis, Tafsir and Fiqh.

A certain saint asked a learned man in dream: Tell me the condition of learning about which you held disputation. He said it has all vanished like scattered dust. Only two rak'ats of prayer at the later part of night has done me benefit. The Prophet said: No people are misguided after guidance except disputation. Then he read the following verse: They did nothing about you but disputation. Rather they are a contentious people. About a verse-'But they in whose hearts there is perversity (3 : 5) the Prophet said that they are a contentious people about whom God said: Beware of them. The Prophet said: You are living in an age when you receive inspiration for actions but soon a people will appear who will be given to disputation. The worst men to God in creation are given to bitter disputes. He also said: Those who have been given to disputation have not been given actions.

SECTION – IV

Harms of the science of polemics and evils of debates and disputations

Know, O dear readers, that after the Prophet, the rightly guided Caliphs were the leaders of the learned in the science of God. They were the eyes of knowledge and were experienced in the legal decisions. They did not take the help of jurisprudents except in cases where consultation was necessary. They decided on the strength of Ijtihad and their decisions were recorded in their lives. After their death, Caliphate went to those who were not so experienced in legal matters and administrative affairs. They were compelled to seek the aid of jurisprudents. At that time, a band of Tabeyins (successors of companions) were alive and they persisted in following strictly the injunctions of religion. Whenever the Caliphs called them, they fled. But some learned men used to mix with the Caliphs and consequently became humiliated. Therefore there were differences of opinion among the learned men and there grew different Mazhabs or sects as a result. There were argumentations and disputations over the intricate questions of religion. They composed also many works on these subjects. This induced the people to take to controversies and disputations.

There are eight conditions of debates

(1) The first condition is that where debate for search of truth is one of Farze Kefayah duties, one who has not already fulfilled his part in duties of Farze Ain should not engage himself in the debates even for searching truth.

(2) The second condition is that one should not consider debates more important than Farze Kefayah duties.

He commits sin who does other works leaving aside a more important Farze Kefayah duty. He is like a man who does not give water to drink to people who are thirsty and facing death even though he has got power to do so, because he remains then busy in giving lessons of cupping. Once the Prophet was asked: When will the people give up enjoining good and forbidding evil? The Prophet said: When flattery will grow in good people among you, kingdom will go to the meanest of you and theology to those who will be corrupt.

(3) The third condition which justifies debate is that the debater should have ability and give decision on his own responsibility without referring to the opinion of Imam Abu Hanifa or any other Imams. He who has not the ability of independent interpretation should not express his opinion but should refer it to an Imam.

(4) The fourth condition which justifies debate is that the subject for decision should be about actual cases that crop up, for example, the question of inheritance and not about future cases. The companions also held consultations as questions arose or were likely to arise in order to arrive at truth.

(5) The fifth condition is that debate should be held in private in preference to open meetings in presence of noted people and in grandeur because privacy is more suitable for clear thinking and to examine what is right and what is wrong.

(6) The sixth condition is that the debater should like truth in the same spirit as a lost thing is searched for. He should not mind whether the truth is found by him or by his adversary. When Hazrat Umar was once giving sermon, a woman pointed out to him his mistake to which he submitted. At another time, Hazrat Ali was asked a question by a man and he replied. When the man pointed out his mistake, he admitted it.

(7) The seventh condition is that the debater should not prevent his adversary from giving up one argument in favour of another and one illustration in favour of another.

(8) The eighth condition is that debate should be held with such person from whom benefit is derived and who is learned.

From these eight conditions, you will be able to distinguish those who debate for the sake of God and those who debate for other purposes.

Third Matter-Evils of Debates

The following evils arise out of modem debates. (1) Envy. The Prophet said: Envy consumes good deeds as fire consumes fuels. A debater is never free from envy and hatred. Envy is a burning fire. One who falls in it gets punishment in the world. Hazrat Ibn Abbas said: Acquire knowledge wherever it is found and don't obey the devils who are prone to disputes. (2) **Pride.** The Prophet said: A believer cannot have pride in him. There is a Hadis Qudsi in which God said: Grandeur is My cloak and pride is My mantle. I destroy one who snatches anything of these two from Me. (3) Rancour A debater is seldom free from the evil of rancour. The Prophet said: A believer has got no rancour. (4) **Back-biting** which is likened by God to the eating of carrion (49 : 12). A debater ascribes to his opponent foolishness, ignorance and stupidity. (5) **Declaration of self-purity.** God says : Don't attribute purity to yourself. He knows best who fears Him (53 : 33). (6) **Spying and prying into the secrets of adversary.** God says: Pry not (49: 12). (7) **Hypocrisy.** A debater expresses his friendship for his adversary outwardly but he cherishes hatred for him inwardly. The Prophet said: When the learned men do not translate their learning into action, when they profess love for one another with their tongue and nurse hatred in their hearts, when they sever the ties of relationship. God sends curse upon them, makes their tongues mute and their eyes blind. (8) **To turn away from truth.** The most hateful thing to a debater is to reject the truth revealed to his adversary and thus he takes to deception and deceit. The Prophet prohibited dispute about, useless things. He said: If a man gives up disputation in matters of unlawful things, a garden will be built for him in Paradise. If a man gives up disputations in matters of truth, a house will be built up for him in the highest Paradise. God said: He is more wrongful than one who devises a lie against God and calls the truth a lie when it comes to him 29 : 68. God said: Who is more wrongful than he who lies against God and treats the truth when it comes to him as a lie. (39:33) (9) Another fault of debate is show **and Battering** the people in an effort to win their favour and to mislead them. Hypocrisy is the greatest disease with which a debater is attacked and it is a major sin. (10) **Deception.** Debaters are compelled to deception. These ten evils are the secret major sins arising out of debates and disputations. Besides these major offences, there arise many other guilts out of controversies leading to blows, kicks, boxing, tearing of garments etc.

The learned men are of three classes. One class comprise those who ruin themselves and also ruin others. Another class make themselves fortunate and make others also fortunate. Such learned men call others towards good. The third class of learned men call ruin to themselves but make others fortunate.

SECTION – V

Manners to be observed by teachers and students. These manners comprise ten duties.

(1) The first duty of a student is to keep himself free from impure habits and evil matters. Effort to acquire knowledge is the worship of mind. It purifies secret faults and takes to God. Prayer is observed by outward organs and as outward purity is not gained except by outward organs, so worship by mind, the fountainhead of acquisition of knowledge, cannot be attained without the removal of bad habits and evil attributes. The Prophet said: Religion is founded on cleanliness. So outward and inward purities are necessary. God says: The polytheists are impure- 9: 28. It is understood from this that purity and impurity are not merely external as the polytheists also keep their dresses clean and bodies clean, but as their mind is impure, so they are generally impure. The inward purity is of greatest importance. The Prophet therefore said: Angels do not enter a house wherein there are dogs. Human mind is a house, the abode of angels, the place of their movements. The blameworthy evils like anger, lust, rancour, envy, pride, conceit and the like are dogs. When dogs reside in a heart, where is the place for the angels? God takes the secrets of knowledge to the hearts through the angels. They do not take it except to the pure souls. Hazrat Ibn Mas'ud said: Knowledge is not acquired through much learning. It is a light cast in heart. A certain sage said:

Knowledge is God-fear as God said: The learned among the people fear God most.

(2) The second duty of student is to reduce his worldly affairs and keep aloof from kith and kin as acquisition of knowledge is not possible in these environments. For this reason, a certain sage said: God has not gifted two minds to a man. For this reason, a certain sage said: Knowledge will not give you its full share till you surrender your entire mind to it.

(3) The third duty of a student is not to take pride or exalt himself over the teacher but rather entrust to him the conduct of all his affairs and submit to his advice as a patient submits to his physician. The Prophet said: It is the habit of a believer not to flatter anyone except when he seeks knowledge. Therefore a student should not take pride over his teacher. Knowledge cannot be acquired except through modesty and humility. God said: Herein there is warning for one who has got a heart or sets up ear while he himself being a witness (50 : 36). The meaning of having a heart is to be fit for receiving knowledge and one who is prepared and capable of understanding knowledge. Whatever the teacher should recommend to the student, the latter should follow it putting aside his own opinion. The people should question only in the matter which the teacher permits him. Here there is an instance of Moses and Khizir. Khizir said: You will not ask me anything I do. Still Moses questioned him and for that he separated him.

(4) The fourth duty of a student is that he should first pay no attention to the difference whether about worldly sciences or science of the hereafter as it may perplex his mind and he may lose enthusiasm. He should adopt first what the teacher says and should not argue about the different mazhabs or sects.

(5) The fifth duty is that a student should not miss any branch of knowledge. He should try to become perfect in them as all branches of learning help one another and some branches are allied with others. If a man does not get a thing, it becomes his enemy. God says: When they do not find guidance, they say, it is an age-long lie (46 : 10). A poet said: A sweet thing is bitter in the month of a patient as sweet water is tasteless to a sick man. Good

knowledge is acquired according to one's genius. It leads men to God or helps him in that way. Each branch of knowledge has got its fixed place. He who guards it, is like a guard who patrols the frontiers in jihad. Each has got a rank in it and each has got a reward in the hereafter according to his rank. The only condition required is that the object of acquisition of knowledge should be to please God.

(6) The sixth duty of a student is that he should not take up all branches of knowledge at a time, but should take up the most important one at first as life is not sufficient for all branches of knowledge. A little learning if acquired with enthusiasm perfects the knowledge of the hereafter or the sciences of the worldly usages and the sciences of revelation, The object of the science of worldly usages is to acquire spiritual knowledge. The goal of the spiritual knowledge is to know God. Our object by this knowledge is not that belief which is handed down from generations to generations. Our object for this knowledge is to acquire light arising out of certain faith which God casts in soul. Such light was acquired by Hazrat Abu Bakr. The Prophet said about Abu Bakr: If the faith of the people of the world is weighed with the faith of Abu Bakr, his faith would be heavy. In short, the highest and the noblest of all sciences is to know God. This science is like a sea of which the rank is that of the Prophet, then of the friends of God and finally that of those who follow them. It has been narrated that the portraits of two ancient wise men were seen on the wall of a mosque. One of them held a piece of paper in which it was written: If you purify everything, don't understand that you have even purified one thing till you know God and know that He is the cause of all Causes and the Creator of everything. In the hand of the second man, there was a scroll in which it was written: I removed thirst before by drinking water and then have come to know God. But when I have come to know God, my thirst was quenched without any water.

(7) The seventh duty of a student is that he should not take up new branch of learning till he has learnt fully the previous branch of learning, because it is requisite for the acquisition of knowledge. One branch of knowledge is a guide to another branch. God says :

who so has been given the Quran recites; it with due recitation (2 : 15). In other words, he does not take up one learning till he masters the previous one. Hazrat Ali said: Don't conceal truth from men, rather know the truth, then you will be the master of truths.

(8) The eighth duty of a student is to know the causes for which noble sciences are known. It can be known from two things, nobility of its fruit and the authenticity of its principles. Take for example the science of religion and medicine. The fruit of the science of religion is to gain an eternal life and the fruit of the other is to gain a temporary life. From these points of view, the science of religion is more noble as its result is more noble. Take up Mathematics and Astrology, the former is noble because the former is more authentic in its foundations. Form this it is clear that the science of the knowledge of God, of His angels of His books and of His prophets is the noblest also the branches of knowledge which help it.

(9) The ninth duty of a student is to purify mind and action with virtues, to gain proximity to God and His angels and to live in the company of those who live near Him. His aim should not be to gain worldly matters, to acquire riches and properties, to argue with the illiterate and to show pride and haughtiness. He whose object is to gain nearness of God should seek such learning as helps towards that goal, namely the knowledge of the hereafter and the learnings which are auxiliary to it. God said: God will raise herewith in rank who are believers and to whom knowledge have been given (58 : 11). God said: They have got ranks to God. In short, the ranks of the learned have got stages, some lower, some higher. The highest rank is that of the Prophets, then of the friends of God and then of the learned who are firm in knowledge and then of the pious who follow them.

(10) The tenth duty of a student is that he should keep attention to the primary object of knowledge. It is not in your power to enjoy bliss of this world and that of the next world together. This world is a temporary abode. Body is a conveyance and the actions run towards the goal. The goal is God and nothing else. All bliss and

happiness lie in Him. So give more importance to the sciences which take to that ultimate goal.

There are three kinds of learnings

(1) One kind of learning is like the purchase of commodities in journey. They are the sciences of medicine, laws (Fiqh) and all other sciences which keep connection with the welfare of the people in the world.

(2) Another class of learning is like the science of travelling in the desert and surrounding obstacles. They purify the mind from evil traits and take it to a high place that does not fall to the lot of any except those whom God shows favour.

(3) The third kind of knowledge is like the knowledge of pilgrimage and its rules and regulations. This is the science of knowledge of God. His attributes and the knowledge of the actions of angels. This is the knowledge which can not be gained except by the agnostics who are close to Him. Those who are lower in rank than them will get also salvation. God says:

As for one who is of those nearest to God, there is happiness, bounty and garden of bliss for him. But as for one who is the companion of the right hand there is peace for him (56 : 87). This is a certain truth which they perceived through contemplations. This is more clear than seeing with eyes. They are confirmed in their faith after seeing for themselves. Others are like those who have got faith but without contemplation and without seeing with their own eyes.

By the soul, I don't mean heart made up of flesh but it is a subtle or secret essence which the bodily senses fail to perceive. It is a spiritual substance from God and has been described sometimes by Nafs, sometimes by Qalb. The material heart is the vehicle for the spiritual essence to remove the veil from it who are firm in knowledge and then of the pious who follow them.

(10) The tenth duty of a student is that he should keep attention to the primary object of knowledge. It is not in your power to enjoy bliss of this world and that of the next world together. This world is

a temporary abode. Body is a conveyance and the actions run towards the goal. The goal is God and nothing else. All bliss and happiness lie in Him. So give more importance to the sciences which take to that ultimate goal. There are three kinds of learnings.

(1) One kind of learning is like the purchase of commodities in journey. They are the sciences of medicine, laws (Fiqh) and all other sciences which keep connection with the welfare of the people in the world.

(2) Another class of learning is like the science of travelling in the desert and surrounding obstacles. They purify the mind from evil traits and take it to a high place that does not fall to the lot of any except those whom God shows favour.

(3) The third kind of knowledge is like the knowledge of pilgrimage and its rules and regulations. This is the science of knowledge of God. His attributes and the knowledge of the actions of angels. This is the knowledge which can not be gained except by the agnostics who are close to Him. Those who are lower in rank than them will get also salvation. God says: As for one who is of those nearest to God, there is happiness, bounty and garden of bliss for him. But as for one who is the companion of the right hand there is peace for him (56 : 87). This is a certain truth which they perceived through contemplations. This is more clear than seeing with eyes. They are confirmed in their faith after seeing for themselves. Others are like those who have got faith but without contemplation and without seeing with their own eyes.

By the soul, I don't mean heart made up of flesh but it is a subtle or secret essence which the bodily senses fail to perceive. It is a spiritual substance from God and has been described sometimes by Nafs, sometimes by Qalb. The material heart is the vehicle for the spiritual essence to remove the veil from it

as it belongs to the science of revelation, a science which is withheld from men and there is no permission to discuss it. What is permissible is the discussion that it is a precious jewel and belongs to the world of spirit and not to the world of matter. God says: They ask you about soul. Say: Soul proceeds from the command of my Lord- 17 : 87. The connection of soul with God is nobler than that of all the bodily limbs. To God belong the creation and the command (7 : 52), but the latter is greater. The command is the most precious thing which can carry the trust of God. It is nobler than the heaven and the earth and what they contain as the latter refused to bear the trust out of fear of the spiritual world. It has come from God and it will return to God. It is the spiritual substance which drives towards God.

Second Subject-Duties of a Teacher

A man has got four conditions in relation to wealth. A wealthy man at first produces commodities. Secondly, he hoards his productions and does not seek the aid of others. Thirdly, he spends it for himself and rests satisfied with it. Fourthly, he spends therefrom for another to get honour. The last is the best. Similar are the conditions of knowledge. It is acquired like wealth and has got four conditions-(1) condition of acquisition of knowledge, (2) condition after acquisition of knowledge, (3) condition wherein he will contemplate and enjoy his achievement, and (4) condition wherein he would impart his knowledge to others and this last condition is the best. He who acquires knowledge and acts up to it and teaches it to the people is noble to the angels of heaven and earth. He is like the sun which illumines itself and gives light to other things. Such a man is like a pot of musk which is full of fragrance and give fragrance to others. He who teaches knowledge to others but does not himself act up to it is like a notebook which does not benefit itself but benefits others or like an instrument which gives edge to iron but itself has got no knowledge_ or like a needle which remains naked but sews clothing for others, or like a lamp which gives light to other things but itself burns. A poet said: Knowledge without action is like a glowing wick, It gives light to others but itself dies burning. Whoever takes up the profession of teaching should observe the following duties:

(1) He will show kindness and sympathy to the students and treat them as his own children . The Prophet said: I am to you like a

father to his son. His object should be to protect the students from the fire of Hell. As parents save their children from the fire of this world, so a teacher should save his students or disciples from the fire of Hell. The duties of a teacher are more than those of parents. A father is the immediate cause of this transient life, but a teacher is the cause of immortal life. It is because of the spiritual teacher that hereafter is much remembered. By teacher, I mean the teacher of the sciences of the hereafter or the sciences of the world with the object of the hereafter. A teacher ruins himself and also his students if he teaches for the sake of the world. For this reason, the people of the hereafter are journeying towards the next world and to God and remain absent from the world. The months and years of this world are so many stations of their journey. There is no miserliness in the fortunes of the next world and so there is no envy among them. They turn to the verse: "The believers are brethren"(49 : 10).

(2) The second duty of a teacher is to follow the usages and ways of the Prophet. In other words, he should not seek remuneration for teaching but nearness to God therefor. God instructs us to say: I don't want any remuneration for this from you (9 : 31). Wealth and property are the servants of body which is the vehicle of soul of which the essence is know ledge and for which there is honour of soul. He who seeks wealth in lieu of knowledge is like one Who has got his face besmeared with impurities but wants to cleanse his body. In that case, the master is made a servant and the servant a master.

(3) The third duty of a teacher is that he should not withhold from his students any advice. After he finishes the outward sciences, he should teach them the inward sciences. He should tell them that the object of education is to gain nearness of God, not power or riches and that God created ambition as a means of perpetuating knowledge which is essential for these sciences.

(4) The fourth duty of a teacher is to dissuade his students from evil ways with care and caution, with sympathy and not with rebuke and harshness, because in that case it destroys the veil of awe and encourages disobedience. The Holy Prophet is the guide

of all teachers. He said: If men had been forbidden to make Porridge of camel's dung, they would have done it saying that they would not have been forbidden to do it unless there had been some good in it.

(5) The fifth duty of a teacher is that he shall not belittle the value of other science before his students. He who teaches grammar naturally thinks the science of jurisprudence as bad and he who teaches jurisprudence discourages the science of traditions and so on. Such evils are blameworthy. In fact the teachers of one learning should prepare his students for study of other learnings and then he should observe the rules of gradual progress from one stage to another.

(6) The sixth duty that a teacher should do is to teach his students up to the power of their understanding. The students should not be taught such things as are beyond the capacity of their understanding. In this matter, he should follow the Prophet who said: We prophets form one

class. We have been commanded to give every man his rightful place and to speak to men according to their intellect. The Prophet said: When a man speaks such a word to a people who cannot grasp it with their intellect , it becomes a danger to some persons. Hazrat Ali said pointing out to his breast: There is much knowledge in it, but then there should be some people to understand it. The hearts of pious men are graves of secret matters. From this, it is understood that whatever the teacher knows should not all be communicated to the students at the same time. Jesus Christ said: Don't hang pearls around the neck of a swine. Wisdom is better than pearls. He who knows it as bad is worse than swine. Once a learned man was questioned about something but he gave no reply. The questioner said: Have you not heard that the Prophet said: He who conceals any useful knowledge will on the Resurrection Day be bridled with a bridle of fire? The learned man said: You may place the bridle of fire and go. If I don't disclose it to one who uderstands it, then put the bridle of fire upon me. God said: Don't give to the fools your property 4:4. There is warning in this verse that it is better to safeguard knowledge from those who might be corrupted by it. To give a thing to one who is not fit for it and not to give a thing to one who is fit for it are equally oppression. A certain poet therefore said:

Should I cast pearls before the illiterate shepherds? They will not understand, nor know their worth.

If God by His knowledge sends one with knowledge, I will give my goods to him, and gain his love. He wastes his learning who gives it to one unworthy. He commits sin who withholds it from one worthy.

(7) The seventh duty of a teacher is that he should teach his backward students only such things as are clear and suited to their limited understanding. Every man thinks that his wisdom is perfect and the greatest fool is he who rests satisfied with the knowledge that his intellect is perfect. In short, the door of debates should not be opened before the common men.

(8) The eighth duty of a teacher is that he should himself do what he teaches and should not give a lie to his teaching. Knowledge can be grasped by internal eye and actions by external eye. Many people have got external eyes but very few have got internal eyes. So if the actions of a teacher are contrary to what he preaches, it does not help towards guidance, but it is like poison. A teacher is like a stamp to clay and a student is like clay. If the stamp has no character, there is no impression on clay. Or he is like a cane and the student is like the shadow of the cane. How can the shadow of the cane be straight when the cane itself is crooked? God said: Do you enjoin good to the people and forget it for yourselves (2:44). Hadrat Ali said: Two men have broken my back, the learned man who ruins himself and the fool who adopts asceticism. The learned man misleads the people through his sin and the fool through his evil action.

SECTION – VI

Evils of knowledge and signs of the learned men of the hereafter

We have enumerated the excellence of knowledge and learned men, but a great warning has come about the dishonest learned men. For this reason, one should know the differences of the learned men of this world and the learned men of the hereafter. What I mean by the learned man of the world is that his object of learning is to live in ease and comforts and to get honour and prestige from the people. The Prophet said: The most severely punished among men on the Day of Resurrection will be a learned man whom God has not blessed on account of his knowledge. The Prophet said: Nobody can be learned unless he puts his learning into practice. He said: Knowledge is of two kinds-knowledge by tongue which is open proof of God for the children of Adam and the science of soul which is useful. He said: In the later days, there will be ignorant worshippers and sinning learned men. He said: Don't acquire knowledge to boast over the learned, nor dispute with the ignorant and gain popularity among the people. He who does this will go to Hell. He said: He who conceals his knowledge will be given by God a bridle of fire. He said: I fear most for one who appears as Anti-Christ than Anti-Christ himself. Someone asked him: Who is he? He said: I fear most for the misguided leaders. He said: He whose knowledge is great but guidance less is away from God. Jesus Christ said: How can you guide the night travellers along the right way when you yourself are perplexed? These and other traditions show that a learned man faces eternal happiness or eternal damnation.

Sayings of Wise Men

Hazrat Osman said: I fear most for this nation the hypocrite learned men. People asked: How can a hypocrite be a learned man? He replied: He has verbal knowledge, but his mind and his actions are ignorant. Hazrat Hasan Basri said: Don't be included within those persons who are learned in wisdom and knowledge but are equal to the ignorant in actions. Khalid-b-Ahmed said: There are four kinds of men-(1) One who has real knowledge and knows that he knows. He is a real learned man. (2) One who has knowledge but he does not know that he knows. Be careful of him. (3) One who has no knowledge and knows that he does not know. Such a man is fit to be guided, so guide him. (4) One who has no knowledge and does not know that he knows not. Leave him alone. Ibn Mubarak said: A man is learned till he searches for knowledge. When he thinks that he has knowledge, he becomes ignorant. Hazrat Hasan said: Death of the heart is the punishment of a learned man. The death of the heart is search of the world with the actions of the hereafter. A poet said:

Woe to one who buys misguidance in lieu of guidance; Woe more to one who buys the world in lieu of the hereafter; Woe still more to one who fosters ir-religion in lieu of religion.

The Prophet said regarding a wicked learned man: Some learned men will suffer such intense agonies of torture that the inmates of Hell will seek refuge on seeing their tortures. They are the wicked learned men. The Prophet said: On the Resurrection Day, a learned man will be brought and will be thrown into Hell. His bowels will gush forth and he will roam with his bowels as a donkey moves round a millstone. The inmates of Hell will move along with him and ask: What is the matter with you? He will reply: I used to enjoin the people to do good but I was not myself accustomed to do it. I used to prohibit them evil but I myself used to do it. God says : The hypocrites will remain in the lowest abyss of Hell (4 : 144) as they refused to accept truth after they acquired knowledge.

There is a story of Balam-b-Bauza about whom the Quran says: Narrate to them the story of one to whom I revealed My signs. He rejected them. So the devil followed him and he became one of those who were misguided. He is therefore like a dog which lulls out its tongue whether you chase it or leave it alone (7:175). This has been said about the wicked learned man. Balam also got God's book but he kept himself busy in worldly affairs and was therefore likened to a dog. Jesus Christ said: The wicked learned man is like a rock which has fallen into the source of a stream. It neither absolves any water itself, nor permits it to flow out and reach the plants. The wicked learned man is also like pipes which come out of a garden full of stench smell as it has got graves of dead men. Its outer part is cultivated but its inner part is full of dead men's bones.

These traditions and historical narratives show that the learned man who is given to lust and worldly love will be disgraced and put to endless tortures and one who is a learned man of the hereafter will get salvation and gain nearness of God.

Signs of the Learned Man of the Hereafter

There are many signs of the teamed man of the hereafter. (1) First Sign. He does not seek the world by his learning. He considers the world as insignificant and the hereafter as great and everlasting. He considers this world and the next world as diametrically opposed to each other like two hostile friends of a man, or like two co-wives. If one friend or co-wife is pleased, the other friend or co-wife becomes displeased. The two worlds are like two scales of a balance, the lower the one falls, the other rises up higher. Or they are like the east and the west. The more one advances towards the east, the more he goes distant from the west. Or the two worlds are like two pitchers, one is full and another empty. The more you pour water from the full pitcher into the empty one, the more the full pitcher will become less and the empty one more in water. There is defect in the intellect of a man who has not come to know that the happiness of this world will soon pass away, as this matter has been established as true by veritable sights and experiences. He who does not recognise the grave nature and stability of the next world is an unbeliever bereft of faith. He who does not consider this world and the next world as opposed to each other does not know the religion of the Prophets and does not believe the Quran from first to last. Such a learned man is not included within the category of the learned men of the hereafter. He who knows these things but does not love the next world more than this world is in the hand of the devil.

God said in the scripture of David: If any learned man loves his passion more than his love for Myself, My treatment with him is that I deprive him of the pleasure of communion with me. O David, don't take the message of God to such a learned man. The world captivated him and he will turn you from My love. Such a man is a robber in the pathway of My servants. When you see such a man who searches Me, he is a true servant, O David, I write one as a man of sound judgement who flees towards Me. I will never punish such a person. For this reason, Hasan Basri said: Death of the heart is the punishment of a learned man and death of the heart means search of this world in exchange of the actions of the next world. Hazrat Ihya-b-Mu'az said: When the world is sought by learning and wisdom, his light goes gradually. Hazrat Sayeed-Musayyeb said: When you see a learned man frequenting the houses of rulers, he is a robber. Hazrat Umar said: When you see a learned man addicted to this world, disregard him for the sake of your religion, because every learned man is addicted to his object of love. The saint Sahal Tastari said: Every branch of learning is worldly except the learning of religion which, if put into practice, is next worldly. Every action without sincerity is faithless. He also said: All are dead except the learned. All teamed men are in a state of stupefaction except those who translate their learning into practice. All the learned men who translate their learning into practice are in error except those who are sincere. Those learned men who are sincere are in fear till they come to know their ultimate good end. Jesus Christ said: How can a man be counted as a learned man who persists in the pathways of this world although his journey is towards the next world? The Prophet said: He who searches learning in which there is pleasure of God but by which he seeks worldly honour will not get fragrance of Paradise on the Resurrection Day. God says of the dishonest learned men: They devour this world in lieu of learning. He described the learned men of the hereafter as God-fearing and given to asceticism. God says regarding the learned men of the world: God took oath from the People of the Book that they would disclose it to the people and would not conceal it, but they threw it behind their backs and sold it for a small price (3 : 184). God says regarding the learned men of the next world: There are such men among the People of the Book who believe in what was revealed to them and what has been revealed to you. They don't sell the verses of God for a small price Their reward is near their Lord (3: 198).

The Prophet said: God sent revelation to a people: Those who learn jurisprudence for an object other than that of religion and those who search the world with the actions of the next world are like those who wear the dress of goat's skin before the people but whose hearts are like the raving wolves. Their tongues are sweeter than honey but their hearts are more bitter than colocynth. They deceive Me and scorn Me. I will create such a calamity for them which will perplex even the patient. The Prophet said: The learned men of my followers are of two kinds. God gives to one kind learning which they distribute among the people and for which they do not covet anything and they do not sell it for a small price. The birds in the horizon, the fish in water, all the animals in the world, and the honourable scribes invoke blessings for them. They will come to God being honoured on the Resurrection Day and they will even get the company of the Prophets.

God gives learning to another kind of men but they are miser to distribute it to the people. They take wealth in its exchange and sell it for a small price. Such people will be brought on the Resurrection Day with bridles of fire and they will raise up shrieks before all the creatures. It will be proclaimed: They are children of so and so. God gave them learning but they were miser in distributing it to the people and took small price in lieu thereof and property in exchange. Thus they will be punished till God finishes the judgment of account.

A more severe punishment will be meted out to the following kind of people. A certain man was a servant of Prophet Moses. He went round saying: Moses, the chosen man of God, told me this. Moses, the confidant of God, told me this. Moses, the intimate friend of God, told me this. Saying these, he became rich and then disappeared. Moses searched for him but his whereabouts were not found. Sometime after, a man came to Moses with a pig with a rope tied to its neck. Moses said to him: Do you know such and such a person? He said: Yes, he is this pig. Moses said to him: O Lord, turn him into his former position. I shall ask him about his condition. God revealed to him. If you remember Me with what Adam and his successors remembered Me, I shall not accept your invocation. I shall inform you how he was changed to this condition. He searched for the world in lieu of religion.

A more severe narration was reported by Mu'az-b-Jabal to the effect that the Prophet had said: One danger of a learned man is that he would prefer talking than hearing, as there is ornamentation and exaggeration in his speech. A speaker is not free from these faults but there is safety and wisdom in silence. There is such a man among the learned who guards his learning but does not like to communicate it to others. Such a learned man is in the first stage of Hell. There is such a man among the learned who is like a king in learning. In other words, if any objection is raised against learning, he becomes angry. He is in the second stage of Hell. There is such a man among the learned who broadcasts his learning and narrates traditions to the rich and not to those who are in need of them. Such a learned man is in the third stage of Hell.

There is such a man among the learned who remains busy with legal decisions and commits mistakes and remains satisfied with one who does divine service. Such a learned man is in the fourth stage of Hell. There is such a man among the learned who delivers lectures quoting the sayings of the Jews and Christians to show his learning. Such a learned man is in the fifth stage of Hell. There is such a man among the learned who delivers lectures with pride and self-conceit and considers his speech as good and when any other man delivers lectures, he sneers at him. Such a learned man is in the seventh stage of Hell.

There is in Hadis: If a man is praised so much that it fills up what is between the east and the west, it is not valuable to God even like the wing of a mosquito. The Prophet said: Don't sit with every learned man. Sit with the learned man who calls towards five matters-towards faith from doubt, sincerity from show, modesty from pride, love from enmity, and asceticism from worldliness.

(2) **Second sign.** The second sign of the learned man of the next world is that his words and actions are the same, rather he does not order an action to be done without first doing it himself. God says: **Will you enjoin the people to do good deeds** but forget them for yourselves (2 : 41)? God says: It is a hateful thing to God that you say what you do not do 61 : God says in the story of Shuaib: I don't wish to do anything which I myself forbid you (9 : 90). God says: Fear God and He will give you knowledge (2 : 282).

God says: Fear God and you will know-(2 : 120). God says: Fear God and listen (5 : 11). God said to Jesus Christ: O son of Mary, take lessons to yourself and then give admonition to others, otherwise you will be ashamed of Me. The Prophet said: I passed by a party of men in the night of my ascension to heaven. Their tongues were being cut with scissors. I asked them: Who are you? They said: We used to give advice to others for good deeds but we used not to do them. We used to prohibit evil deeds to others, but we used to do them.

The Prophet said: The corrupt learned men and illiterate worshippers will be the cause of destruction of my people. The Prophet once came to his companions and said: Take to learning as far as possible, but God will not give its rewards till you translate it into action. Jesus Christ said: He who teaches good but does not translate it into action is like a woman who commits fornication in secret and becomes pregnant but when her pregnancy is exposed, she becomes repentant. God will disgrace one before all people on the Resurrection Day who does not act according to his learning. Hazrat Mu'az said: Beware of the learned man's error, because he is the most honoured one among the people and because the people follow his error. Hazrat Umar said: Three things will cause the end of time. One of them is the error of the learned men. Hazrat Ibn Mas'ud said : Soon there will come a time over the people when sweetness of heart will vanish. At that time neither the teachers, nor the taught will get any benefit from learning. The hearts of the learned will be hard like a hard stone Rains will fall on it from the sky but it will slip away therefrom. The reason is that the hearts of the learned will be addicted to the love of this world in preference to that of the next world. God will then rob them of the fountain of wisdom and extinguish the light of guidance from their hearts. They will say to you by their tongue 'Fear God' but sin will be exposed in their actions. Tongue will then become dry and heart hard. The only reason is that the teachers will teach except for the sake of God. There is written in the Torah and Bible: Don't search for learning which you do not know till you do what you know. Hazrat Huzaifa said: You are now in an age wherein if you give up one tenth of what you know, you will perish, but their will soon come an age wherein if a man does one-tenths of what he knows he will get salvation.

The simile of the learned man is that of a judge. The Prophet said: Judges are of three classes. One class of judges judge with justice and with knowledge of truth and they will go to Paradise. Another class of judges judge unjustly with or without knowledge of truth and they will go to Hell. Another class of judges judge contrary to the laws of God and they will go to, Hell. The Prophet said: The devil sometimes will prevail over you on account of knowledge. It was questioned: O Prophet of God, how will it happen? He said: The devil will say: Search for knowledge but don't put it into practice till you acquire it. So he will remain busy with acquisition of knowledge but will remain without action up to his death and at the time of his death he will have no action. Hazrat Ibn Mas'ud said: The Quran was revealed in order that men may direct their lives according to its teachings. Direct your life according as you read it. There will soon appear such men who will keep it like an arrow and they are not good among you. The learned man who does not act up to his knowledge is like a patient who describes the qualities of a medicine without using it or like a hungry man who describes the taste of a food without eating it. God said: Woe unto you for what you utter. The Prophet said: What I fear most for my followers is the errors of the learned and the arguments of the hypocrites about the Quran.

(3) **Third sign.** Another sign of the learned man of the next world is that his mind would be directed towards such learning as will be useful for the next world and give encouragement to pious deeds. He will avoid those learnings which will bring lesser benefit and wherein there are much arguments. He who shuns the learning of practice and remains busy in arguments is like a sick man who suffers from many diseases, but when he fears death, he goes to an experienced physician and asks him many questions of the qualities of drugs and complexities of medical profession but he does not ask him about his diseases. This is the height of foolishness.

One day a man came to the Apostle of God and said: Teach me

some of the strange things of knowledge. He asked him: What have you done with the beginning of knowledge? The man said: What is the beginning of knowledge? The Prophet replied: Have you known God? He §aid: Yes. He asked: What have you learned about this truth? He said: What God willed. The Prophet said: Have you known death? He said :Yes. He said: How have you prepared for it? He said: What God willed. The Prophet said: Go and gain experience of these things first and then I shall teach you some of the strange things of knowledge.

A student should be like Hadrat Hatem Asem who was the disciple of Hadrat Shaqiq Balakhi. He once asked Hatem: How long are you in my company? Hatem said: For the last 33 years. He said: What have you learned from me during this period? Hatem said: I have learned only eight things. Shaqiq said: You have not learned except eight things. He said: Yes, O dear teacher, I have learned nothing except eight things. I don't wish to speak falsehood. He said: Describe those eight things to me. Let me hear them. Hatem began to describe them.

First, I looked around and beheld that every man has got an object of love and he lives with that thing until his death. When he goes to the grave, it becomes separate from him. I pondered over the following words of God– "We are for God and to Him we shall return." So I have made good deeds as my object of love. When I will go to the grave, my good deeds will accompany me to the grave. The sage Shaqiq said: O Hatem, you have done well.

Second, I have pondered over the following words of God: "As for one who fears the majesty of his Lord and refrains his soul from lust, paradise is his resting place— 79:40. 1 have come to know that the words of God are true. I have tried my utmost to suppress my lust and remained satisfied with obeying the injunctions of God.

Third, I looked around the people and found that ever one values what he possesses. Then I turned to the following words of God: What is with you will end and what is with God will last- 16: 98. Than I began to give unto God whatever valuable things fell into my hands.

Fourth, I looked around and saw that everyone puts his trust in his wealth and properties, his name and fame and his honour and glory and found that there is nothing in them. Then I looked towards the following words of God: "The most honourable of you to God is one who is the most God-fearing among you"- 49: 13. Then I intended to accept God-fear in my life till I am honoured by God.

Fifth, I looked around the people and found them slandering and cursing one another because of envy and hatred and then I looked towards the words of God: "It is I who distributed their subsistence among them in this world's life"- 43 : 71. So I gave up envy and hatred and realised that subsistence comes from God and then I disliked the people more.

Sixth, I looked to the people and found them ungrateful to one another and even some of them kill others and then I looked towards the following words of God: The devil is your foe and so take him as foe- 35 : 6 . So I took the devil as a foe and ceased to have enmity with the people.

Seventh, I turned to the people and found everyone seeking his livelihood and for that debasing himself and committing unlawful things and then I looked towards the following words of God: There is no animal in the earth of which the provision is not upon God- 11 : 8 . Finding that I am one of the animals whose provision is upon God, I turned towards the duties prescribed by God and entrusted my fate unto Him.

Eighth, I turned to the people and found that everyone placed his trust in something created, some in his wealth, some in his profession, some in his industry and some in the health of his body and then looked towards the following words of God: If a man relies on God, He is sufficient for him- 65 : 3 Then I relied on God and He is sufficient for me.

On hearing Hatem, Hadrat Shaqiq exclaimed: Hatem, may God prosper you. I examined the Torah, the Bible, the Zabur (Psalms) and the great Quran and found that all these centre round these eight things and he who puts them into practice follows these four books.

In short, the learned men of the hereafter seek and acquire

knowledge but the learned men of the world are engaged in acquiring wealth and name and fame and give up those learnings for which God sent the Prophets.

(4) **Fourth sign.** Another sign of the learned man of the next world is that he has got no attraction for various kinds of foods and drinks, luxury in dresses, furniture and houses, but rather he adopts moderate course in all these things following the earlier sages and he is best satisfied with the least of everything. The less a man is attracted towards luxuries , the more he will be close to God and the more he will be in association of the learned men of the hereafter and in rank.

Abdullah-b-Khawas used to keep company with Hadrat Hatem Asem and he said: Once I with 320 pilgrims went to Rayy along with the sage Hatem Asem. We had food stuffs with us and not food. We went to a merchant who was well known for love of the poor. We became his guests that night. He said next day to the sage Hatem: Have you got any necessity with me? I wish now to go to see an ailing theologian. Hatem said: Visiting the sick is no doubt meritorious but looking after the poor is worship. I will go along with you. The sick man was Muhammad-b-Maqatil, judge of Rayy. When we came near his gate, we looked at his lofty and beautiful palace. Hatem thought for a moment and then said: Is this the condition of the house of a learned man? After permission, we entered the house and found it very beautiful and spacious with carpets spread all over the floor and screens of varied colours hanging. The judge lay down on a soft mattress and a servant was standing with a fan near his head. The merchant asked about his health but Hatem stood silent. Being requested to sit, he did not sit but asked the judge: From whom have you got your learning? He said: From the companions of the Apostle of God. He asked him: From whom did the companions learn? He said: From the Apostle of God. He asked: From whom did the Apostle of God learn? He said: From Gabriel and he learned from God. Hatem asked: Have you found in their learnings that to God the rank of a man whose palace is high and spacious is greater? He said: No. He asked: What then have you found? The judge said: I found therein that a man who renunciates the world, turns his attention towards the next world, loves the poor and proceeds towards the hereafter has got a great rank near God. Hatem said to the judge: Whom have you followed, prophets or their companions, or the pious men, or Pharaoh and Namrud who erected lofty buildings with bricks? The dishonest learned men like you are fools. Then he went away from that place.

Ibn Maqatil's sickness became thereafter acute and the inhabitants of Rayy came to know what passed between him and Hatem. They said to Hatem: The palace of Tanafusi and Qazawin is more lofty and spacious. Hatem went there on his own accord and said to Tanafusi: May God have mercy on you! I am a foreigner and I wish that you should teach me the elements of my religion and the particulars of ablution. Tanafusi said: Yes, O lad, bring a pot of water. When it was brought, Tanafusi made ablution and washed each limb thrice and said : This is thus. Hatem said: I am making ablution in your presence. Then he began to wash each limb four times. Tanafusi said: O Shaikh, you have been extravagant and washed your hands four times. Hatem said: O glorious God, I have been extravagant for washing my hands four times, but you do not consider yourself extravagant for what you are in all these luxuries. Tanafusi then came to know that he had no necessity of learning from him ablution. Thereafter he did not come out to the people for forty days.

Hatem once went to Baghdad and there Imam Ahmad went to see him and asked him: What will ensure salvation from the world? Hatem said: You are not safe in this world unless you possess four characteristics-(1) overlook the ignorance of man, (2) conceal your ignorance from them, (3) seek their good, and (4) don't seek anything from them.

When the sage Hatem went to Medina, some of its inhabitants went to him and he asked them: O people, what is the name of this city? They said: It is the city of the Prophet of God. He asked: Where is the palace of the Prophet of God? I shall observe my prayer therein. They said: He had no palace except a small cottage wherein he rested. He asked: Where are the palaces of his companions? They said: They had no palaces. They had only cottages in this world for rest. Hatem said: O people, this city then is the city of Pharaoh. They brought him before the Governor and said: This man is a foreigner and says that this is the city of Pharaoh. The governor asked him: Why do you utter this? Hatem said: Don't be hasty in judgement upon me. I am a foreigner. Then he narrated the whole conversation between him and some Medinites. Then he said: God said: You will find in the Prophet of God an excellent example (33:21) Whose example have you adopted, example of the Prophet or of Pharaoh ? They then left hire. These are the stories of Hatem Asem.

In short, use of ornamentation in permissible things is not unlawful but it creates fondness for these and to give them up at the end becomes difficult. The Prophet did not lay stress for renunciation of the world. It has been narrated that Caliph Yahya-b-Sayeed once wrote to Imam Malek-b-Anas saying: In the name of God, the Most Merciful, the Most Compassionate and blessings on Prophet Muhammad. From Yahya-b-Sayeed to Malek-b-Anas: I have been informed that you put on fine clothes , eat delicious foods, sleep on soft couches and keep a doorkeeper at your door. You sit in the assembly of learning and people come to you from distant places. They have taken you as Imam and they are satisfied with your words. O Malek, fear God, take to humility. I write to you this letter as an admonition. None has seen its contents except God. Imam Malek wrote back saying: I have received your letter and it has come to me as an admonition, kindness and a sign of good conduct. May God bless your piety and reward you for your advice. I seek His help. There is no power and might except by His help. We do what you have mentioned but beg forgiveness of God for them. God said: Who has made unlawful the fineries of God which God has gifted to His servants and clean and pure foods- 7 : 32 1 know certainly that abstinence from these things is better than indulging in them. Don't give up writing to me. Peace be on you. See then the sense of justice which Imam Malek showed. He did not make the fineries of the world unlawful but admitted that abstinence from luxuries is better.

(5) **Fifth sign.** Another sign of the learned man of the hereafter is

that he keeps himself distant from the ruling authorities and avoids their company, because this world is sweet, ever-new and its bridle is in their hands. He who comes near them is not free from their pleasures and harms. They are mostly unjust and do not obey the advices of the learned men. The learned man who frequents them will look to their grandeurs and then think God's gift upon him as insignificant. To keep company with the rulers is the key to evils. The Prophet said : He who lives in desert becomes hard-hearted, he who follows them becomes unmindful and he who frequents the rulers falls into danger. He said also: Soon you will have rulers to whom you will bear allegiance or not. He who rejects his allegiance to them will be saved and he who hates them will be safe but God will keep him distant who remains satisfied with them and follows them. He was asked: Shall we fight with them ? The Prophet said: No, till they pray.

Hazrat Huzaifa said: Be careful of the place of danger. He was asked. What is it? He said: The palaces of the rulers. Some one of you will go to a ruler, approve his lies and say that he possesses an attribute which he does not actually possess. The Prophet said: The learned are the representatives of the Prophets to the people till they do not mix with the rulers. When they mix, they commit treachery with the Prophets. So beware of them and don't mix with them. Hazrat Sayeed-b-Musayyeb said: When you see a learned man frequenting the house of a ruler, beware of his company as he is a thief. Hazrat Aozayi said: There is nothing more hateful to God than a learned man who frequents the house of a ruler. The Prophet said: The learned men who frequent the houses of rulers are worst and the rulers who frequent the houses of the learned men are best. Hazrat Maqhul said: He who learns the Quran and becomes expert in religious learning but comes to the company of the rulers out of greed is immersed in the sea of Hell-fire. When you see a learned man loving the world, convert him to your religion because I have learnt it by experience.

Hazrat Hasan Basri said: There lived before your time a man who was born in Islam and enjoyed the company of the Prophet. He is Sa'ad-b.-Abi Waqqas. He did not frequent the houses of rulers and hated it. His sons said to him: Those who are like you in following Islam and keeping company with the Prophet frequent the houses of rulers. It would have been better if you frequent their houses. He said: O dear sons, the world is a corpse and the people surround it. By God. I will not be a partner to it even if I am able to do it. They said: O father, you will then die of starvation. He said: O sons, I would rather starve to death than die as a great man with hypocrisy. Hazrat Hasan used to say to the opposing parties: By God, know that earth will consume the flesh and fat but not faith. Hazrat Umar-b-Abdul Aziz wrote a letter to Hasan Basri saying:

(6) **Sixth sign.** Another sign of the learned man of the hereafter is that he does not give Fatwa or legal decision in a hurry but tarries to be relieved of it. When he is asked about a matter known to him from the Quran, Hadis, Ijma and Qiyas, he gives opinion. When he has doubt, he says: I don't know. When he is asked about a matter about which he has formed an opinion through Ijtihad, independent interpretation and speculation, he is careful not to commit himself but refer the matter to someone else who is more capable than himself. According to one tradition: There are three roots of learning, the express word of the Quran, the lasting usage of the Prophet (and another root is unknown to me-reporter). The sage Shubi said: 'I don't know' is half of learning. He who remains silent for God owing to his ignorance gets reward not less than that of the man who does not remain silent, because to confess one's ignorance is the most difficult thing. Such was the condition of companions of the Prophet and the earlier sages. When Ibn Umar was asked any question, he would say: Go to the ruler, because he has taken the affairs of men. Hazrat Ibn Mas'ud said: He who gives opinion as soon as a question is put to him is mad. He also said: 'I don't know' is the shield of a learned man. If he commits mistakes, it would amount to murder.

Ibrahim-b-Adham said: There is nothing more formidable to the devil than a learned man who manifests his knowledge both openly and silently. The devil says: Look to this man. His silence is severe to me than his speech.

Some wise man said: There are Abdals (worshippers) in the world.

Their meal ends when they are still hungry. They sleep when it overcomes them. Their words end only in necessary talks. In other words, they do not speak unless asked and they remain silent when sufficient reply is obtained from others.

When compelled, they reply. Ibn Umar used to say: Do you wish to use us as a bridge over which you wish to cross over to Hell. Abu Hafs Nishapuri said: A learned .man is he who fears the day of questions, who fears that he will be asked on the Resurrection Day: Wherefrom have you got this answer? The Prophet said: I don't know whether Uzair was a Prophet or not, whether Tubba was accursed or not, whether Zul-Qamair was a Prophet or not. When asked about the best and worst places on the earth, the Prophet said: I don't know. But the Almighty God said to me that the best place is mosque and the worst place is market. When Hazrat Ibn Umar was asked ten questions, he replied only one and not others. Hazrat Ibn Abbas replied nine and did not reply one. Someone said that among the jurists, the greater number were men who used to say 'we don't know' than the numbers who used to say `we know'. Sufiyan Saori said: Malek-b-Anas Ahmad-b-Hanbal, Fuzail, Bashar and others were among the former. Abdur Rahman-b-Abi Laila said: I met in this mosque 120 companions of the Prophet among whom there was none who when questioned to express an opinion would not have wished that someone else would reply to it. It is narrated that when somebody presented something to someone of Ahle Suffa, he would give it to another who would give it to another and so on, until it finally came back to the first one. Now see what was the condition of the learned men of that age and what is the condition now.

The Prophet said: Let not the people seek legal decision except from three persons, a ruler or a person to whom power is delegated or a religious man. Some one said: The companions used to refer to one another about four things **Imamate (leadership), Wasiat (legacy), safe (keeping), and Fatwa** (legal decision). Someone said: One who hurriedly used to give opinion was a less learned man. The activities of the companions and their followers were confined only to four things-reading the Quran, building mosques, Zikr of God and enjoining good, and forbidding evil. They heard the Prophet say: There is no good in most of their secret talks except only in his who enjoins alms-giving or what is right or concord among men. Hadrat lbn Hussain said: Any question of legal decision, when put to them, used to be placed before Hazrat Umar who used to call all the warriors who took part in the battle of Badr for consultation. The Prophet said: If you see a man adopting silence and asceticism, take advice from him, as he is not free from wisdom.

The learned men are of two kinds, a learned man for the public who is a Mufti or giver of legal decision and a companion of the ruler, and another learned man for Tauhid and good deeds and he resides in solitude. It is said that such a learned man was Imam Ahmad-b-Hanbal who was like the river Tigris and everyone used to take benefit from him. The sage Bashr-b-Hares was also like him. He was like a covered well of fresh water visited by a single person at a time. A wise man said: When knowledge increases, loquacity decreases.

If any question was put to Hazrat Abu Darda, he used to give no reply. When Hazrat Anas was asked anything, he used to say: Ask our leader Hazrat Abbas. When Hazrat Abbas was asked, he used to say: Ask Hares-b-Zaid. When lbn Umar was asked anything he used to say: Ask Sayeed-b-Musayyeb.

(7) **Seventh** sign. The seventh sign of the learned man of the next world is that his main object of anxiety is to learn secret knowledge, observation of the heart, knowledge of the paths of the hereafter, to travel thereon and to have abiding faith in finding self-mortification and observation, because self-mortification leads to Mushahadah or contemplation and lets flow the fountain of wisdom through the intricate details of the science of heart. Reading of books and learning of sciences are not sufficient for it but this wisdom appears as a result of hard labour. It opens if one sits in loneliness with God with a mind turned with humility of spirit towards God and through self-mortification, observation and watching. This is the key of

Ilham or inspiration and the fountainhead of Kashf or secret knowledge. Many students who have been learning for a long time could not move more than what they heard. There are many students who cut short their education and remain busy in action and observation of the heart. God opens for them the niceties of wisdom for which the wisdom of the wise becomes perplexed. For this reason, the Prophet said: If a man acts according to his learning. God gives him such a knowledge as was unknown to him. It was also mentioned in one of the books of ancient ages: O children of Israel. don't say that knowledge is in heaven. Who will bring it down to the earth? Don't say that knowledge is in the lowest abyss of the earth? Who will dig it out? Don't say that knowledge is far beyond the ocean. Who will bring it after crossing it?

Know, O dear readers that knowledge is in your hearts. Take its lesson from those who have got knowledge of soul or heart and make one's character like that of the Truthful and then knowledge will spring forth in heart, so much so that it will immerse him therein. Sahal Tastari said: The learned men, the worshippers and the ascetics departed from the world with their hearts locked up. They can not be opened except by the hearts of the truthful and martyrs. Then he recited this verse of God: To him are the keys of unseen things. None knows them but He (6 : 59). Had it not been for the fact that the light to the heart of one who has a heart with inner light determines the outward or esoteric knowledge, the Prophet would not have said: If they seek justice of you (thrice), ask your heart. The Prophet said that God said: A man continues to come close to Me with optional divine servings till I love him. When I love him. I become his ears with which he hears, etc. So many are the subtle meanings of the mysteries of the Quran that appear in the hearts of those persons who have devoted themselves to Zikr and meditation of God. It is not found in the commentaries and it also did not appear in the hearts of the reputed commentators. It appears as a result of the meditation of a devotee. When its meaning is presented to the commentators, they take it as good and realise that they are the news of a pure soul and a gift of God arising out of sincere devotion and reflection. The condition of secret knowledge, the science of practical religion and the subtleties of the flow of thoughts of the heart is similar. Each of these beneficial learnings is an ocean of which the depth is beyond reach. Each disciple gets its clue in proportion to his ability and good deeds.

Hazrat Ali said in the course of a long discourse about such men: Hearts are like different vessels and the best vessel is that which holds good things. Men are of three kinds-the divine learned men, the travellers to the path of salvation, and the ignorant people calling towards evils who are swayed by every passing wind. Their hearts are not illumined by the light of knowledge and stand not on its firm foundation. Knowledge is better than wealth. It guards you, but you guard wealth. Knowledge increases by expense, while wealth decreases Learning is knowledge by which religion is learnt and by which allegiance is obtained in your lifetime and which becomes a good thing to be remembered after your death. Knowledge is a judge and wealth seeks justice. Along with death, the benefits of wealth disappear, but the benefits of knowledge remain. All people are dead, but the learned are alive and will live as long as time shall last. Then taking a deep breath and pointing to his breast Hazrat Ali said: Alas, here is abundant knowledge, but I find none to carry it. I don't find any trusted seeker but I find such men who seek the world with the weapon of religion and attribute to the friends of God the gift's of God and give prevalence of His proof over His creations, make subdued the seekers of truth, but on the first onslaught of opposition doubt arises in their minds. They lose their insight owing to their scepticism and keep themselves busy in indulgences. They amass wealth and hoard it. O God, thus will knowledge perish when its people will die. The world will not be free of men who will establish religion secretly and openly in order that the proofs of God are not obliterated. They will be few in number but they will be great in honour. They will be lost openly, but their pictures will reign in hearts. God will preserve His religion through them. They will leave the religion for their successors and will plant it in the hearts of the young. The real nature of knowledge will be disclosed with their help. They will get good news from the life of sure faith. They will make easy what the rich think difficult and they will make clear what the heedless think obscure. They will keep company with the world with their bodies, but their souls will be kept hanging in lofty places. They are servants of God among His people, His trustees and deputies on the earth. Then he wept and said: How eager I am to meet them. These are the attributes of the learned men of the next world which can be gained by constant actions and sincere efforts.

(8) **Eighth sign.** Another sign of the learned man of the next world is that he is sincere and upright for making his faith firm and strong as firm faith is the root of religion. The Prophet said: Sure faith is belief in its entirety of perfect faith. So it is necessary to learn the learning of faith, after which the path of the heart will be opened. For this reason the Prophet said: Learn sure faith. In other words, keep company with those who have firm faith, hear from them the learning of sure faith, follow them always, so that your faith may become firm as their faith became firm. A little sure faith is better than many actions. When two persons, one of whose sure faith was good but whose sins more and another whose actions were more and faith little, were mentioned to the Prophet, he said: There is no man without sin. One whose intellect is short and faith sure cannot be injured by sin, because whenever he commits sin, he repents and seeks forgiveness. Thus his sins are expiated and his virtues remain intact and he enters paradise. For this reason, the Prophet said: Among the things you have been given, the least is firm faith and determination for patience. Whoever is given a special share of these two, has got faith even if he misses prayer at night and fasting by day. Luqman advised his son: O dear son, action is not possible except through firm faith in religion. A man cannot act except in proportion to his sure faith and his action does nut decrease except when his sure faith decreases. lhya Ibn Mu'az said: Tauhid (monotheism) has got light and Shirk (polytheism) fire. The light of Tauhid for the sins of monotheism is more warm than the fire of polytheists for their virtues. Here light means sure faith. God referred to those who have sure faith several times in the Quran and pointed out also that through faith they receive His blessings.

The reply to the question - What is meant by Yeqin or sure faith is as follows. The philosophers and the scholastic theologians say that its meaning is faith in objects beyond doubt. There are four states of a person when he is eager to know the truth of a thing. Firstly, when truth and falsehood are equal in the mind of a person. Such a state is called doubt. Secondly, if mind inclines more to a thing out of the two states and if mind knows that it may be otherwise, the first state will be stronger. For instance, if you are asked about a man who is in your sight pious and God-fearing, whether he will be punished or not, your mind inclines more to his not being punished as there are outward signs of his piety. Nevertheless you admit the possibility that something which requires punishment has been concealed in his secret life. This admission is mixed with your first inclination and creates in your mind conjecture. The third state is that the mind is strongly inclined to a thing and opinion adverse to it cannot come to it. This is called I'tiqad or belief approaching certainty. This is the conjecture of the general public about religious matters.

The fourth state is sure or certain faith in a matter without the least doubt in it. This is called 'Yeqin'. For instance, when a wise man is asked: "Is there anything eternal in existence" he cannot suddenly reply to it as the eternal thing is not subject to conjecture or perceived by the senses and it is not like the sun and the moon of which the truth can be perceived by eyes. So the existence of an eternal thing cannot suddenly be said to be true without thought. The truth of an eternal thing is not such as the truth that two is greater than one or as the truth that nothing can occur without a cause. Knowledge of these things come out spontaneously without the necessity of any thought. So true belief in the truth of an eternal thing does not come spontaneously in the mind. Those who have knowledge of an eternal thing tell the people of it and the people believe it and stand on it. This is called I'tiqad or faith. This is the state of all common people.

But there are such men who establish the truth of an eternal matter by such proof as follows. If there be no existence of an eternal thing, then all things are originated or created. If all the things are created, they come without cause or some of them come to existence without cause. This is impossible and that which leads to impossibility is itself impossible. Therefore the mind is compelled to believe in the existence of something eternal. All things fall under one of the three categories. (1) All existing things are eternal, (2) or all existing things are originated or created, (3) or somethings are eternal and somethings are originated. If all things are eternal, the object is attained as the truth of eternal things has been established by proof. But if all things are created, it becomes impossible as the existence of a thing becomes without a cause. In that case, either the first or the third position is established. The knowledge thus obtained through reasoning such as above or through the mind instinctively as the impossibility of any created thing coming into existence without a cause or through traditions as the knowledge that there is existence of Mecca, or through experimentation such as our knowledge that cooked scammony is purgative, or through some evidences as we have already stated, is called Yeqin or certain faith. 'The ordinary meaning of Yeqin is belief without doubt.

The second meaning of Yeqin is that of the jurists, sufis and most of the Darned men. It is not to look at a thing with conjecture or doubt. For instance, it is said that so and so has got weak faith about death, although there is no doubt in it. Another instance is that so and so has firm faith in earning wealth, although a time comes when he cannot even earn his livelihood. Thus whenever anything prevails over the mind and enjoins one to do and prohibits him not to do is called Yeqin or certain faith. All people believe firmly about death and it is free from doubt, but there are men who do not turn their attention to it and there are men who engage all their thoughts towards preparation for death. Such men are called men of strong faith. For this reason, some one said: I have seen nothing so certain and at the same time completely unheeded as death. According to this, faith may be described either with strength or with weakness. What I wish to impress is that the object of the learned man of the hereafter is to make his faith strong, certain and firm as it is a medicine of doubt, so that it becomes so strong in his mind that it can rule over him.

Thus it is clear from what has been described above that Yeqin can be described in three meanings-as to strength and weakness, increase and decrease and clearness -and vagueness.

What the Prophets said from the first to the last is a subject of certain faith. Yeqin is a work of special Marfat. These matters appertain to Shariat and I am mentioning some of these matters which are the roots of certain faith.

(1) **Tauhid.** This is to believe firmly that all things come from the Cause of all causes, with no attention to the secondary causes-but to the First Cause. It is not to look to the means or intermediaries but to the original and primary cause. It is that all causes come from Him and that everything is within His control and power. It is that everything is subject to His will and nothing has got any will of its own. If one has got sure faith in this Tauhid, his wrath on others, hatred for others and jealousy for others vanish away and His will remains supreme in his mind. Then to him, the means or intermediaries become like hand and pen. He does not express gratefulness to hand and pen as he considers them as weapons and means. This certain faith is highest in rank. Then he understands that the sun, moon, stars, animals, plants and all creatures are subject to His order, that the pen moves under the control of the writer who moves them. (2) From this, his faith that God provides every man with subsistences grows strong. God says: There is no moving animal in the earth whose provision is not upon God - 9 : 8 . He believes that what has been preordained for him must come to pass. The result of this certain faith is that he will not regret for anything he loses. (3) Then he believes firmly in the following: Whoever does an atom weight of good will find it and whoever does an atom weight of evil will find it -99 : 7. That is a faith of reward and punishment. As there is connection of bread with satisfaction of stomach and punishment with sins or poison with loss of life, so he finds connection of good deeds with rewards and of evil deeds with punishment. As there is greed to satisfy hunger whether its quantity is large or small, so he strives to do all acts of worship, whether few or many. Just as a man avoids poison regardless of quantity, so a man avoids sins, major or minor. Belief in its first meaning is found among all believers, while certain belief of the second meaning is found only in the favourites of God. The stronger the faith, the stronger is carefulness and the more are the religious actions.

Fourthly, he believes that God watches him in all circumstances and sees his currents of thoughts in mind and machinations of the devil. This certain faith is in accordance with the first interpretation. The object is noble according to the second interpretation as it is the faith of a Siddiq. In this case, he observes all the etiquettes in loneliness as he observes them

before an emperor. For this reason, he makes his heart more pure and clean than his body. In this condition, shame, fear, humility, peace, modesty and all other praiseworthy qualities appear in him. So certain faith is the root and its branches are many.

(9) **Ninth sign.** Another sign of the learned man of the next world is that he becomes humble and adopts silence. The effect of God-fear appears on his body, dress, character, movements, speech and silence. If any man looks at him, it reminds him of God and his nature and character are proofs of his actions. His eyes are a mirror of his mind. The signs of the learned man of the hereafter are recognised in his face, tranquility, modesty and freedom from pride and vanity. A certain wise man said: God has not given a man a garment better than the garment of God-fear. It is the garment of the Prophets, Siddiqs, Pirs and the learned men. The sage Sahal Tastari divided the learned into three classes. (1) One class are those who are well acquainted with the commands of God but not punishment of God has not given a man a garment better than the kind of learning is God-fear which cannot be inherited. (2) Another class are those who have got knowledge of the commands of God and His punishments and they are the ordinary believers. (3) Another class are those who have knowledge of God, His commands and punishment. They are Side's , and God-fear and humility become strong in their minds. Hadrat Oman said: Acquire knowledge and therefore acquire tranquility, gravity and patience. Humble yourselves before your teacher and let your students do the same before you. Be not among the proud learned men lest your knowledge encourages ignorance. There is in a tradition: There are such good men among my followers who rejoice getting the mercy of God and weep secretly for fear of His punishment. Their soul is in the earth but their wisdom is in the hereafter. They walk with modesty and come close to God through the means of his grace. Hasn't Hadrat

Basra said: Patience is the vizier of knowledge, kindness its father and humility its garment, Bashir-b-Hares said: If a man seeks to rule by knowledge, the nearness of God keeps enmity with him, as he is detested both in heaven and earth. There is a stony that a certain wise man of Bans Israil composed 360 books on wisdom for which he was called Hakim (wise). God then revealed to his Prophet: Tell so and so, the earth has become full of your hypocrisy and you have not sought My pleasure therein. So I accept nothing of it. The man became repentant and gave it up. He began to mix with the people and roamed in the streets befriending all the children of Israil and he humiliated himself. God then revealed to their Prophet: Tell him: You have now carved My pleasure.

It has been narrated that the Prophet was asked: O Prophet of God, which action is best? He replied: To avoid evil and to make your tongue wet with the remembrance of God. He was asked: Which companion is best? He replied: The companion who helps you when you remember God and reminds you when you forget. He was asked: Which companion is worst? He replied: The companion who does not remind you when you forget. If you remember, he does not help you. He was asked: Who is the most learned man among the people? He replied: The most learned man among them is he who fears God most.

He was asked: Inform us about the best men among us, so that we may keep company with them. The Prophet said: Those who remind you of God whenever they are seen. He was asked: Who **are** the worst among men? He said: O God, I seek Thy pardon. They said: Tell us, O Apostle of God. He said: The corrupt learned men. The Prophet said: Those who have been the most God-fearing in the world will be the most secure in the hereafter. Those who have wept much in the world will laugh most in the hereafter. Those who have suffered most in the world will be happiest in the hereafter.

Hazrat Ali said in his sermon: This is my responsibility and I am pledged for the following: The crops of nobody will wither if they were planted with piety. The roots of no tree will get thirsty if they were raised with righteousness. The most ignorant man is he who knows not the honour of God-fear. The worst man to God is one who gathers knowledge from every quarter and yet remains covered in the darkness of trials. The worst man calls such a man a learned man, while he has not lived a single day in learning. He gets up in the morning from sleep and searches for increase of wealth. He goes after greater knowledge little knowing that a little knowledge of right kind is better than a great deal of knowledge which detracts man from God. He lives in doubts and scepticism like living in the spider's web and does never know whether he committed mistake or not.

Hazrat Ali said: When you hear the word of knowledge, remain silent and don't mix it with frivolous talks. It will yield no fruit. Someone said: If a teacher possesses three qualities, gifts become perfect on a student, patience, humility and good conduct. When a student possesses three qualities gifts become perfect on a teacher, intelligence, good manners and keen understanding. In short the qualities which the Quran mentions are found in the learned men of the hereafter as they learn the Quran for actions and not to acquire name, fame, power and prestige. A certain wise man said: Five qualities inferred from five verses of the Quran are the signs of the learned men of the hereafter, God-fear, humility, modesty, good conduct and love of the hereafter more than that of the following verse: Of His servants, the learned fear God most (35 : 25). Humility is based on the following verse: They are humble to God and they barter not His verses for a small price (3 : 198). Modesty is based on the following verse: And lower your wing for the believers (15 : 88). Good conduct is based on the following verse: You have become gentle to them on account of the mercy of God (3 : 153). Asceticism' is based on the following verse: But they to whom knowledge has been given said: Woe to you, the reward of God is better for one who believes and does good deeds (28 : 80).

When the Prophet read this verse: If God wishes to guide anyone, He expands his breast for Islam (6 : 125), he was asked as to the meaning of expansion of breast and he said: This is light. When it is cast into heart, it expands. He was asked: Has it got any sign?

The Prophet replied: Yes, to be separate from this world of deceit, to turn to the hereafter and to prepare for death before it actually comes.

(10) **Tenth sign.** Another sign of the learned man of the hereafter is that he studies the learning of practice and avoids such learnings as destroy actions, keep mind anxious and provoke evils. The root of religion is to be careful of evil deeds. For this reason, a poet said:

> *I have not known evil for evil's sake,*
>
> *I have not known it but to live.*
> *He who is ignorant of the evil of men,*
> *Falls unto it although he is wise.*

Hasan Basri was the man whose words has the greatest similarly to those of the Prophet and whose ways of life nearest to those of the companions. He was asked: O Abu Sayeed, you utter such words which nobody knows except you. Wherefrom have you got them? He said: From Huzaifah. Huzaifah was asked: You utter such words which no companion heard except you. Wherefrom have you go them? He said: From the Messenger of God. He was always asked about good deeds but I used to ask him about evil deeds, so that I may not fall therein. The companions were wont to ask the Prophet: O Apostle of God, what are the rewards of one who does such and such good deeds? I used to ask him: O Apostle of God, what corrupts the deeds? So Hazrat Huzaifah had special knowledge about hypocrisy, hypocrites and subtleties of dangers and difficulties.

The natural way of the actions of the learned men of the hereafter is to make efforts about the different conditions of heart but this knowledge is now rare. When ever anything of it is presented to a learned man, he expresses wonder at it and says that it is the deception of one who believes sermons. A poet said:

> *The true path is one out of many paths.*
> *Very few are sojourners to this path.*
> *Their goal is obscure, they are unknown.*
> *Slowly and steadily they march to their destination.*

People are indifferent to their goal.
Ignorant also are they of the true path.

It has been said that at Basra there were 120 men of scholastic theology regarding speech and Zikr but there were only three men regarding the knowledge of Yeqin or certain faith and the conditions of soul and secret attributes. They were Sahal Tastari, Shu'bi and Abdur Rahman.

(11) **Eleventh sign.** Another sign of the learned man of the next world is that he relies on his insight and knowledge which enlighten his heart and not on books and what he learns from others. His object of following is what the law giver said and enjoined. The companions believed blindly what they beard from the Prophet and they put it into practice. He from whose soul screen has been removed and whose soul has been illumined with the light of guidance is an object to be followed and he should not follow others besides him. For this reason, Ibn Abbas said. There is nobody except the Apostle of God whose knowledge is not sometimes followed and sometimes rejected. One sage said: We placed in our hearts and in our eyes what we received from the Prophet. We accepted something of what came from the companions and rejected something. Their successors were mere men like ourselves. The companions were superior, because they saw the circumstances under which the Prophet had lived and saw with their own eyes the revelation of the Quran and hence their rank is higher as their minds were imbued with it. The light of Prophethood was so strong on them that it saved them from many sins. They were not satisfied with the words of others. Their minds were distant from books and manuscripts which were not in vogue in their times, nor in the time of their successors. These books were compiled first in about 120 Hijra after the death of the companions and some of their successors specially after the death of Hazrat Sayeed-b-Masayyeb, Hasan Basri and other pious successors. Hazrat Abu Bakr and one party of the companions did not like to collect even the Quran in a book form for fear that the people would not commit the Quran to memory and lest the people depend only on this. Then Hazrat Umar and some companions gave advice to put into writing. Thus Hazrat Abu Bakr had the

Quran collected in one book. Ahmed b-Hanbal was critical of Malik for his composition of Al-Muatta and said: He has done what the companions did not do.

It has been said that the first book in Islam was written by Ibn-Juray on dialects of the Quran and historical sayings based on what he heard from Mujahid, Ata and the students of Ibn-Abbas at Mecca. Then Muammer-b-Rashed composed a book in Yemen on traditions and practices of the Prophet. Then came the book Muatta of Iman Malik and the Jami of Sufiyan Saori. Then in the fourth century many books on scholastic theology and argumentation were written::. When the people were inclined to these books, Yeqin or certain belief began to diminish. Thereafter the science of heart, research into the qualities of soul and the learning of safety from the stratagem of the devil began to disappear. Thus it became the custom to call the scholastic theologians and storytellers who embellished their words with ornamentation and rhymed prose. Thus the learnings of the next world began to decrease.

(12) **Twelfth sign.** Another sign of the learned man of the next world is that he saves himself from innovations even though the people are unanimous on innovations and novelties. He is rather diligent in studying the conditions of the companions, their conduct and character and their deeds. They spent their lives in jihad, meditation, avoidance of major and minor sins, observation of their outer conduct and inner self. But the great object of thought of the learned men of the present time is to teach, compose books, to make argumentation, to give Fatwa, to become mutawalli of Waqf estates, enjoy the properties, of orphans, frequent the rulers and enjoy their company.

Hazrat Ali said: The best of us is one who follows this religion. In short if you follow the companions of the Apostle of God, no blame will attach you even if you act in opposition to the people of this age. Hazrat Hasan Basri said: Two innovators have appeared in Islam, a man of bad judgment who holds that paradise is for those whose judgment is like mine, and a rich man who loves this world and searches it. Reject these two. God saved the learned man of the next world from these two kinds of persons.

The Prophet said: Word and guidance act two matters. The best word is the word of God and the best guidance is the guidance of the Prophet. Beware of innovation, because it is the worst thing. Every innovation is heresy and every heresy is sin. Beware don't think that the end will be delayed. Your hearts may become hard. Whatever is ordained is impending. Beware, what has passed will not return. The Prophet said in a sermon: Blessed is he whose concern for his own faults keeps him away of finding faults of others, who spends out of his lawful earning, keeps company with theologians and the wise and spurns the sinners and the wicked people. Blessed is he who humbles himself, makes his conduct refined, heart good and does not do harm to the people. Blessed is he who acts up to his knowledge, spends his surplus wealth, abstains from superfluous talks, follows sunned and does not introduce innovations.

Ibn Masud said: In latter days, good guidance will be better than many actions. He also said: You are now in an age when the best of you is one who is quick in doing good deeds, but soon there will come an age when the best of you will be one who will be firm in faith and remain silent toward doubt. Hazrat Huzaifa said a more wonderful saying : your good deeds of this age are the evil deeds of the past age and the evil deeds of this age will be considered as good deeds of the next age. You will be in good deeds till you know the truth. The learned man among you will not conceal truth. He said the truth, because most of the good deeds of this age were reprehensible at the time of the companions. The good deeds of our age is the embellishment of mosques, excess in ablution and bath, huge expenses in the construction of buildings for mosques, spreading of soft and fine rugs in mosques etc. The early Muslims seldom placed anything for their prayer. Hazrat Ibn Mas'ud truly said: You are living in an age when passion is harnessed by knowledge, but soon there will come over you a time wherein passion will have priority over knowledge. Imam Ahmad-b-Hanbal used to say: People have discarded knowledge and followed strange things. How little is their learning. God is our helper. Imam Malik said: In past times people were not in the habit of questioning as they do nowadays and their learned men did never say that such a thing is lawful and such a thing is unlawful and the question of unlawfulness never arose, as their condemnation of unlawful thing was open.

Abu Sulaiman Darani said: Nobody who gets any inspiration for something good should attempt to do it unless it is confirmed by a tradition. Let him then praise God for he has got what was in his mind. When the Caliph Marwan introduced the custom of a pulpit in the 'Id prayer, Hazrat Abu Sayeed Khudri said to him: O Marwan, is it not innovation? He said: It is not innovation. It is better than what you know. Many people assemble here. I wish that my sound should reach them. He said: By God, you don't know better than what I know. By God, I will not pray today behind you. He declined to pray behind him saying that he Prophet used to stand with a stick in his hand at the time of 'Id prayer and deliver sermon.

There is a well known Hadis: Whoever introduces such an innovation in our religion which is not there is an evil man. There is in another Hadis: The curse of God, angels and all people is upon one who deceives our people. He was asked: O Prophet of God, what is the deception of your people? He said: God has an angel who proclaims every day saying: He who oppresses the religion by introducing an innovation in opposition to the usages of Prophet in relation to one who commits it, is like a man who changes the reign of a king in relation to one who opposes his particular order. The latter crime can be forgiven but there is no pardon of one who changes the regime. A certain learned man said: Truth is heavy. He who increases it transgresses and he who decreases it fails and he who keeps attached to it is satisfied. The Prophet said: Adopt the middle course. He who goes in advance retards it and he who remains behind advances. God says: Avoid those who make their religion a sport and pastime (6 : 69). God says: Have you seen one who considers his evil as good and it appears to him alright? What has been introduced as innovation after the companions and what is unnecessary appertain to sport and pastime.

These are the twelve signs of the learned men of the next world any every quality was found in the learned men of early ages. Be therefore one of the two. Either be imbued with these attributes or be repentant after admitting your sins and faults. But never be the third one, as in that case doubt will arise in your mind. If you take the weapons of the world in lieu of religion, follow the conduct of the transgressors and if you take to ignorance and refusal of faith, you will reside with those who are doomed to destruction and despair.

SECTION – VII
Intellect and its Noble Nature

The noble nature of knowledge has been revealed through intellect. Intellect is the source and fountainhead of knowledge and its foundation. Knowledge is like the fruit of a tree and it flows from intellect, or like the light of the sun or like the vision of the eye. Why should it not be honoured when it is the cause of fortune in this world and the next? What is there to distinguish between beasts and men except intellect? Even a ferocious beast which has got more strength than man fears a man at seeing him as it knows that he may put him into snare on account of his intellect.

For this reason, the Prophet said: Just as the rank of the Prophet upon his followers, so is the rank of an old man over his people. This is not for his wealth or for his long body or for his great strength but for his ripe experience grown out of intellect. For this reason, you find the ignorant near the quadrupeds and they were about to kill the Prophet. But when they saw his noble countenance, they feared him and there shone on his face the brilliance of his prophethood although it was latent in his soul in the same manner as intellect. My object is to show the honour of intellect from the Quran and Hadis. Intellect has been termed as Nur or light in the following verse: God is the light of the heavens and the earth. His light is like a niche etc. (24 : 35). He named benefitting learning arising therefrom as spirit, revelation or life.

God said: Thus I have revealed to you spirit by My command (42 : 5). God said: Have I not given life to one dead and have I not created light for him with the help of which he can mix with the people -6:122. Whenever God mentioned about light and darkness, He meant knowledge and ignorance.

God said: He will take them from darkness into light (5:180). The Prophet said: O people, acquire knowledge from your Lord and advise one another with intellect. Known what you have been enjoined and what you have been prohibited. Know that intelligent man is he who obeys God although his face is ugly, his body dwarf, his rank low and appearance shabby. An ignorant man is he who disobeys God though his appearance is beautiful, his body long, his conduct good and his speech fluent. He who disobeys God is not more intelligent than an ape or a pig. Don't mix with those who received honour for love of the world as they are doomed. The Prophet said: The first thing God created is intellect. He said to intellect: Comer near and it came near. Then He said to it: Go back and it went back. Then God said: By My honour and glory, I have created nothing in my sight more honourable than you. Through you I take, through You I give, through you I give reward and through you I punish.

Once a party of men were praising a man before the Prophet and praised excessively. The Prophet asked: How is his intellect? They said: We shall inform you after seeing his diligence in prayer and other good deeds. Why do you ask us about his intellect? The Prophet said: The ignorance of an ignorant man is more harmful than the transgression of a sinner. On the Resurrection Day, a man will be raised to the rank of nearness to God in proportion to his intellect. The Prophet said: Nobody earns a better thing than intellect. It shows him path towards guidance and saves him from destruction. The intellect of a man does not become perfect and his religion firm till his faith does not become perfect. The Prophet said: A man acquires the rank of praying all nights and fasting all days through good conduct. The good conduct of a man does not become perfect till his intellect is not complete and when his intellect becomes perfect he obeys God and disobeys his enemy the devil. The Prophet said: Every thing has a root and the root of a believer is intellect and his divine service will be in proportion to his intellect. Have you not heard the words of the sinners in Hell: Had we heard and understood, we would not have been the inmates of Hell.

Hazrat Umar asked Tamim Dari: What is the supreme authority

among you? He said: Intellect. He said: You have spoken the truth. I had asked the Prophet as I asked you and he had replied as you replied. Then the Prophet said: I asked Gabriel: What is the main thing? He said: Intellect. Hazrat Bara'a-b-Azeb said: I asked many things to the Prophet. He said: O people, for everything there is a mainstay and the mainstay of man is intellect. He who among you learns a thing by proof and argument is the best in intellect among you. Hazrat Abu Hurairah said: When the Prophet returned from Uhud, he heard him say: So and so is such and such. The Prophet then said: You have got no knowledge about these men. They asked. O Prophet of God, how? He said: Each man has got rank according to the intellect God has given him. Their victory and their hope were in proportion to their intellect. So they reached to their different ranks. On the Resurrection Day, they will get those ranks according to their intention and intellect.

The Prophet said: Angels have been earnest and diligent in their obedience to God through their intellect, while the believers among the children of Adam have endeavoured to that effect in proportion to their intellect. He who is more earnest in obedience of God's commands is greater in intellect. Hazrat Ayesha asked: O Apostle of God, for what thing do the people in the world get excellence over one another? He said: For intellect. I asked: In the next world? He said: For intellect. I asked him: Will they not get their rewards in proportion to their actions? The Prophet said: O Ayesha, do they act, except in proportion to their intellect? Their actions will be in proportion to their intellect and they will get reward in proportion to their actions.

The Prophet said: Everything has got a weapon and the weapon of a believer is his intellect. Everything has got a mainstay and the mainstay of man is his intellect. Everything has got a support and the support of religion is intellect. Every people have got a goal and the goal of this people is intellect. Every people have got a missionary and the missionary of the worshippers is intellect. Every merchant has got merchandise and the merchandise of the diligent is intellect. Every entity has got a permanent house and the basis of the house of Siddiqs is intellect. Everything has got a basis and the basis of the next world is intellect. Everyone has got an offspring to whom he is ascribed and mentioned and the offspring of the Siddiqs to which they are ascribed and mentioned is intellect. Every journey has got a tent for shelter and the tent of a believer is his intellect. The Prophet said: He who is greatest in intellect among you is most fearful of God and the greatest observant of what has been ordered and prohibited even though he does not do much optional worships among you. The Prophet said: The believer who is most loved by God is he whose sole goal is to obey the commands of God, to admonish His servants, to complete his intellect and to admonish himself. He who acts according to that the few days of his life gets success and salvation.

Truth about Intellect and its Division

Intellect is a word which has got four meanings.

First meaning. It is an attribute for which man can be distinguished from other animals. It shows the path to theoretical learnings on mastering the abstract disciplines. Haris-b-Asad said in defining intellect that it is a natural attribute by which theoretical sciences are grasped and understood. It is like a light which falls into the heart and helps it to understand things. He who denies this meaning and limits intellect to understand only the necessary sciences is wrong, as he who is indifferent to the sciences and he who is asleep are both classed by him in the same rank. They have got this instinct though they are not learned. Just as life in them helps them to move their bodies at sweet will, so also intellect is so much intermingled with some men that it helps them towards acquisition of theoretical learnings. Had it been possible that the natural intellect, sensation and power of understanding of a man and an ass are equal without difference, then it would have been possible that an ass and a lifeless thing are equal regarding life with no difference. Just as according to natural law, an ass has been helped with life, so according to natural law, a man and a beast have been differentiated in the matter of theoretical learnings by intellect. Intellect is like a mirror which can be differentiated from other things having bodies by their special attribute regarding form and colour. This special attribute is a polisher. Forehead can be differentiated from eye as it has not been given the special quality of sight as in case of eye. As there is connection of eye with sight, so also there is the connection of this natural quality of intellect with learning. Just as there is connection of sun's rays with sight, so there is connection of Shariat with intellect with a view to express and spread learning.

Second meaning. According to this meaning, intellect is wisdom which appears even in childhood, as a boy knows by instinct that two is greater than one, that an individual cannot remain in two different places at the same time and that a lawful thing is not the same as an unlawful thing.

Third meaning. Intellect means according to this knowledge acquired through experience. Thus he who is taught by experience and schooled by time is called a man of intellect and he who lacks these qualifications is called ignorant.

Fourth meaning. When the natural power of a man reaches such point by which he can know the result of actions and for which the present pleasure of sexual passion is controlled, it is said that he has got intellect. Such a man is called an intelligent man. Such a man acts not by dictates of passion but by the ultimate result of an action.

The first meaning of intellect is its base and fountainhead. The second meaning is its branch and near the first meanings. The third meaning is the branch of the first and second meanings. The fourth meaning is the ultimate result of intellect and distant goal. The first two arise as natural causes and the latter two are acquired. Hazrat Ali said:

> *Knowledge is of two kinds, natural and acquired,*
> *Acquired knowledge is useless without the other.*
> *Just as the light of the sun rendered useless,*
> *When the light of the eye is closed.*

The first meaning is understood from the following Hadis. The Prophet said: God has not created anything more honourable than intellect. The fourth meaning is understood from the following Hadis: When a man comes close to the doors of religion and good deeds, he comes close to intellect. The Prophet said to Abu Darda: Increase intellect, then your nearness to Lord will increase. Abu Darda said: May my parents be sacrificed to you, how will it be in my case? The Prophet said: Avoid illegal things prohibited by God and fulfil the obligatory duties ordered by God, you will then become a man of intellect. Do good deeds, your honour and fame will increase in this world and you will gain for that proximity to your Lord and honour in the next world.

Hazrat Abu Hurairah and others went to the Prophet and said: O Prophet of God, who is the most learned of men? He said: The wise. They asked him: Who is the best worshipper among men? He said: The wise. They asked him: Who is the most excellent of men? He said: The wise. They asked him: Is not he the wise man who is best in conduct, whose eloquence is well-known, whose hand is full of charity and whose rank is exalted? The Prophet said: These are the treasures of the life of the world but the hereafter is for the God-fearing The wise man is God-fearing though he is abject and despised in the world.

The Prophet said: The wise man is he who believes in God, believes in His Prophet as true and obeys His commandments. It appears from this that intellect is the name of natural instinct. It is however appeared to knowledge as a thing is known by its fruit. A learned man is one who fears God, as fear of God is the fruit of learning. Thus the word intellect, if applied to any fruit, becomes like a natural attribute. Knowledge does not come from outside. It lies under intellect as a natural course. It is like water hidden in earth. If a well is dug, water comes out of it and no new thing is poured over it. Similarly there is oil latent in almond seeds and in roses. To this effect, God says: When your Lord took out progeny from the children of Adam from their backs and then took witnesses 'Am I not your Lord', they all said: Yes (7: 171). This means confession of their souls, not verbal promise by tongue. God says about this matter: If you ask them "Who created you", they would certainly answer "God" (43 : 87). In other words, their souls will bear witness about it. God says: The natural religion of God upon which He created men (30 : 22). In other words, the natural religion of every man is upon a thing that he should have faith in one God and know the natural attribute of each thing. In other words, this attribute is latent in him. So Iman or faith is hidden in the heart of every man.

Viewed from this angle, men are of two kinds. To one kind of men Iman was presented but they forgot it and they are unbelievers and to another kind of men who cultivated their souls and remembered it. These people are like those who forgot a thing after remembering it and afterwards it is reminded to them. God says for this: So that they may remember (14 : 25) , that those with understanding may remember (38: 28) . Remember the gifts of God upon you and your covenant with Him (5 : 10). 1 have made the Quran easy for remembrance. Is there any one who will remember it (54. 17) ?

Soul is like a horseman and body like a horse. The blindness of the horseman is more serious and harmful than that of the horse. The power of internal insight is more than that of external sight. Thus God said: His soul fulfilled not what he saw-: 11 . And thus I showed Abraham the kingdom of the heavens and earth (6 : 75). The opposite of inner light and insight is blindness. God says: It is not the eyes that are blind but the souls which are in breasts(22 : 45). God says: He who is blind in the world will be also blind in the hereafter.

These secrets were revealed to the Prophet, some through insight and some through sight and both were called sight. He whose insight is not ripe acquired nothing but husk of religion, These attributes are called intellect.

Intellectual Disparity of Men

As the lands are of several kinds, so also there is disparity of intellect in different individuals by instinct. This disparity of intellect in different individuals is also understood from a tradition. Abdullah-b-Salam narrated that the Prophet at the end of a long sermon described the Throne and stated that the angels asked God: O God, hast Thou created anything greater than the Throne? He said: Yes, intellect. They asked: How great is it? He said: Alas, your intellect cannot grasp it. Can you count the number of sands:

They said: No. God said: I have created intellect in different minds as numerous as sands. Some men have been given one grain, some two, some three, some four, some over one Farq, some one Wasq and some more.

This disparity of intellect is found in all its meanings as described above except the second, namely axiomatic knowledge, such as the thing that two are greater than one, that an object cannot remain in two different places at the same time or that a thing cannot be both eternal and originated. Intellect with reference to the three other meanings is subject to disparity. With regard to the fourth meaning of intellect, namely controlling power, disparity of men is clear and evident. For instance the power of control of appetite and sexual passion is different indifferent individuals even it is different in the same individual at different stages of life. A wise man will be able to overcome appetite more easily than an ignorant and illiterate man. A young man may fail to overcome sexual appetite but when he grows old, he is able to do it.

The disparity is also due to the differences in knowledge of a subject. Thus a man having special knowledge of medicines may refrain from some harmful foods while a lay man fails to do that simply because he lacks in medical knowledge. Similarly a learned man is more competent to give up sin than an ignorant man.

FOUNDATION OF BELIEF

SECTION – I

Belief in God

Praise be to God, the Creator, the First, the Last, the Doer of whatever He wills, who guides His servants towards the true path, who makes Himself known to men that He exists by Himself without any partner, He is single without any associate, the Eternal without any before Him and without any beginning, the Everlasting without any end. He is the First, the Last, the External and the Internal, the All-knowing. The following beliefs about God are necessary

(1) **To believe in His Transcendence.** He is without body and form, free of restriction, limitation and resemblance, not divisible. Nothing is like Him and He is not like anything. He is not limited by measure, space and time. He is free from diligence, rest and change. Everything is in His grasp. He is above Arsh, above heaven and above everything. He is nevertheless below the deepest depth, yet He is near, very close to a thing, nearer to the jugular vein of a man. He is not in anything and nothing is in Him. He is beyond space and beyond time. His is now as He was before. He expresses Himself through His creatures and not by existence. He is free from change, increase or decrease.

(2) **To believe in His power and existence.** He is Ever-living, All-powerful, Almighty, the great Destroyer. He is free from faults and failures, slumber, sleep, disease, death. He is the Lord of the entire universe, angels and everything. The heavens are rolled in His hands. He is unique in creation and unrivalled in ever new creations. He fixed the provision and death of created beings and

nothing can escape from His power. His power and might are above counting.

(3) **To believe in His knowledge.** His knowledge is without limit and He knows everything. Whatever happens between the deepest abyss of the earth to the highest heaven is within His knowledge. The smallest atom in the earth or in heaven is not outside His knowledge. He knows the creeping of an ant on a solid stone in intense dark night or in the movement of a mote in the air. Everything open and secret is within His knowledge. Every thought in mind, every contrivance of the devil and every thought good or bad is within His knowledge. His knowledge is eternal and unlimited without any increase or decrease and without any defect.

(4) **To believe in His will.** Nothing comes into being small or great, good or evil, benefitting or not benefitting, faith or infidelity, known or unknown, profit or loss, sin or virtue without His order, power and will. What He wills comes into being. What He does not will comes not into being. Not a glance of the eye, not a stray sudden thought in mind is outside His will. He does what He wills. There is none to rescind His command, there is no obstacle to it. There is no refuge of one who is disobedient to him. There is none to follow His command without His will. If mankind, jinn, angels and devil want to remove an atom from its proper place, they won't be able to do it without His will. His will lies naturally in His attributes which are unlimited. There is no precedence or subsequence of any event from its appointed time.

(5) **To believe in His hearing and sight.** He hears and sees. His hearing and sight are all pervading. Nothing however scanty can escape His hearing and nothing however subtle can go from His sight. Distance is no bar to His hearing and seeing, rather distance and nearness are all equal to Him. Darkness can not obstruct His sight. He sees without eye, catches without hands and creates without instrument. His attributes are not like those of the created beings, His being is not like that of the created.

(6) **To believe in His words.** God speaks without sound. It is eternal, ancient and self-existing unlike the talks of the created. His talk is without sound. It has got no connection with circulation

of air. It does not take the help of words and language through the movement of lips. The Quran, the Bible, the Gospel and Psalms are His created books to His Prophets. The Quran is recited by tongue, written on papers and preserved in heart, nevertheless it is eternal existing with the eternity of God. Hazrat Moses heard His words without sound and language and the righteous will see Him in the hereafter without body and space.

(7) **To believe in His actions.** There is no creator of actions except He and nobody is outside His judgment. He created everything in its best of make and form and no other form is better than it. He is wise in His actions and just in His judgments. His justice is not comparable to that of men. Whatever exits in the world, men, jinn, angels, devils, heaven, earth, animals, plants, inanimate things comes out of nothing but by His power. He existed in eternity by Himself and there was nothing along with Him. Thereafter He originated creations not because of His necessity. He has got no fatigue or languor. Whatever He does is from a sense of justice, not of oppression or injustice. Obedience to Him is binding on all His creatures and He expressed it through His Prophets. He gave them miracles and conveyed His injunctions and prohibitions through them.

(8) **To believe in other world.** It is to attest to the prophethood of Muhammad. God sent the unlettered Quraishite Prophet Muhammad as an apostle to all the Arabs and non-Arabs, to the jinn and men and by his law he abrogated all other laws. He gave him superiority to all other Prophets and made him leader of mankind and did not make complete any faith with the words of Tauhid till it was followed by the attestation that Muhammad is His servant and apostle. He made compulsory to believe whatever he said about this world and the next world. He does not accept the faith of a man unless he believes in these articles of faith along with the following.

(a) **To believe in Munkar and Nakir.** They are two terrible angels. They will make the dead one sit up with his soul and body and ask him about his religion and his Prophet. This is the first examination after death. (b) To believe in the punishment of grave as true. (c) To believe in the Balance with two scales and a tongue the magnitude of which is like the stages of heaven and earth. Therewith the actions of men will be weighed. The weight would be like a mote or mustard seed to establish exact justice. (d) To believe in the Bridge. It is a bridge stretched over Hell, sharper than the edge of the sword and thinner than a hair. The feet of the unbelievers will slip and they will fall down into Hell. The feet of the believers will be firm upon it by the grace of God and so they will cross it to Paradise. (e) To believe in the Fountain. It is a fountain of the Prophet. The believers will take drink from it and enter Paradise after crossing the bridge. Whoever will drink therefrom once will never be thirsty. Its water will be whiter than milk and sweeter than honey. There will be so many pitchers around like so many stars in firmament. (f) To believe in the judgment. Some will render little account, some great and some will enter Paradise without account. They will be in the neighbourhood of God. Those who believe in Tauhid will come out of Hell after their due punishment in Hell. (g) To believe in the intercession of the Prophets, then the learned, then the martyrs, then the rest of the believers. They will have the right of intercession in proportion to their ranks to God. (h) To believe in the goodness of the companions, first of Abu Bakr, then of Umar, then of Osman and then of Ali. You will have good idea about them and praise them as God and His Apostle praised them.

Excellence of Belief

What has been said above about belief is applicable to a boy in his early years in order that he may commit them to memory. Its meaning will be gradually unfolded to him. The first duty of a boy is to commit them to memory, then to understand them and then to believe them and then to know them as certain and sure. It comes to his mind as a matter of course without proof. The root of faith of the ordinary people is Taqlid or blind belief in authority. True it is that the belief which is based on authority is not free from some weakness, but when it is certain and sure, it becomes perfect. To achieve this end, one should not resort to scholastic theology but to reading the Quran, Tafsir and Hadis and to understand their meaning, because in that case the light of divine service appears in him, and the advices of the pious, their company, their character and conduct, their God-fear and their asceticism spread effect in his mind. Instruction to the boy is like the sowing of seed in his heart. The above actions are like the serving of water and tending to seed. It grows, becomes strong and thrives to a tree and its root becomes strong and firm and its branches rise high. The boy should also be guarded against argumen tation and speculation as their harms are greater than their benefits. To make faith strong by argumentation is like striking a tree with an iron matter. To teach by proof is one thing and to see proof by eyes is another thing. If the boy wants to be included within the travellers of the hereafter with Taufiq or God's grace as his friend, the doors of guidance are opened up for him till he remains engaged in actions attached to Godfear and restrains himself from passions and lusts making efforts in discipline and self-mortification. Owing to these efforts, a light from God falls in his heart as God says: Whoso strives for Us, We shall guide them in our paths, for God is assuredly with those who do right- 29: 69. That is the most valuable jewel and the ultimate goal of the saints and favour ites of God. That is the secret matter which rested in the breast of Hazrat Abu Bakr and for which he was superior to all others. The expression of this secrecy has got different stages.

It will be open to one in proportion to one's efforts and striving and the more one makes his soul clean and pure. It is like the learning of the mysteries of medicines, jurisprudence and other sciences. They differ in proportion to the differences of intellect and knowledge. As there is no limit to these stages, there is also no limit to the degrees of secrets.

SECTION – II

Proof of Belief

Iman or belief is founded upon four pillars, each of which has got ten bases:

(1) **First pillar.** It is the knowledge of essence of God and it is

established upon ten bases. They are the knowledge and belief that God is existing, eternal, ancient, without form, without body, without length and breadth, without any special direction, occupying no space, object of vision in the next world and He is one without any partner.

(2) **Second pillar.** It is to have knowledge of His attributes and to believe them. It is founded on ten bases-He is All-powerful, All-knowing, living for ever, willing, hearing, seeing, speaking, eternal in words, knowledge and will and free from changes of events.

(3) **Third pillar.** It is to have knowledge and faith in His works which are established over ten bases. They are that men's actions are created, willed and fixed by God, that He is kind to creatures free from imposing works beyond power of men, that He punishes men, does what He wills, that there is nothing obligatory on Him, that He sent apostles and that our Prophet was helped by miracles and that his prophethood will last till the Day of Resurrection.

(4) **Fourth pillar.** It is to believe in the things accepted on authority and it is based on ten things. It is to believe in the truth of Resurrection, questions by Munkar and Nakir, punishment of grave, the Balance, the Bridge, Paradise, Hell, the true Imam, excellence of the companions in accordance with chronological order and qualifications of being an Imam.

FIRST PILLAR

The basic principles of faith for knowledge of God.

(1) The first basic principle is to have knowledge of the existence of God. The first light which illumines faith and the first thing to be followed is the Quran and there is no word better than the word of God. God says: Have I not made the earth a couch, mountains its tents? I have created you of two sex and ordained your sleep for rest, night as a mantle and day for gaining livelihood. I created above you seven solid heavens and placed therein a burning lamp and I sent down waters in abundance from clouds that I might bring forth by it corns and herbs and gardens thick with trees (78 : 6). God says: In the creation of the heaven and the earth and in the

alternation of night and day and in the ships which pass through the sea with what is useful to man and in the rain which God sends down from heaven, giving life by it to the earth after its death and by scattering over all kinds of earth and in the change of the winds and in the clouds that are made to do service between heaven and earth, are signs for those who understand (2 : 159). God says: Don't you see how God created the seven heavens one over the other, placed therein the moon as a light and the sun as a torch and God caused you to spring forth from the earth like a plant. He will turn you back into it again and will bring you forth main (71 : 14). God said: Don't you see the germ of life? Is it you who created it or I? I have decreed death among you and I shall not be overcome to change your forms and create ycu what you know not (56 : 58).

It is clear that if he who has got a little intellect and ponders over these verses and looks to the wonderful creations of the heavens and the earth will realise that without a great Designer these workmanship are impossible. The human soul naturally testifies that God exists and that everything is governed by His Laws. For this reason God says: Is there any doubt about God, the Creator of heavens and earth ? (14 : 11) The Prophets were therefore sent by Him to call the people towards monotheism 'there is no deity but God.' They were not commanded to say: For us there is one God and for the world another God, because such a thing was inborn in their minds from the time of their birth. God said: If you ask them who has created the heavens and the earth they will reply 'God'. God said: Turn your face then towards the true faith, the natural religion whereon God created men 30 : 30. Therefore there are testimonies of the Quran and human nature which are sufficient proofs. All other proofs are unnecessary but still we shall prove by the proof of knowledge that God exists.

Proof of Knowledge

A new thing cannot come into existence without a cause. The world is an originated new thing and it did not come into existence without a cause. That a thing cannot come into existence without a cause is clear, for such a thing belongs to a certain definite time and it also comes to our intellect that it comes at a fixed time without precedence or subsequence, because of the urgency of its fixed time. The world is a new or originated thing. Its proof is found in the fact that it is not free from motion and rest which are the characteristics of every new material thing. Even motion and rest are two new originated things not free from changes. The world and whatever exists in it are originated things. There are three matters in this argument. Firstly, a body is not free from motion and rest. It requires no meditation. Secondly, motion and rest themselves are originated things. Its proof is that one comes after another. It is found in all bodies. What is static can move and what is moving can become static according to the dictates of intellect. If any of the above two things is predominant over the body, it becomes a new even. A new thing is originated because of its emergence, an old thing is distant because of its extinction. If the eternity of a thing is established, its extinction is impossible as we shall prove it by the subsistence of the creation. Thirdly, what is not free from changes is an originated or new thing or whatever is not independent of originated things is itself originated. Its proof is that if it were not so, the world before every new thing may change which has got no beginning and unless these new things come to nought, the turn for the present new things to come into being would never come. But it is impossible for a thing which has no end to come to nought.

Another reason is that if there is no end of the motion of heavenly bodies, three conditions would arise-their numbers would be either odd or even, or both odd and even, or neither odd nor even. The last two are impossible, as positive and negative are united therein, since the affirmation of one is the negation of another and negation of one is the affirmation of another. They cannot be even, as even number becomes odd by the addition of one. That which has no end cannot be even without change. They cannot be odd, because the number becomes even with the addition of one. How can it change into odd when its number has got no end? From this, it is concluded that the world is not free from changes and therefore it is an originated thing. When it is an originated thing, it requires a Creator to bring it into existence.

(2) **The second basic principle** is the knowledge that God is eternal. He has got no beginning and no end; He is the final of everything and before everything living or dead. Its proof is this. If he were an originated thing and not eternal. He would have need of a Creator who would also have need of a Creator. Thus it would have continued without end. Whatever comes in succession ends in an ancient creator which is the first. For this reason, the Creator is the First and the Last, the Creator of the world and its Fashioner.

(3) **Third basic principle**. It is that God is everlasting without end. He is the first and the last, the open and the secret. When the attribute of eternity has been established his end becomes impossible. Its proof is this. If He had an end, He would have remained in two conditions, either he would come to nought by Himself or through an opposing annihilating agent. If it is possible for a thing which is self-existing to come to nought, it is also possible for that thing to come into existence. The reason is that if a thing requires a cause to come to existence, it also requires a cause to come to nought. It is not possible that a thing comes to nought after meeting with an opposing agent. If that thing which comes to nought is eternal, how does the form of existence of a thing become? It is not also possible that an originated thing coming before an eternal thing loses its identity and existence. God is eternal as we have learnt it from previous discussions. How then did He exist in eternity with His opposites? If the opposite is an originated thing, its existence from eternity is impossible.

(4) **Fourth basic principle.** It is that God is without form, not occupying any space and free from space, motion and rest. Its proof is this. Every form occupies a space and moves and stays in it. Body has got motion and rest which are the character of originated things. What is not free from changes is an oiginated thing. If any form is limited by space and is eternal, it is understood that the substance of the creation of the world is eternal. If a man says that God has got body and occupies space, he commits blunder for using such word and not for its meaning.

(5) **Fifth basic principle.** It is that God is not composed of a body having different substances. When He does not occupy any space,

He has got no body as every body is limited by space and composed of different substances. The substances of the body are not free from division, composition, motion, rest, form and quantity. These are the qualities of an originated thing. If it were possible to believe that the Creator of the world has got a body, then it would be possible to attribute divinity of the sun and the moon and other heavenly bodies. If a designer wishes to make a body without the substance of body, he will commit mistake.

(6) **Sixth basic principle.** God has got no length and breadth as these are attributes of a body which is an originated thing. Its Creator existed from before it. So how will He enter in a body as He existed by Himself before all originated things and there was nobody along with Him. He is All-knowing, Almighty, Willing Creator. These attributes are impossible for a body. He exists by Himself without the substances of a body. He is not like any worldly thing, rather He is ever-living, everlasting and nothing is like Him. Where is the similarity of the Creator with the created, the Fashioner with the fashioned? Hence it is impossible that anything is like Him.

(7) **Seventh basic principle.** It is that God is not confined within any direction as He created directions, either above or below, right or left, front or behind. He created two directions for man, one rests on earth called the direction of feet and one above his head. What rests above head is above and what rests below feet is below. To an ant, below the roof, the above portion is its lower side and the lower side is its upper side though they are contrary in our case. He created for man two hands one right hand and another left. Accordingly there is right hand direction and the left hand direction. Then there are front direction and back direction. When direction is an originated thing, how can He be governed by that? Along with the creation of men, directions have been created. There is nothing above God, because He has got no head and the word 'above' is connected with head. There is nothing below Him as the word 'below' is connected with feet and God has no feet. If He is above the world, there is a direction opposite to it and every opposite thing has got a body like it or similar to it. But God is free from it. He is unique, He is the Designer.

(8) **Eighth basic principle.** It is that God is seated upon His Throne, that is upon power. It is not inconsistent with the attribute of His grandeur and the symptoms of origination and annihilation. This is what is meant by the following verse of the Quran: Then He ascended to heaven and it was then but smoke-(41 : 10). It means His dominion and power as the poet said:

Bishr has gained power in Iraq,
Without sword and shedding blood.

The people of truth accepted this interpretation as the people of untruth were compelled to accept the interpretation of these words of God: He is with you wherever you are (57 : 4). This means that He encompasses everything. This is supported by the following Hadis: 'The heart of a believer is within two fingers of the Merciful,' meaning within His power or might. It is also supported by the following Hadis: 'The Black Stone is the right hand of God in the earth,' meaning it is established on honour in the earth. If its meaning is taken literally, the result would be impossible. His taking rest on the Throne means this. If it is taken literally, it becomes possible to believe that He has got a body and the Throne is also a body limited by space. It is impossible.

(9) **Ninth basic principle.** It is that although God is free from form, space and direction. He is an object to be seen in the hereafter as He said: On that day shall faces beam with looking towards their Lord (75 : 22). He is not visible in this world as God said: Vision does not comprehend Him, but He comprehends vision (6: 103), also because of the following verse: God addressed Moses saying: You cannot see Me (7 :109). I don't understand how the Mutazalites hold that God is visible in this world also though Moses could not see Him. Insight is a kind of Kashf and knowledge, and Kashf is more clear than knowledge. When God has got connection with knowledge and not with direction, He has got connection also with insight without any direction. As God sees His creation though not in front, the creation also sees Him though not in front. As it is possible to know Him without modality or form, it is also possible to see Him likewise.

(10) **Tenth basic principle.** It is that God is without any

partner, single without any like. He is unique in ever new creations, innovations, and inventions. There is nothing like Him. The Quran says: Had there been any other God therein, they would have gone to ruin (21 : 22). If the first God willed something, the second would have been compelled to aid the first and thus he would have been subordinate to him. This means that he would have no supreme power. If the second is to oppose the first, he would be powerful and the first would be weak rather than an Almighty God.

SECOND PILLAR OF FAITH
God's Attributes based on Ten Principles

(1) **First basic principle.** It is that God is Almighty as He said: He is power over all things (15 : 120). He is truthful as the world is perfect with His designs and well regulated. He who sees a garment of silk of which the weaving and texture are fine and says that it has been made by a dead man or a man who has got no power, would be lacking in natural intellect and is utterly foolish.

(2) **Second basic principle.** It is that whatever exists is within His knowledge and under His control. Even an atom in heaven and earth is not outside His knowledge. He is truthful in all His promises and has got knowledge of everything. This is attested by the verse: Does He not know who has created? He is subtle, cognizant (77 : 14). Take this proof by your intellect that there is nothing like of what He created with wonderful design. This shows the deep knowledge of the Designer and wonderful intricacies. He is the end of praise and guidance as He described Himself.

(3) **Third basic principle.** It is that God is Ever-living, because it has been established that He has got knowledge and power and that He has got life. If it were conceived that a powerful and knowing designer is without life, then it is possible also to doubt the lives of animals in spite of their motions and rest. This is the height of foolishness.,

(4) Fourth basic principle. It is that every action happens according to the will of God. In other words every existing thing lives

according to His will. He is the original Creator and repeats creations and whatever He wills, He does. When every action happens according to His will, the opposite thing also comes into being according to His will. So power leads His will to two different directions.

(5) Fifth basic principle. It is that God is hearing and seeing and it is impossible to evade His sight and hearing. He is the bridge of mind and lies secretly in thoughts and reflections. The thinnest sound of the creeping of a black ant on a solid stone in the deep darkest night does not evade His hearing. How will it not be when His sight and hearing are perfect beyond doubt and there is no decrease of this power? How can the power of the created become perfect in relation to the power of God? How can a designer become perfect in relation to the great Designer? How can a portion become equal to one whole?

(6) Sixth basic principle. It is that God speaks without words and sounds and letters. It does not resemble the speech of other beings. In reality His speech is speech of the mind. Just as speech of mind has got no sound or words, so His speech has got no sound or words. A poet says:

Speech is of the mind.
Tongue is the vehicle of mind.

He who cannot conceive it is a fool. Pay no attention to one who does not understand that the eternal is that before which nothing existed. Thus in the word 'Bismillah' the word `B' precedes `S' and consequently 'S' cannot be eternal. God has got a secret for leading some men astray as He says: There is no guide for one whom God misguides (13 : 33). Whosoever thinks it impossible the Prophet Moses heard God's words which had no sound or words, it becomes impossible for him to believe that he will see in the next world such a thing as has got no body though he understands that a thing can possibly be seen which has got no colour, body or size, even though he has not seen such a thing. Similarly conceive of hearing what is applicable to sight. If you understand that God has got knowledge of everything, understand it also that along with His being, He has got attribute of speech. Understand it also that all the words represent His speech. If it is possible to conceive of the existence of the seven heavens and Paradise and Hell all written in a small piece of paper and that Tardier of men is preserved in the minutes part of heart and seen with an eyeball without the things existing in the eye ball, it is also possible to conceive the speech of God as being read with tongue, preserved in mind, written on paper, but the essence of speech does not come down on these things, because if it comes down on paper on account of writing, then the essence of fire would come down on paper on account of its writing and would burn it.

(7) **Seventh basic principle.** It is that the words emanating from God are eternal along with His attributes, since it is impossible that He is subject to change. Rather it is necessary that His attributes should become eternal as His being is eternal. He is without change and without novelty. He exists with His attributes from eternity. What is not free from change is originated. Origination is an attribute of body as it is subject to change and the attribute of body is also subject to change. How can the Creator be sharer with it in the attribute of change? For this it can be said that He is eternal. His words are eternal but our words and sounds are new and originated.

(8) **Eighth basic principle.** It is that His knowledge is eternal. Whatever occurs in His creation is within His knowledge from eternity and not His new knowledge. Whenever any animal is born, His knowledge about it is not new but eternal and ancient. For instance, if I know that laid will come at sunrise, his arrival at sunrise and to welcome him would be owing to that foreknowledge and not for any new knowledge. The eternal knowledge of God should be understood in this way.

(9) **Ninth basic principle.** It is that His will is eternal. His will to make an event at the appointed time has ,got connection with His eternal knowledge, because if there is rise of a new will, it remains confined to the place of event. If His will rises in another object and not in His being, He cannot will just you cannot execute an action which is not in yourself. How can you do it when it depends on the will of another which again depends on the will of another

and so on to infinity and there is no end to it. If it is possible for a will to come into being without another will, it would be possible for the world to come into being without a will.

(10) **Tenth basic principle.** It is that God is wise by His knowledge, living with His life, mighty with His power willing with His will, speaking with His words, seeing with His light and hearing. These attributes belong to His eternal attributes. If one says that He is wise without wisdom, his words will be like those of a man who says that he is wealthy without his wealth, learned without his learning and the object of learning. Learning, object of learning and the learned man are inseparable, as murder, murderer and one murdered are inseparable. As murder can not be conceived without the killer and one killed, a learned man cannot be conceived without learning and an object of learning.

THIRD PILLAR OF FAITH

Knowledge of the Action of God involving Ten Principles

(1) **First basic principle.** It is the knowledge that every event in the world is His action, creation and invention. There is no creator of it except He. He well regulated the creation and gave it its due power and motion. All the actions of His servant are His creations and keep connection with His power, confirming thereby His words -God is the creator of everything (9 : 102). God created you and what you make(37 : 96). Whatever is your conversation, hidden or open, He truly knows the innermost recess of your hearts. "What! does He not know when He has created, when He is the subtle, the cognizant?" He ordered men to take precaution in their actions, words, secret matters and thoughts as He knows the orientation of their actions and gave proof of His knowledge by creating creations. How will He not be the Creator of the actions of men when He has got full power without any decrease? His power is connected with the movements of men. All motions are similar and are connected with power of God. What then would prevent its connection in the case of some actions and would not prevent it in the case of other actions when all are similar ? How

could animals be independent of the Creator when the wonderful workmanship of spiders, bees and other animals amaze the wisest and intelligent minds? Who has got power of speciality in these creations except God? Then animals themselves do not know the benefits they produce. So they cannot be called the causes of workmanship. Now think that all creations bow down to One who is the Creator of the heavens and the earth.

(2) **Second basic principle.** It is that God being the Creator of the power of men, does not prevent them from doing voluntary actions by way of acquisition, for God created power and the container of power, choice as well as the container of choice. Power is an attribute of a man though it is the creation of God and not acquired by man. Motion is also the creation of God and an attribute of man acquired on the strength of power, because the power with which he was created is his attribute, but motion is connected with the attribute of power and for this reason of connection, it has been named power of motion. The power of motion is not the result of compulsion on any man as he can move according to his will and knows the difference between compulsion and volition. How can this motion be his creation when he does not know the different parts of acquired actions and their numbers? When these two matters are disproved, namely the matter that actions are the result of compulsion and the matter that they are the result of volition, there remains the middle position which is this that actions are voluntary in a fixed manner through power of God by invention and through the power of a man by acquisition. God has no necessity of keeping connection with the container of power in the matter of creation because the power of God is eternal and its connection with the world is eternal.

(3) **Third basic principle. It** is the knowledge that though the actions of man are his acquisitions, they are nevertheless not outside the will of God. Neither a twinkling of an eye, nor a sudden rise of thought in mind in the visible and invisible world occurs except through His order, power and will. Good or evil, benefit or loss, belief or infidelity, knowledge or ignorance, success or failure, guidance or misguidance, sin or virtue, Shirk or Iman come from Him. There is none to reject His command, none to disobey his

decree. He guides whom He wishes and misguides whom He wishes. There is none to question Him of what He does, but the people will be questioned (21 : 33). All say: What He wills occurs and what he does not will does not occur. God says: If God willed, He would have guided all men rightly (3 : 30). Had I wished, I would have given every soul its guidance (31 13). He who thinks that God does not will sins and evils as they are evils and that it is the devil who wills them is cursed. Tell me how a Muslim can deny the supreme rule of God. If the power of a village chief is curtailed, he will think it dishonourable. He will think it derogatory to his position if actions are conducted according to the wishes of his enemy in the village. The result will be that many will be out of his control. Now it is seen that evil deeds are predominant in men. If every sin is done against the will of God, God's helplessness is seen. When it is established that all actions of men are creations of God, it follows that the evil actions are also the result of His will.

Question may be asked how God commands to do what He does not wish and how He prohibits what He wishes. In reply we shall say that command is one thing and will is another thing. Thus if a master beats his slave, the ruler rebukes the

master for beating his slave. The master shows reason that his slave does not obey him. As a proof he orders his slave to arrange the bridle of his horse before the ruler though he knows that the slave will not obey it. If he does not order him, his objection before the ruler does not stand and if he wishes that his order should be obeyed it amounts to his murder. It is impossible.

(4) **Fourth basic principle.** It is that God is generous in inflicting trouble on men by His command. Neither creation, nor imposition of obligations is necessary for Him although the Mutazalites hold that they were necessary for the welfare of men. But this is impossible since He is the only being to enjoin and prohibit. How will it be limited by compulsion? The object of compulsion is of two things, such a work which if given up will cause harm in future as it is said that it is compulsory on men to obey God who will punish him in the hereafter by the fire of Hell; or it is to avoid such present harm which is injurious as it is said that to drink water for

a thirsty man is compulsory so that he may not die. Secondly it is such a work the negation of which seems impossible. Thus it is said that the existence of a thing which is known is necessary because if it does not exist, it becomes an impossibility. If it occurs, knowledge becomes ignorance.

(5) **Fifth basic principle.** It is that God can inflict on man what is beyond his capacity. If it were not possible, it would have been impossible for , men to pray for removing it. The people prayed: O our Lord, lay not on us that for which we have no strength- 2 : 246 This is against the belief of the Mutazalites.

(6) **Sixth basic principle.** It is that God is free to punish a man in spite of his virtues and to reward a man in spite of his sins. The Mutazalites hold the contrary view. God has got freedom of action among His servants and it is impossible that His servants will oppose His freedom. Tyranny means to dispossess a man from his possession but it is impossible in the case of God as He does not dispossess others in view of the fact that the kingdom of heaven and earth is His. It is proved by this. Slaughter of animals is infliction of pain on animals and men Various tortures inflicted on animals have not been preceded by any offence or crimes committed by the animals. If it is said that these animals would be raised up again and rewarded for this which is incumbent upon God, then we would say that every ant killed under feet and every bug crushed would be brought back to life. It would violate the dictates of reason and law as nothing is incumbent upon God.

(7) **Seventh basic principle.** It is that God does with regard to men what He wills and it is not incumbent on Him to do whatever is good for them. It has already been stated that nothing is compulsory on God but His dealings are not intelligible to men, because there is nobody to question Him what He does but men are subject to questions. The Mutazalites say that it is incumbent upon God to do whatever is salutary for men.

(8) **Eighth basic principle.** It is that to have knowledge of God and to obey His commands are compulsory on men, not on account of the reason as the Mutazalites say, but on account of

Shariat. Shariat declared poisonous serpents beyond death, while reason in realising what Shariat foretells thinks it possible and urges that precautions should be taken against any possible punishment. But reason itself does not lead to that knowledge of harm. If a man warns by saying: A lion stands behind you, he should at once take to his heels without searching reason.

(9) **Ninth basic principle.** It is that sending Prophets to men is not impossible. Some say that there had been no use in sending them, because reason renders it unnecessary. This is false, because reason does not support the actions which will lead to salvation in the hereafter just as it does not guide them to discuss the medicines which are useful for health. The necessity of Prophets for men is like that of the physicians for men. The integrity of the physicians is known by experience and the truthfulness of the Prophets is known by miracles.

(10) **Tenth basic principle.** It is that God sent Muhammed as the last Prophet and as an abrogator of all previous laws of the Jews, Christians and the Sabians and God helped him with open miracles and wonderful signs, such as splitting up the moon into two parts, the praise of the pebbles, causing the mute animals to speak, water flowing from his fingers etc. The open miracle with which he guided the Arabs is the Quran as the beauty of the language throughout the Quran is unparalleled and the Arabs could not surpass it in spite of their eloquence and rhetoric. Though the Prophet was illiterate and did not learn how to read and write, yet God informed him in the Quran about the histories of the previous nations, the informations which he gave about the previous nations in the Quran being an illiterate person, the prophecies he made about the future events and the clue he gave to the unknown things are his miracles. For instance God says: You will enter the sacred mosque if God wills having your heads shaved and your hair short (48 : 27). The verse: The Romans have been vanquished in a land nearby but after their defeat they defeat them in a few years (30 : 1). The object of these verses is to prove the truth of the messenger of God by miracles.

Fourth Matter

To believe the Hadis of the Prophet involving ten basic Principles.

(1) First basic principle. It is to believe in the Resurrection of the dead and the Day of judgment as in the traditions. It is a settled fact like the beginning of our creation. God said: People say: Who shall give life to bones when they are rotten? Say, He shall give life to them who gave them life at first (36: 73). The beginning of creation is the proof of its resurrection. God said: Your creation and your resurrection are like a single soul-(31 : 27). Resurrection is the second stage of men and is possible like the first stage of creation.

(2) Second basic principle. It is the question of Munkar and Nakir which has been mentioned in traditions and therefore to believe it is compulsory. The second life will be in such a place where he will be questioned. This is possible naturally, as the stillness of the dead man's corpse or its failure to hear the questions put to it will refute it, because a sleeping man is openly still and dead-like but his soul feels pain and pleasure at that time in dream. Its effect can be seen when he wakes up from sleep. The Prophet used to hear the words of Gabriel and see him but the man surrounding him did not hear his words or see him. As God did not give them such power of sight and hearing, they did not see and hear.

(3) Third basic principle. It is to believe in the punishment of the grave as it has come in Shariat. God said: They will be exposed to Me morning and evening and on the Resurrection Day. The supporters of Pharaoh will be given severe punishment (40 : 49). This is possible and to believe it is compulsory. Animals have got special organs to feel pains and pleasure even though they are eaten by ferocious animals.

(4) Fourth basic principle. It is to believe that the Balance is true. God said: I will set up just balance on the Judgment Day (21: 48). God said: Those whose balances will be heavy will get salvation, and those whose balance will be light will be losers (7 : 7).

(5) **Fifth basic principle.** It is to believe in the Bridge which is spread on the back of Hell, thinner than a hair and sharper than the edge of a sword. God said: Guide them to the bridge of Hell and tell them to wait there, as they will be questioned (27 : 23). It is possible, because He who makes the birds fly in the horizon can take the people to travel on the Bridge.

(6) **Sixth basic principle.** It is the belief that Paradise and Hell have been created by God. God said: Vie in haste for pardon to your Lord and a Paradise, vast as the heavens and the earth, is prepared for those who fear God- 3 : 127. This proves that Paradise and Hell are created.

(7) **Seventh basic principle.** It is to believe that the rightful Imams after the Prophet are Hazrat Abu Bakr, then Umar, then Osman, and then Ali and that the Prophet's attention was not upon any particular Imam. As to the struggle which took place between Muawiah and Ali, it was the result of differences of opinion to discover truth by ljtehad. Hazrat Muawiah did not do it for leadership. Hazrat Ali considered that the mode of punishment of the murderers of Osman was to be belated as they got relations in the army. Hazrat Muawiah considered that their arrest was better as their influence might help further bloodshed.

(8) **Eighth basic principle..** It is to believe the excellence of the companions in accordance with their chronological order in which they succeeded the Prophet and the real excellence is in the sight of God and that it did not come to anybody except to the Holy Prophet. Several verses to that effect in praise of the companions were revealed and there are a number of traditions

(9) **Ninth basic principle.** It is to believe that an Imam, in addition to his qualifications of his being a Muslim, mature and intelligent must have five other qualities-(1) he must be a male, (2) he must be a God-fearing man, (3) he must be learned, (4) he must be competent, (5) he must belong to the tribe of Quraish as the prophet said: The leaders are from the Quraish. When these qualities are found in a man, he is fit to become an Imam or ruler provided majority of the people swear allegiance to him. Those

who oppose the majority of the people are rebels and it is incumbent to bring them under control.

(10) Tenth basic principle. It is that if a man who is invested with the power of rule is found lacking in God-fear and learning and if there is fear of disturbance and trouble in case of his removal, then his rule will stand, because if he is removed, two conditions will arise. (l) Another man will be reinstated in his place or the post will remain vacant. In the first case, the harms which will be caused to the Muslims in general will be greater than the harms of one who has got no God-fear and learning in him. The qualities of leadership are for the greater good of the people.

These four pillars involving forty basic principles are the articles of belief. He who believes in these things follows Hale Suntan or the people of the ways of the prophet.

SECTION – III
Rules of Articles of Belief

This section comprises three questions- (1) significance of the word 'Belief' and 'Islam', (2) whether belief increases and decreases, and (3) the meaning of 'belief' according to the early Muslim sages.

(1) **First question.** There is difference of opinion regarding the meanings of Islam and Imam, but there are three questions in that connection-(a) literal meanings of the words, (b) their technical meanings in the Quart and traditions, and (c) functions of the terms according to jurisprudence.

(a) **Literal meanings.** Imam means belief or confirmation of truth. God said: You have mot brought faith in Me (12 : 17) meaning you do mot believe Me as true. Islam means submission and surrender and avoidance of unbelief, rebellion and disobedience. Heart is the special seat of Imam or confirmation of truth and tongue is its interpreter. Islam means submission and surrender and confirmation by tongue. The word 'Islam' is sure comprehensive and 'Imam' is a special term. Imam is a part of Islam. Imam is Islam, but every Imam is mot Islam.

(b) The second question relates to interpretation of the words Imam and Islam. Chariot used the words in three different ways both (a) in one meaning, (b) in two meanings, or (c) in two meanings mixed together. (a) The one meaning is sup ported by the verse: I have taken out the believers who were in the city and I did mot find in it but only one house of Muslims (51 : 35). In fact there was only one family of Muslims God said: O my people, if you believe God, them put your trust in Him if you are Muslims (10 : 84). The Prophet said: Islam is built upon five pillars. He answered it when questioned about Iman. (b) As to the two meanings of the words, God said: The desert Arabs say: We have believed. Say, you have not believed, but say: We have accepted Islam (39 : 14). This shows that they surrendered outwardly. Gabriel once asked the Prophet: What is Iman and what is Islam? The Prophet replied in two different meanings. These meanings are mixed together. Islam is the work of mind, words and actions, while Iman is an action of mind or to confirm truth by mind.

(c) The third meaning relates to rules of Shariat which governs the two terms: One relates to the hereafter and another to this world. The former is to bring out men from Hell-fire and not allow them to remain there forever. The Prophet said: Whosoever has in his heart the belief to the weight of an atom will be brought out of Hell-fire. What sort of Iman is this? Some say it is inward belief and some say it is verbal confession. Some say it is actions according to Islam. It is again said that he who combines himself all these three elements will be taken out of Hell. With regard to the second element, a man will also be taken out of Hell although he committed some major sins. He is called Fasiq or a great sinner. The third element is confirmation of faith by mind and attestation by tongue but not followed by actions. Regarding confirmation of truth by mind at death before verbal confession by tongue, such a man also will be taken out of Hell as the Prophet said: He who has an atom of belief in his heart will be taken out of Hell. Regarding verbal confession by tongue of Kalema Shahadat but not confirmation by mind, there is no doubt that such a person will remain forever in Hell.

(2) **Second question.** Iman is subject to increase and decrease. It

increases by good deeds and decreases by evil deeds. There is existence of a thing which has got increase or decrease and nothing grows or diminishes of itself. So there is existence of Iman which increases by good deeds and decreases by evil deeds. God says: He increased their belief. God says: In order to increase their belief along with their belief. The Prophet said: Belief increase and decreases. This law is applicable to every attribute of mind. Mind appertains to the unseen spiritual world and the action of organs appertains to this world. There is subtle tie between these two worlds and some men think that the two worlds are the same. He who has seen both the worlds perceived the real nature of things. This is the first meaning. Regarding the second meaning of increase and decrease of belief, the Prophet said: Belief has got more than seventy branches. He also said: When a fornicator fornicates, he ceases to be a believer at the time. So there is action along with belief which shows that it increases and decreases. Regarding its third meaning, it is sure and certain belief which can be seen by Kashf, expansion of breast and deep insight. Mind is not satisfied till it has got faith like the fact that two is more than one, that fire burns and that the world is created. So this is the highest stage of belief after increase.

(3) **Third question.** It is with regard to the answer. 'I am a believer if God wills, on a question put to one- "Are you a believer?" The reply should not be "I am a true believer or I am a believer to God." These qualifications are correct or put forward for four reasons, two of them come from doubt and two do not come from doubt. The first reason which does not come from doubt is the care taken for fear of showing oneself pure. God says: Don't impute purity to yourself. God says: Have you not seen those who hold themselves to be righteous (4: 52)? A certain wise man was asked: What is detestable talk? He said: To praise oneself. The second reason for the u.;e of these qualifications is courtesy and to entrust all actions to the will of God. God says by way of instruction to the Prophet (18 : 23); Don't say of anything; `I will do it tomorrow' without saying `if God wills.' The third meaning keeps connection with doubt when one says: I am a true believer if God wills. There is doubt whether the man is a perfect believer because God said: True believers are those only

who believe in God and His Apostle and afterwards do not doubt and who fight with their lives and properties for the cause of God. These are the truthful-(94 : 15). It has been expressed also in verses (133.2:172; 58: 12;57;10). The Prophet said: Belief has got seventy branches. The fourth reason arises also from doubt. It is the fear of bad end, for no one knows what will be his end, good or bad.

These are therefore the different reasons for qualifying answer to the question: Are you a believer?

MYSTERIES OF CLEANLINESS

The Holy Prophet said: Religion is founded on cleanliness. He said: Cleanliness is the key to prayer. God said: Therein are men who love purity and God loves the pure (9:109). The Prophet said: Cleanliness is one-half of belief. God said: God desires to make you clean and to complete His favours on you (5 : 7).

Those who possess insight understand by these sayings that the most important thing is the purification of the heart. If the tradition 'cleanliness is one-half of faith' is limited only to the external cleanliness of physical organs by water and not also to the purification of the heart which may entertain evil designs and thoughts, its meaning then will be distant and it is impossible.

Purity has got Four Stages

(1) The first stage is the purification of the external organs from excrements and filths. (2) The second stage is the purification of the body organs from sins and faults. (3) The third stage is the purification of the heart from evil traits and evil vices. (4) The fourth stage is the purification of the inner self from everything except God. This is the stage of the Prophets and the saints. Every item of cleanliness is half of action, because the object of the actions is the glorification and greatness of God. In reality God's knowledge is not attained unless the heart is purified of all things other than God. For this reason, God said: Say 'God', then' leave them to play in the useless talks (6:91). There can be no two things in mind at the same time and God also has not created two minds in the same man. The object of the actions is to adorn the mind with praiseworthy qualities and religious firm faith. It is well known

that. the mind will not be adorned with those qualities till the blameworthy evils and false faith reign in it.

To purify the mind from these evils comprises half of its actions and the first half is pre-requisite for the second. In this sense, purity is said to be half of belief. So to purify the bodily limbs from the prohibited things is the first half and to strengthen it with religious acts is its second half. These are the stages of belief and every stage has got its rank. Nobody will attain a 'higher stage. unless he first goes through the lower one. He can not attain real purity of heart till he purifies it from the blameworthy vices and adorn it with the praiseworthy qualities. He can't purify the heart till he purifies his organs from prohibited things and makes it firm with religious acts. The more honourable is the object, the more difficult is the attainment of that object. The longer is the road that leads to it, the greater are the obstacles. Don't think that this can be attained with ease and without efforts. He who is blind to these stages of purity will not understand the above mentioned four stages. He will understand the lowest stage of cleanliness. It is like the outer husk of a crop or like skull in relation to brain. He understands that the outer cleanliness is the desired object and makes exaggeration in it and spends much time and wealth in advertising (Istinja) in cleanliness of cloth, body and in the use of water and thinks that the noble purity comprises these outward and external cleanliness. The early Muslims concentrated their entire attention and energies on the purification of their hearts and were lenient in their outward cleanliness. Even Hadrat Omar, being placed in a high position, made ablution with the water from a jar which belonged to a Christian woman. The companions were accustomed not to wash their hands after eating from the remains of fat and food but to wipe them out against the arches of their feet and regarded the use of soap as innovation. They used to say prayer kneeling and prostrating directly on the ground in the mosque and walk barefooted on the roads. They used to use pebbles after calls of nature.

Abu Hurrah and some inmates of Suffa said: We ate meal and when the prayer time came, we wiped our fingers against the pebbles and proceeded to say prayer. Hazrat Omar said: We did not know the use of soap at the time of the Prophet and the hollows of our feet were our towels. It is said that the first four innovations after the Prophet were the use of sieves, soap, tables and eating to satiety. The efforts of the companions were towards the purification of the heart to the extent that some one among them said: It is better to say prayer with shoes than without shoes because when the Prophet took off his shoes with uncleanliness at the advent of Gabriel, the companions also took off their shoes. He told them: Why have you taken off your shoes? One of them named Nakhyi said: Perhaps someone in need may pass by and take these shoes. In fact, they walked barefooted, sat on the mud and sand, prayed directly on the floors of the mosque. They used to eat bread of coarse wheat which the animals trod with their feet and sometimes polluted with their urine. They made no efforts to avoid small impurities.

These things have now changed. The people termed cleanliness for ironed cloth and say that it is the foundation of religion. One group spend most of their times in beautifying their bodies just like a new bride but their minds are full of evil thoughts, pride, self-conceit, ignorance, show and hypocrisy. He who cleanses with stones after calls of nature, walks barefooted in mud, prays in mosque on the floor, walks on the rugs without leather over shoes or makes ablution with water belonging to an old woman, is attacked furiously and he is termed as impure.

The following are three matters of external purity-(1) purification from impurities, (2) purification of the body from excrements, and (3) purification from bodily growths, such as pairing of nails, cutting off hairs, circumcision, removal of the hairs of pubes and the like.

SECTION – I
Purification from Impurities

There are three matters in this; the things to be removed, the means of removal and the meaning of removal. That which shall have to be removed is of three kinds, inanimate objects, animate objects and parts of animate objects. As to inanimate objects, all are pure except wine and intoxicating things. As to animate objects, all except dogs and pigs and their young ones are pure. When an animal dies, it becomes impure except fivelocusts, fish, worms in food-stuffs, dead animals which have no flowing blood like flies, beetles and the like. As to purity from inanimate objects, it is of two kinds, the first is what is cut off from an animal and its law is the same as that of dead bodies. Hair is not impure. Bones, however, become impure after death. The second is what is changed after entering into belly. They are all impure. What emits from the body not after change is pure, such as sweat and tears. Things which have a fixed seat and are subject to change are impure, such as saliva, mucus of nose except the seed of life like semen, eggs, blood, pus, feces, urine are impure. Nothing is exempted of these impurities except five things-(1) the remains of odour after abstersion with pebbles are exempted, (2) whatever cannot be avoided such as mud in the streets and the dust of dung in spite of their impurities is exempted, (3) what is attached to the leather socks of impurities of the streets is exempted after it has been wiped against earth, (4) the blood of fleas and the like little or much on shirt is exempted except when it goes beyond the ordinary limits, and (5) blood of itches and pimples is exempted.

The Means of Removal of Impurities The means of removal of impurities are either condensed or liquid things. The condensed or soild things are pebbles of abstersion. Pebble purifies it if it is itself pure and dried. It should be hard, pure, dry and free from illegality. Liquid thing is water with which impurities are cleansed. Only pure water can remove impurities. The water, when mixed with impure thing and does not change its colour is pure, but if its colour, taste and odour are changed, it becomes impure. The Prophet said: When water is sufficient to fill two pitchers, it caries no impurities, if less, it carries impurities and does not remain pure. This is applicable in case of stagnant water. If flowing water mixes with impure things and becomes changed, it then becomes impure.

Some incidents together with urgent need and necessity strengthen the belief that only change in water was taken into consideration by the Prophet. The following words of the Prophet support it:

Water was created pure and nothing makes it impure except that which changes its colour, taste and smell.

Manner to remove impurities. If the impurity is not a matter of touch, it is sufficient to run water over all its parts. If the impurity is physical, it should be removed. If its taste remains, it indicates the persistence of the physical matter. The same is true of the persistence of colour. If it sticks, it is exempted provided it is thoroughly rubbed. If taste persists, the persistence of its physical matter is perceived.

SECTION – II
Purification of Body from Excrements

It comprises abstersion, ablution, bath and purification with sand. We are now stating the manner of their performance in the prescribed order. The following are the rules of answering the calls of nature. If one is pressed by calls of nature, he should go from the view of men and take shelter behind something. He should not uncover his private parts before he sits down and should not face or keep back Ka'ba, sun or moon but there is no harm when he is within a room. He should not sit in a meeting place of the people, urinate in stagnant water, under a fruit free, or in a hard surface and windy place. He should sit on his left leg. When entering a room, he should advance his left leg first and then his right leg and should not urinate while standing. Hadrat Umar said: While I was urinating standing, the Prophet told me: O Umar, don't pass urine standing. Hazrat Ibnul Mubarak said: There is no harm in urinating in a bathroom if the water goes out flowing. The Prophet said: Let nobody among you urinate in a bathroom and then make ablution as many machinations come from it. None should take with him anything which contains the name of God or his Apostle. On entering room, he should say: I seek refuge in God from the accursed devil, the filthy, the impure, the abominable, the pernicious. On leaving it, he should say : all praise is due to God who has removed from me what was harmful to me and left for me what is useful. Before sitting, he should take pebbles with him. He should not wash his private part with water in the first place.

He should take utmost pains in cleansing his penis from urine by shaking it to and fro three tines. Hazrat Salman said: The Prophet taught us everything even how to cleanse after calls of nature. He prohibited us to cleanse with bone, our dung or face the Ka'ba.

Manner of Abstersion

He will perform abstersion with three stones. If the orifice is cleansed therewith, it is good and if not more stones may be used. The Prophet said: Let one who uses stones use odd numbers. He shall take stones in his left hand, place it in the fore part of his orifice and run it over with horizontal and circular motions to the rear part. Thus it will continue from the rear part to the fore part. Taking the third stone, he should ran it around the orifice. He should then move to another place and perform the act of abstersion with water. At the end of abstersion, he should say: O my God, purify my heart from hypocrisy and make my private part pure from indecencies. He should then wipe his hand against earth or wall till odour is removed therefrom. The use of stones and water are both desirable. It is related that when God revealed the verse (9 :109); "Therein are men who love purity and God loves the pure", the Apostle of God said to the people of Quba: What is the purity for which God has praised you? They said: We are accustomed to use both stones and water after calls of nature.

Manner of Ablution

He shall commence with the use of tooth-stick. The Prophet said: Your mouths are the pathways of the Quran. Cleanse them therefore with stick. The Prophet said: Prayer after the use of tooth-stick is better than prayer without its use by seventy -five times. He said : Had it not been difficult for my followers, I would have ordered them to use tooth-stick before every prayer. He said: Why should I not see you with yellow teeth? The Prophet was accustomed to use tooth-stick several times every night. Hazrat Ibn Abbas said: The Prophet has so repeatedly commanded us to use toothstick that we thought that soon a revelation would come for its use. The Prophet said: Use tooth-stick, as it purifies the mouth and pleases God. Hazrat Ali said: Use of tooth-stick increases memory and removes phlegm. The companion of the Prophet used to keep tooth-stick in their ears even at the time of journey.

It is desirable to use the tooth-stick before every prayer and every ablution, before and after sleep, after eating anything of unpleasant smell. After the use of tooth-stick, face the Ka'ba for ablution and then say: In the name of God, the Merciful, the most Compassionate. The Prophet said: There is no ablution for one who does not take the name of God, that is complete ablution. He should then wash his hands three times and should say: O God, I ask Thee for luck and blessing and seek refuge to Thee against ill-luck and destruction. He shall rinse his mouth thrice with water and say afterwards: O God, help me to read Thy Book and glorify Thy name. Then he shall take up water and cleanse his nose thrice and say: O God, grant me to enjoy the fragrance of paradise while Thou art pleased to promise it to me. At the time of throwing dust from nose, he should say: I seek refuge to Thee from the stench of Hell and from the evil of the world. He will then wash his face thrice from ear to ear and from flat portion of head to fore part of the chin. As he washes his face, he should say: O God, make my face white and bright with Thy light on the day when Thou will make the faces of Thy friends bright. He should then wash his arms up to the elbows three times. The believers will come on the Resurrection Day with brightness on their foreheads, wrists and ankles from the effect of ablution. The Prophet said: Whosoever is able to cleanse the fore part of his head, let him do so. He should then wipe his head by soaking his hands in water. Thrice he should do it and say: O God, cover me with Thy mercy and shower upon me Thy blessings. He shall then wipe his ears both outside and inside with fresh water thrice. He should then wipe his neck with fresh water because the Prophet said: Wiping the neck from behind will save one from breach of trust on the Resurrection Day. Then he should wash his right foot thrice and left foot thrice. When he will finish ablution thus, he should raise his head towards the sky and say: I testify that there is no deity but God. He is one and there is no partner for Him. I testify also that Muhammad is the servant and Apostle of God.

There are several undesirable things in ablution-to wash each limb more than three times. The Prophet said: Whoever goes beyond three times transgresses. He said: Soon there will appear among my people those who will exaggerate in ablution and invocation.

Excellence of ablution. The Prophet said: Whoever makes ablution well and prays two rak'ats of prayer in such a way that nothing of the world occurs in his mind, goes out of his sins in such a manner that he comes out as it were from the womb of his mother. The Prophet said: Should I not inform you what atones sins and raises ranks'?-performing ablution in distress, to step towards the mosques and to wait for the next prayer after a prayer. This is the "bond". **He repeated** it three times. The Prophet said after washing each limb: God does not accept prayer except this ablution. He performed ablution after pouring water twice on each limb and said: God will reward him twice. He performed ablution of each limb thrice and said: This is the ablution of the Prophets before me and of Abraham. The Prophet said: Whosoever remembers God at the time of his ablution, God purifies his whole body and he who does not remember God, is not purified except those places where the water was applied. The Prophet said: Whosoever makes ablution after ablution, ten merits are recorded for him. The Prophet said: Ablution after ablution is like a light. The Prophet said: When a Muslim in ablution rinses his mouth, the sins come out of his mouth. When he blows his nose, the sins come out of his nose. When he washes his face, the sins fall down from his face, even from his eye brows. When he washes his two hands, the sins fall down from his two hands, even from beneath his fingernails. When he wipes his head, the sins come out of his head, even from his two ears. When he washes his feet, the sins come out of his feet, even from beneath his toes. Then he goes to the mosque and prays. Those become additional. There is in another tradition: One who makes ablution is like a fasting man. The Prophet said: Whosoever performs ablution well and then says looking to the sky: I testify that there is no deity but God and He has no associate and I testify that Muhammad is the Apostle of God, eight gates of Paradise are opened up for him and he will enter therein through whichever gate he wishes.

Manner of Bath

One shall place the vessel with water to his right and then after taking the ;name of God wash his hands thrice and remove any impurity he has from his body. He shall then perform ablution in the manner already described with the exception of washing of feet. He shall then pour water on his head thrice, over the right side thrice, over his left side thrice. He shall then rub his body in front and back including beard and hairs. He is not required to make ablution after bath provided he has performed it before bath.

Bath is compulsory in four cases, in case of emission of semen, in case of copulation, after masturbation and after child birth. Other baths are sunnat, such as baths on two 'Id days, Friday, at the time of Ihram, at the time of waiting at Arafat, at the time of entry into Mecca, on the last three days of pilgrimage at the farewell circumambulation, at the time of conversion to Islam, after recovery from swoon and after washing a dead body.

Manner of Tayammum

The manner of purification with sand is as follows. If the use of water does harm to a person, if water is not found on search, or if there is danger in reaching the place of water such as fear of ferocious beast, or fear of enemies, or if the water is even insufficient to quench thirst, or if the water is in possession of another and the price is high, or if he is ill, or has got wound and water will do harm, then he should wait till the time of compulsory prayer comes. He should then proceed to use pure soil with intention of Tayammum. He should put his right palm over the sandy soil and lift it to his face, wipe it and intend to observe prayer. It should be done only once. Then he shall again place his left palm over the sand and wipe his right hand and then place his right hand to the elbows over the sand and then wipe his left hand up to the elbows. By this Tayammum, only one prayer at a time can be done.

SECTION – III

Cleansing the external bodily growths and discharges. These are of two kinds, the discharges and the wet excretions of the body and bodily growths. These excretions are eight in number.

(1) That which attaches to the hairs of head such as dirt and lice should be removed by washing, combing and the use of ointment. The Prophet used to oil his hairs and comb them on every alternate days and ordered his followers to do the same. The Prophet said: Oil your hairs on every alternate days. He also said: Let one honour his hairs. It means: Keep them clean of filth and arrange them. Once a man came to the Prophet with dishevelled hairs and ruffled beard and he said: Has he got no oil wherewith to arrange his hairs? Then he said: One of you comes as if he is a devil. (2) Filth which collects in the holes of ears. This filth should carefully be cleansed. (3) Filth in the nose should be removed by inhaling and exhaling. (4) The Filth which collects between the teeth and the tip of the tongue should be removed by tooth-stick and the rinsing of mouth. (5) Filth which attaches to the beard should be removed and the beard should be combed. There is a well known tradition that the Prophet either at home or in journey never parted with his tooth-stick, comb and mirror. Hazrat Ayesha said that the Prophet said: God loves a man who adorns himself whenever he goes out to meet with his brethren. (6) The Filth which collects in finger joints should be removed and the Prophet ordered his followers to cleanse them specially after eating. (7) The Filth which collects in nails of fingers should be removed. The Prophet ordered that the manicuring of nails, plucking the hairs of armpits and shaving the pubes should be done once every forty days. Once revelation stopped coming to the Prophet. When Gabriel came to him, he asked him the reason and Gabriel raid: How can revelation come to you when you have not cleansed the filth from your knuckle and nails and filth of mouth by tooth-stick? (S) Filth of the whole body collected through perspiration and dust of path ways should be removed by bath. There is no harm to enter public bathroom for that.

Second Kind of Filths

These are bodily growths and are of eight kinds. (1) **Hairs of head.** There is no harm in shaving the hairs of head for one who desires to be clean and there is no harm in keeping them provided he oils them and keeps them arranged and combed. (2) **Hairs of moustache.** The Prophet said: Cut off your moustaches, in another narration, spare your moustaches. In another narration, trim your moustaches and spare your beards. In other words, let your moustaches extend to the upper hip. Shaving of moustaches was never mentioned in the tradition, while trimming so closely as to resemble shaving has been narrated by the companions. There is no harm in leaving the ends of moustaches to hang down. The Prophet said: Cut off your moustache along a tooth-stick. The Prophet said: Spare the beard and let it grow. The Prophet **said: Do** the opposite as the Jews used to spare their moustaches and trim their beard.

(3) **Hairs of armpits** should he removed once every forty days either by plucking or by shaving. (4) **Hairs of pubes** should be removed once every forty days either by shaving or by the use of a depilatory. (5) **Nails** should he manicured because of their ugly appearances and also because of the dirt which collects underneath them. The Prophet said: O Abu Hurairah, manicure your trails as the devil sits therein when they are long. (6-7) **Navel cord and foreskin of genital organ,** The navel cord is cut off at the time of birth of a child. The Prophet said: Circumcision is Sunnat for a male and meritorious for a female. Excess should be avoided· in the case of a female. The Prophet said to Umm Atiya: O Umm Atiyya, be moderate in circumcision and cut off only a small portion of clitoris, for it is better to preserve femininity and more welcome to masculinity. (8) **Length of beard.** There are differences of opinion regarding the length of the beard. Some say that it is to be kept up to the grip and there is no harm in cutting beyond the grip. Hazrat Umar and some Tabeyins used to do it. Hasan Basri and Qatadah said that to spare it to grow long is better as the Prophet said: Spare your beards.

It has been said that the bigger the beard, the smaller the intellect.

There are ten undesirable practices regarding beard. These are dyeing the beard black, bleaching it with sulphur, plucking it, plucking the grey hairs, trimming it, augmenting its size, keeping it dishevelled, combing it for show of people, making it black for show of youth, making it grey to attract honour and dyeing it red or yellow. Dyeing it with black colour is prohibited as the Prophet said: The best of your youths is he who follows the old among you and the worst of your old is he who follows the youth among you. The Prophet said: Black dye is the sign of the inmates of Hell. The first man who used black dye was Pharaoh. The Prophet said : There will appear in later ages people who will dye their beards black like the peak of pigeons. They will not get the fragrance of Paradise. Dyeing the beard yellow or red is permitted. The Prophet said: Yellow is the colour with which the Muslims dye their beards and red is the colour with which the believers dye their beards. Henna can be used for red dye and saffron and Philyrea for yellow dye. Bleaching the beard with sulphur to give the appearance of advanced age, to attract veneration and to have their testimony accepted is undesirable. To shave beard is Makruh or undesirable. So also plucking grey hairs because the Prophet prohibited it as it is a light for a believer.

PRAYER

Prayer is the pillar of religion and safeguard and root of religious belief and the chief of religious actions. The chapter is divided into seven sections.

SECTION – I

Excellence of Prayer

Excellence of Azan. The Prophet said: Three persons will remain on the Resurrection Day on the mountain of black musk. They will have no fear of account and they will have no anxiety till they become free from what is near men. (1) One who recites the Quran to seek the pleasure of God and leads the prayer of the people who remain pleased with him. (2) One who proclaims Azan in a mosque for pleasure of God and call the people towards the path of God. (3) One who is given trouble in the world regarding his livelihood but does not give up the actions of the next world in searching it. -The Prophet said: If a man, jinn or anything hears the Azan of a Muazzin, he will testify for him on the Resurrection Day. The Prophet said: The hand of the Merciful remains on the head of a Muazzin till he finishes his Azan. God says: If a man calls towards God and does good, who is better than him in preaching? This was revealed regarding a Muazzin. The Prophet said: When you hear Azan, say what Muazzin says. Say at the time of Hai aa las salah-"There is no might and strength except through God." When he says: prayer has begun, say "May God establish the prayer and keep its tongue so long as the heaven and earth exist." When at the time of Fajr prayer it is recited "prayer is better than sleep," say "you have spoken the truth, you have spoken good and given admonition." Say when the Azan is finished: "O God. Lord of this. perfect invitation, and ever living prayer, grant position, means and honour to Muhammad and raise him up to the position of glory which Thou hast promised him."

Excellence of Compulsory Prayer

God says: Prayer is compulsory on the believers at the appointed times. The Prophet said: God has made compulsory for His servants prayer for five times. If a man observes them and does not leave anything out of their duties, there is covenant for him from God that He will admit him in paradise. If a man does not observe them, there is no covenant from God for him. If He wishes, He may punish him and if He wishes, He may admit him in paradise. The Prophet said: Prayer, five times is like a flowing canal of pure water by the side of one's house. He takes bath five times daily in it. Will you see any impurity in his body? They said: No. The Prophet said: As water removes impurities, so prayer for five times removes sins. The Prophet said: Prayer for five times expiates the Alas of a man till he does not commit major sins. The Prophet said: The distinction between us and the hypocrites is our presence at morning and night prayers and their absence at these two prayers. The Prophet said: If a man meets God after destroying his prayer, God will not look towards his virtues. The Prophet said: Prayer is the pillar of religion. He who gives it up destroys the pillar. The Prophet was once asked: Which action is best? He said: To pray at the appointed times. The Prophet said: If a man protects his prayer for five times with full ablution and at appointed times, these will be proof and light for him on the Resurrection Day. He who destroys his prayer will rise with Pharaoh and Haman.

The Prophet said: Prayer is a key to paradise. He said: God has not made anything compulsory dear to Him for his servants after Tauhid than prayer. Had there been anything better than it, he would have fixed it for the angels. They took from Him the organs of prayer, Some bow, some prostrate, some stand, some sit. The Prophet said: He who gives up prayer intentionally becomes an infidel. In other words, he becomes near coming out of faith as his firm tie becomes loose and his pillar falls down just as when a man comes near a town it is said that he has reached the town and entered it. The Prophet said: He who gives up prayer intentionally, becomes free from the covenant of Muhammad. The Prophet said: O Abu Hurairah, enjoin on the members of your family to pray as you can't conceive wherefrom God will supply you provision.

Excellence of fulfilling the duties of prayer

The Prophet said: Compulsory prayer is like a scale. He who measures out in full takes full. The Prophet said: If two men of my followers stand in prayer, it seems that their prostrations are the same but the spirit of their prayer is like the distance of the heaven and earth. He hinted at their God-fear. The Prophet said: God will not look to a man on the Resurrection Day who does not make his backbone erect between his bow and prostration. The Prophet said: If a man turns his face towards another direction in prayer, God will turn his face in to that of an ass. The Prophet said: if a man says prayer at its appointed time, establishes ablution, makes his bow and prostration perfect and has got God-fear, it will become bright and rise upwards and say: May God guard you as you have guarded me. If a man does not pray at its appointed time, does not make ablution well and does not make perfect his ruk'u and prostration and God-fear, it will become dark and rise upwards and say: May God destroy you as you have destroyed me. God will keep it folded as old cloth is kept folded. The Prophet said: The word thief applies to one who steals in prayer.

Excellence of Praying in Congregation

The Prophet said: The rewards of a prayer in congregation is twenty-seven times more than the prayer said alone. The Prophet did not see once some persons joining prayer in congregation and said: I wished that I should give order to some one to lead the prayer and oppose those who have not joined in prayer and burn their houses. In another narration: I oppose those persons who do not pray in congregation and order that their houses should be burnt with fuel. If a man among them had known what rewards there are in night prayer, he would have surely been present at night prayer. There is in Hadis: He who remains at night prayer prayed as it were half the night. He who remains present in the morning prayer prayed as it were the whole night. The Prophet said: He who prays a prayer in congregation fills up his neck with divine service. Hazrat Sayeed-b-Musayyeb said: I reached the mosque before Azan for 20 years consecutively. The sage Waseh said: I want three things in the world (1) such a brother who will keep me straight if I become crooked, (2) such livelihood as can be earned without begging, and (3) such a prayer in congregation of which the faults are forgiven to me and excellence is written for me. Hazrat Ibn Abbas said: He who does not respond to Azan does not hope for good and no good is expected from him. The Prophet said: If a man prays in congregation for forty days and does not lose even Takbir, God writes for him two salvations-one salvation from hypocrisy, and another from Hell.

Excellence of prostration.

The Prophet said: There is nothing except prostration which can take one near God. The Prophet said: There is no such Muslim whom God does not give a rank in lieu of his one prostration and remove one sin from him. A man asked the Prophet: Pray that I may be included within the party of your intercession so that He may give me mercy of your intercession in paradise. The Prophet said: One who prostrates will gain the nearness of God, as God says: Prostrate and seek nearness. God says: There are signs in their foreheads as an effect of prostration. It is said that this sign is effected as a result of dust that is attached to forehead at the time of prostration . Some say that it is the light of God-fear as it is expressed outwardly from a secret place. This is the correct view. Some say that it is the light that will be seen on their forehead on the Resurrection Day on account of ablution. The Prophet said: When a man prostrates, the devil does away from him weeping and saying: Alas! He has been ordered to prostrate and he has prostrated. So there is Paradise for him. I have been ordered to prostrate but as I have disobeyed it, there is Hell for me. It is narrated that the Caliph Abdul Aziz used not to make prostration except on the ground. Hazrat Abu Hurairah said: Prostration takes a servant near God and he makes invocation at that time.

Excellence of God-fear.

God says: Pray to remember Me. God says: Don't be one of the heedless. God says: Don't come near prayer when you are intoxicated till you do not understand what you say. Some say that intoxication means a great anxiety. Some say that it means attachment to the world. There are many worshippers who do not drink wine but they do not know what they say in prayer. The Prophet said: If a man prays two rak'ats without any thought of the world therein, his past sins are forgiven. The Prophet said: Prayer is the embodiment of modesty, humility, entreaties, repentance, raising of hands and utterance of words "O God, O God," He who does not do it, is a cheat. There is in earlier scriptures that God said: I don't accept the prayer of every one. I accept the prayer of one who humbles himself before My glory, does not take boast in doing My service and gives food for My sake to the hungry and the poor. I have made prayer compulsory, ordered for Haj and Tawaf for My remembrance. If you have got no fear of God in your mind, what is the value of your Zikr? The Prophet said: When you pray, pray in such a manner that you are bidding farewell. He said: Fear God, He will teach you. God says: Fear God and know that you must meet Him. The Prophet said: He who does not restrain himself from indecency and evil deeds in prayer keeps away from God. Prayer is munajat or invocation. How can it be with heedlessness? Hazrat Ayesha said: The Prophet used to talk with us and we also used to talk with him. When the time for prayer came, he did not as it were recognise us and we also did not recognise him, as we remained busy in declaring the glory of God. The Prophet said: God does not respond prayer of a man who does not observe it with his mind and body. When the Prophet Abraham stood in prayer, the voice of his mind could have been heard from a distance of two miles. When the sage Sayeed Tanukhi prayed, his two eyes used to shed tears which flowed down his beard. The Prophet once saw a man in prayers sporting with his beard and said: If he and his mind had God-fear, his organs also would have God-fear. It is narrated of Moslem-b-Yasar that whenever he wished to pray, he used to say to his family members: You hold conversation, I will not hear you. It is said that when he was praying in the congregational mosque, one corner of the mosque once suddenly fell down for which the people gathered there, but he could not know it till he finished his prayer. When the time of prayer came, the heart of Hazrat Ali used to tremble and his colour became changed. He was questioned: O Commander of the faithful, what has happened to you? He said: It is time of trust of God which was entrusted to the heavens, earth and mountains but they became fearful of it and refused to bear it, but I am bearing it when it is has come to me. When Hazrat Zainal Abedin, son of Hazrat Hussain, performed ablution, his colour turned pale. His family members asked him: What troubles you at the time of ablution? He said: Don't you see before whom I am going to stand? Hazrat Daud used to say in his Munajat: O my Lord, who lives in your house and from whom you accept prayer? God revealed to him: The man who lives in My house and from whom I accept prayer is one who humbles himself before My glory, passes his life in My remembrance, controls his passion for My sake, entertains a stranger and shows kindness to the aggrieved. His light will sparkle like the rays of the sun in the sky. I respond to him if he calls me. If he invokes Me, I accept it. I give him patience in his ignorance, remembrance in his carelessness and light in his pride. His simile among the people is the simile of Firdous in high gardens. His river does not become dry and his face does not become changed.

Once Hatem Asem was asked about prayer and he said: When the time of prayer comes, I make full ablution, come to the praying place and wait there till my neighbours come there. Then I stand for prayer, face the Ka'ba with Bridge under my feet, Paradise by my right Side and Hell by my left side, angel of death behind me and think that this is my last prayer. Then I stand between fear and hope, recite Takbir, make Ruk'u with humility, prostrate with fear and sit on my left waist and spread my sole of feet and keep my right side on my toes. I don't know whether my prayer has been accepted or not.

Excellence of Mosque and Praying Place

God says: Those who have got faith in God and the next world inhabit God's mosques. The Prophet said: If a man constructs a mosque for God, He constructs for him a palace in Paradise. The Prophet said: If a man loves mosque, God loves him. He said: When one of you enters a mosque, let him pray two rak'ats before he sits. He said: There is no prayer for mosque except in mosque. He said: Angels like ore of you until he keeps seated in his praying place. They say: O God, send blessings on him. O God, have mercy on him, forgive him till he keeps his ablution or gets out of mosque. The Prophet said: There will be some people among my followers who will come to mosque and sit in groups. They will like to talk of this world and its matters. Don't sit with them. God has got no necessity of them. He said: God said in some of His books: Mosques are my houses in the world and My neighbours are those people in them who are habituated to go there. Good news is for one who keeps his house pure and then meets Me in My house. He said: When you find a man visiting mosque always, bear witness that he has got faith. He said: Random talks in mosque consumes virtues as animals eat grass. Hazrat bearers of the Throne seek forgiveness for him till the light exists in the mosque. Hazrat Ali said: When a man dies, praying, cloth in the world and his good deeds raised high in the sky weep for him. Then he said: The heaven and earth did not weep for them and wait for them. Hazrat Ibn Abbas said: The world weeps for him for forty days.

SECTION – II

Open Actions in Prayer

After the removal of the impurities of body, place, cloth and places of shame, make ablution, stand facing the Ka' ba and keep some open space between the two feet. Keep your head erect or bend a little and close the eyes. If you cast your look, cast it to your place of prostration. Then make niyyat, then raise both the hands up to the ears uttering Allah o Akbar-God is greatest. Thereafter recite the formula: Glory to Thee, O God, there is Thy praise and blessed is Thy name, exalted is Thy Majesty and there is no deity besides Thee. I seek refuge to God from the accursed devil and I begin in the name of God, the most Compassionate, the most Merciful. Then recite the opening chapter of the Quran and then at least three verses of the Quran. Then saying 'God is greatest,' bow down and recite three times 'Glory to my Lord the Great' and then fall in prostration on the ground and recite three times 'Glory to my Lord, the Great.' Then sit down and then again fall prostrate and recite the formula as above mentioned and then stand erect. Thus finish one unit of prayer. Then repeat another unit in this manner, sit and recite. All invocations are for God and all services and pure things. Peace be on thee O Prophet, and the mercy of God and His blessing. Peace be on us and on the righteous servants of God. I bear witness that there is no deity but God that Muhammad is His servant and His Messenger. Then if you do not pray four such units make the following of invocation: O God, make Muhammad and the followers of Muhammad successful as Thou didst make successful Abraham and his followers, for surely Thou art the praised, mighty. O God, bless Muhammad and the followers of Muhammad as Thou didst bless Abraham and the followers of Abraham. Surely Thou art the praised, the mighty. Then close up the service followed by an invocation of your choice.

SECTION – III

Internal Conditions

Prayer should be observed with humility of mind. God says: Pray to remember Me. Presence of mind is opposed to absence of mind or heedlessness. If one is heedless throughout his prayer, how can he say prayer with the purpose of remembering God? God says: Don't be of the heedless. He says: Prayer is modesty and humility. There in there is injunctions, prohibitions and blocks. The Prophet said: If a man does not refrain from thoughts of obscene and evil things, it does not add to it but distance'. There are two kinds of prayer of a heedless man The Prophet said: There are many praying men who do not gain anything in their prayer except fatigue and efforts. The prayer of a heedless man has been spoken here. The Prophet said: Nothing is written for a praying man except what he understands in his prayer. Its speciality is that there are entreaties and seekings to God in prayer. Munajat with inattention is not considered as Munajat. There are God's remembrance in prayer, Quran reading, bow, prostration, standing and sitting. God's remembrance means prayer and Munajat to Him. Without them, it ends in voice and tongue.

The object of fasting is to bring under control belly and sexual passion, or else it ends in depriving this - body from food and drink. Body is tried by the troubles of pilgrimage. Troubles are given to mind if Zakat is paid out of wealth and thus mind is tried. There is no doubt that the object of these religious act is to remember God. If that object is not attained, there is no use in prayer, as it is very easy to move the tongue with inattention. The object of word is to talk and it does not occur exempt in mind. It does not exist in mind without humility of spirit and presence of mind. If you recite in prayer: 'Show us the right path', and if you are inattentive at that time, it is only the movement of your tongue and nothing else. The object of Quran reading and God's remembrance is to praise and glorify God and to entreat Him and invoke Him with humility of spirit, but if his mind remains absent at that time and does not know that He is present with whom he is speaking, it must be understood that his tongue moves only owing to habit but he is far away from the object of prayer to enliven God's remembrance and with that to make firm the tie of faith.

Sufyan Saori said: The prayer of one who has got no God-fear becomes void. Hasan Basri said: The prayer which is not said with attention hastens towards punishment. The Prophet said: There are many praying men whose prayers are written to the extent of one-sixth or one-tenth. In other words, the portion of prayer which is said with attention is only written. The sage Abdul Wahed said: The portion of prayer which is said with humility of mind is accepted. This is the consensus of opinion of the sages. In short, earnestness of mind is the life of prayer.

Life of Prayer and its Internal Condition

There are many works signifying the life of prayer, humility of mind, understanding what is said, honour, hope and shame. (1) The meaning of humility or presence of mind is that the action and word must be the same in mind and there should be no other thought therein. When there is no other thing in mind which is concentrated only to one thing, there is earnestness or presence of mind. (2) When mind is not present in prayer, it does not remain idle and is concentrated to the thoughts of the worldly affairs with which it is immediately concerned. So there must be firm belief that prayer is a stepping stone to the next world which is everlasting. Presence of mind is gained only when it is realised and the world is considered as a merely temporary abode and insignificant.

(3) To understand the meaning of words uttered and to engage intellect to understand their meanings. The medicine of removing various thoughts that come in mind in prayers is to cut the root or to remove the reasons which cause different thoughts. He who loves a thing remembers that thing. For this reason, he who loves things other than God is not free from diverse thoughts in prayer.

(4) Honour of God is a condition of mind. It rises out of acquaintance of two things. The first thing is the knowledge of the glory of God. This is the root of faith, because the mind of one who does not firmly believe in His glory, is not given encouragement to honour Him. The second thing is to think oneself helpless and insignificant. From the knowledge of these two things, helplessness, modesty and fear of God arise and as a result honour for God arises in mind.

(5) Fear of God is a condition of mind which arises out of knowledge of God's power and His rewards and punishments. You must have knowledge that if God would have destroyed all past and present, nothing of His sovereignty would have reduced. It is to he seen along with that whatever dangers and difficulties God gave to His Prophet and friends, these are different from those on kings, rulers and emperors. The more the knowledge about God, the more would be the fear of God.

(6) Hope in God arises out of firm faith in the following matters-knowledge of God's mercy and gifts, knowledge of His creation and remembrance of Paradise through prayer.

(7) Shame arises out of knowledge of neglect in divine service and

inability to fight for God. Human mind becomes humble in proportion of certainty of faith.

For this reason Hazrat Ayesha said: The Prophet talked with us and we also talked with him but when the time of prayer came, he could not recognise us and we did not recognise him. It is narrated that God said to Moses: O Moses, when you want to remember Me, remember Me in such a way that your limbs tremble and that you hold Me dear at the time of remembrance and rest satisfied.

When you remember Me, keep your tongue behind your mind. When you stand before Me, stand before Me with fearful mind like the meanest slave and speak with Me with the tongue of a truthful man. God revealed to him: Tell your disobedient followers to remember Me. I took oath upon Myself that I shall remember one who remembers Me. When Abraham stood for prayer, voice of his heart was heard from a distance of two miles. An individual will be forgiven in the next world according to the qualities of his mind and not of his body. Nobody will get salvation except one who comes with a sound mind.

Profitable Medicine for making Mind Humble

Know, O dear readers, that a believer will declare God's glory and fear Him, hope in Him and be ashamed to Him for his sins. After his faith, a believer will not be free from these conditions. Although the strength of his mind will be according to the strength of his faith, yet there is no other cause except the following ones for the absence of his mind; random thoughts, heedlessness, absence of mind in Munajat and absentmindedness in prayer. This heedlessness in prayer arises out of engagement of mind in various thoughts. The medicine of keeping the mind present is to remove all thoughts and primarily to remove the root of these thoughts. There are two bases of this root : external root and the internal root.

External root. Thought catches what the ear hears or the eye sees and mind turns towards that thought. This causes to produce other thoughts. So the root of thought is eye and then the root of one thought is another thought. He whose niyat is fine and aim high cannot be diverted by what occurs in his organs or limbs, but he who is weak falls a prey to it. Its medicine is to cut off these roots and to shut up the eyes, to pray in a dark room, not to keep anything in front which may attract attention and not to pray in a decorated place or a decorated and painted praying cloth. For this reason, the sages used to do divine service in dark, narrow and unspacious rooms.

Internal root is very difficult. The thoughts of worldly matters are not confined to one subject. It goes from one thought to another. If they shut up their eyes, it does not do them any benefit. The way to remove them is to take one's mind to understand what is recited in prayer and to stick to it after giving up all other thoughts. The Prophet once told Osman-b-Ali Shaiba: I forgot to tell you to cover the screens of variegated colours in the room, because there should remain nothing in the house which can divert attention from prayer. If the rise of thoughts is not stopped by this method, then there is another easy method to prevent it. That is to cut off the root cause of the disease. It has been narrated that Abu Zaham presented a valuable dress of variegated colours to the Holy Prophet. He put on it and said prayer. Afterwards he took it off and said: Take it to Abu Zaham as it has diverted my attention from prayer The Prophet had a ring of gold in his band before it was unlawful. He threw it away when he was on the pulpit and said: My sight has fallen on it. It is said that Hazrat Abu Talha once prayed in his own garden which pleased him so much that he forgot how many rak'ats he prayed He mentioned it to the Prophet and said: O Prophet of God, I wish to gift this garden. The Prophet said: Give it to whom you like. Once a man was praying in his garden in which dates were hanging. It pleased him so much that he forgot how many rak'ats he prayed. He mentioned it to Hazrat Osman who said: Spend it in the way of God. Hazrat Osman purchased it for fifty thousand coins. Thus they used to cut off the root of their thoughts and expiated the loss in prayers. This is the medicine for cutting the root of the disease of mind. To bring sexual passion under temporary control is not so benefitting. Its root must be cut as it baffles the whole prayer. The following illustration is given. In a certain tree numerous sparrows used to make tremendous noise as they had their nests in it. A traveller began to drive them away being disgusted with their noise. They fled away for the time being but came again to make greater noise. If he wants to get himself relieved of the noise permanently, he should cut the tree. The sparrows will make noise till the tree lasts. Similarly attachment to a thing may temporarily be removed from mind, but it will come again and disturb the mind. Attachment to the world is the root of all thoughts, the primary cause of all iosses. If one wants a peaceful mind in prayer, he should cut off all attachments of the world. If one is engaged in worldly matters, he should not expect to get taste in invocations.

Meaning of different items of prayer. Azan. When you hear the call to prayer, think of the general call on the Resurrection Day and look to your external and internal matters when replying and make haste. Those who respond in haste to this call, will get reply with mercy on that fearful day. So keep your mind on Azan.

Meaning of cleanliness. When you make your praying cloth pure and clean and your body clean of impurities, don't be indifferent to make your mind pure. Make it pure of impure ideas and thoughts as for as possible. Repent for what you have failed to do and determine not to do it in future. So make your heart pure as it is the object of sign of your Lord.

Meaning of covering private parts. The meaning of covering private parts is to cover your private parts from the sight of men. God looks to your heart. So cover the faults of your heart and know that it is not secret from the sight of God. Your repentance, shame and fear will expiate it. Stand before God just like a fugitive slave who returned to his master being repentant with humility of spirit and bent down head.

Meaning of facing the Ka'ba. The meaning of turning your face towards the Ka'ba is to turn your mind towards God after taking it off from all directions and all evil thoughts. Move the external organs to move your secret mind and keep them under control of mind. Keep the face of your mind towards God alone with the face of your body. The Prophet said: When a man stands in prayer and directs his hope, face and mind towards God, he comes out of his prayer as on the day his mother gave birth to him.

Meaning of standing in prayer. Its external meaning is to stand before God with body and mind. You shall bend down your head which is higher than your other limbs. The meaning of this bending down of your head is to bend down your mind free from all self-conceit and pride. Know that you are standing before the mighty and greatest Emperor. You fear king but you don't fear God although He is fit to be feared most. For this reason Hazrat Abu Bakr asked the Prophet: How should we be shameful to God? He said: You should be shameful to God just as you become shameful to see the most God-fearing man among you.

Meaning of Niyyat. Promise firmly that you will respond to God's orders through prayer, make it perfect and make niyyat sincerely for Him and keep an eye with whom you are speaking secretly, how you talk and for what matter. At this time your head should perspire, your limbs should tremble and the colour of your face should become changed.

Meaning of Takbir. When your tongue utters Takbir, let not your mind speak falsehood. Your mind should correspond with your tongue in declaring Him to be the greatest. If you have got in mind something which is greater than God, God will attest that you are a liar.

Meaning of opening Dua. 'I turn my face towards the Creator of heavens and earth'. To :urn face towards the Ka'ba means to turn it towards God. God exists everywhere and so to turn towards the Ka'ba means to turn towards the only object of your life, towards the Almighty after giving up all things. When you recite 'I am not of the polytheists,' your mind harbours then secret shirk as God says: If any body wishes to meet with his Lord, let him do good deeds and do not set up any partner in His divine service! This was revealed with respect to a person who wants divine service and also the praise of men. So take care of this shirk. When you utter-'My life and my death are for God,' know then that this condition is of the slave who safeguards the existence of his master in lieu of his existence. When you utter-'I seek refuge in God,' you should give up your low desires and temptations. You should then take firm resolution to take refuge to the fort of God giving up the fort of the devil. The Prophet said: God said 'There is no deity but God' is My fort. He who enters My fort is safe from My punishment. God protects one who has got no deity but God. He who takes his low desires as his deity lives in the fort of the devil and not in the fort of God.

Meaning of Quran reading. Reading this matter, men are of three classes-(1) he who moves his tongue but his mind is heedless, (2) he who moves his tongue and his mind follows his tongue, this is the rank of the fortunate, (3) he whose tongue is directed first towards understanding the meaning and then his mind takes his tongue as its servant. Tongue will give expression of mind.

Meaning of other items. When you utter- 'I begin in the name of the Most Compassionate, the Most Merciful', seek first the favour of God. When you say 'Thou are the Lord of Judgment Day', understand then that there is no sovereignty except His sovereignty and fear His Judgment. Express your helplessness by saying. "Thee do we worship" and understand that religious acts do not become easy except with His assistance.

It is said that when Zarrah-b-Auf finished reciting 'when the trumpet will be blown,' he fell down senseless and died. When Ibrahim Nakhyi heard this verse, 'when the sky will be rent asunder' he began to tremble seriously. So read the Quran slowly and attentively so that it becomes easy to understand. The Prophet said: God remains with the praying man till he does not look to and fro'. As it is your duty to protect your head and eyes, so it is compulsory on you to restrain your mind in prayer from thoughts other than God. When you look towards any other thing, remember then that God sees your condition. If you are absent minded at the time of munajat, it is very bad. Keep the fear of God within your mind. Hazrat Abu Bakr used to stand in prayer just like a statue. Some used to remain in Ruk'u like a motionless stone, so much so that birds sat on his head. The Prophet said: Pray as if it is your farewell prayer, having in mind fear and shame owing to defects in prayers and fear that your prayer may not be accepted, that it may be thrown on your face with your express and secret sins. There is in Hadis that when a man stands in prayer God lifts up the screen between Him and His servant and faces him. The angels climb upon his two shoulders and pray in horizon along with him and say 'Amen' along with his invocation. They spread virtues over the scalp of his head from above the horizon. A proclaimer proclaims: If this invoker had known to whom he is invoking, he would not have looked to and fro. The doors of heaven are opened up for a praying man and God takes pride before His angels for the praying men. So the doors of heaven are opened up for him and the face of God comes before his face. In other words, his Kashf is opened. He said: The softness, weeping and victory which a praying man sees in his mind, bespeak of the advent of God in his mind. When His nearness is not the nearness of space, there is no meaning of it except the nearness of mercy, guidance and removal of evils.

God says: Those believers got salvation who fear God in their prayers. Then He praised them with their speciality of prayer. It is connected with God-fear. Then he described the qualities of those who got salvation through prayer, as God says: Those who guard their prayers. Then He says: They will inherit the garden of Firdous. They will abide therein. If tongue is moved with inattention, can this reward be achieved? The praying one will inherit the gardens, they will directly see divine light and they will enjoy the happiness of nearness.

Stories of the Prayers of God-fearing Men

Know, O dear readers, that God-fear is the result of real faith and belief. He who has been given it, fears God in and out of prayer, when he remains alone and even at the time of calls of nature, because he who fears God knows it well that He knows the condition of mind and his sins and faults. Fear grows in the mind of one who knows this and it is not limited only in prayer. It is narrated that a sage did not raise up his head for forty years being ashamed and fearful of God. The saint **Rabia-b-Qasem** used to close up his eyes so tightly that the people would think that he was blind. He used to go to the house of Ibn Mas'ud for twenty years. Whenever his female slave saw him, she used to say to her master: Your blind friend has come. At this Hazrat Ibn Mas'ud used to laugh. Whenever he used to knock at the door, the female slave would come to him and see him with closed eyes. Hazrat Ibn Mas'ud told him : Give good news to those who are humble, By God, had the Prophet seen you, he would have surely been pleased with you. One day he went with Ibn Mas'ud to the shop of a blacksmith. When he saw him blowing and fire coming out, he at once fell down senseless. Ibn Mas'ud sat near his head up to the prayer time but still he did not regain his senses. Then he bore him to his house and he did not recover senses till his prayer for five times passed away. Ibn Mas'ud sat by his head and said: By God this is real God-fear.

The saint Rabia said: I did not observe such prayer in which I had other thing in mind except what I uttered and what was said to me. Hadrat Amr-b-Abdullah feared God in prayer very much. When he prayed, his daughter beat drum and the women of the house held conversation but he did not hear them. One day he was told: Does your mind think any matter in prayer? He said Yes, it thinks about its stay before God and going from this world into another world. He was told: Do you see what we generally see about the affairs of the world?' He said: I consider it better that my teeth should go from one side to another than what you see. This is not attention in prayer.

Moslem-b-Yasar was one of them. It is said that while he was one day praying within a mosque, one of its comers fell down but he did not come to know of it. The limb of a certain pious man was damaged and it required operation but it was not at all possible. Some said: When he prays, he will not be able to feel its pangs. Accordingly the limb was operated while he was engaged in prayer. Some said: Prayer belongs to the next world. When you enter prayer, go out of the world. Hazrat Abu Darda said: It is the rule of religion that when a man goes to prayer, he should perform all his necessary things, so that his mind becomes free from thoughts. The Prophet said: The prayer of a man is not written except its one-third, half, one-fourth, one-fifth, one-sixth or one-tenth. He said What is said in prayer with understanding is only written for him. Hazrat Umar once said from his pulpit: The head of two sides of a man becomes grey, yet he does not observe prayer for pleasure of God. He was asked: How does it occur? He said: His God-fear, modesty and his self-surrender for God do not become perfect. Abid Ahiya was once asked: What is the meaning of heedlessness in prayer? He said: One commits mistakes in his prayer and does not know how many rak'ats he has prayed. The sage Hasan Basari said in its explanation: He forgets the time of prayer. Jesus Christ said: God says: My servant gets salvation by observing compulsory duties, but he gains My nearness by doing optional duties. The Prophet said: God says: My servant will not get salvation till he fulfils the compulsory duties.

SECTION – IV

Imamate

There are six duties of Imam before prayer. (1) He shall not be an Imam of a people unless they give consent to it. If they differ, an Imam would be elected by a majority. If the minority are religious and good, their opinion should be followed. There is in **Hadis:** The prayer of three persons will not ;go up beyond their heads—(a) a fugitive slave, (b) a woman whose husband is displeased with her, and (c) an Imam with whom his people are dissatisfied. The Imam is a guarantee for his followers. (2) When a man is given option between Azan and Imamate, he should prefer Imamate as the office of an Imam is better than that of a Muazzin. Some say that Azan is better as there are many merits of Azan. The Prophet said: An Imam is a surety for his followers and Muazzin is an object of trust. He said: The Imam is an object of trust. When he bends down, the followers bend down and when he prostrates, they prostrate. He said: When he fulfils the prayer, it is for him' and for them also. If there is defect in it, it goes against him and against them also. For this reason, the Prophet said: O God, show the straight path to the Imams and forgive the Muezzins.

The Prophet said: Paradise becomes sure for one without account who is Imam for seven years. He who proclaims Azan for forty years will enter into Paradise without account. The Prophet, Hazrat Abu Bakr and Umar used to fix salary for an Imam. The

Prophet said: One day of a just ruler is better than divine service for seventy years. The Prophet said: Your Imams are your intercessor. He said: Your Imams are representatives of God on your behalf. If you wish to purify your prayer, place in front the best man among you. Some earlier sages said: There is no better man after the Prophet than the learned except the praying Imams, as they stand between God and His servants, some with Prophethood, some with learning and some with prayer, the pillar of religion. By this proof, the companions elected Abu Bakr as their Imam. They then said: We have considered that prayer is a pillar of religion. So we shall select such person for our religion on whom the Prophet was pleased for this pillar. They did not select Bilal as the Prophet selected him for Azan. It is reported that a man asked the Prophet: Give me clue to such an action which will lead me to Paradise. He said: Be Muezzin. He said: I can't do it. He said: Then be Imam. He said: I can't do it. He said: Then pray behind an Imam.

(3) The Imam shall observe the times of prayers and shall pray for pleasure of God in their earliest times. The Prophet said: The Imam who prays at the last time of a prayer, does not miss it, but what he misses in its earliest time is better than the world and its treasures. It is not good to delay prayer in expectation of a greater number of men. One day, there was tome delay for the morning prayer on the part of the Prophet when he was in a journey. The companions did not wait for the Prophet when he made delay in making ablution. The Prophet then said: You have done better. Do it always.

(4) Act as an Imam for the sake of God and fulfil with good manners the trust of God in the other conditions of prayer and act as an Imam with sincere intention and don't take for it remuneration. The Prophet said to Osman-b-Affan: Appoint such a Muezzin who will not take remuneration for his Azan. Azan guides to the path of prayer and it is better not to receive its remuneration. Hazrat Sufiyan said: Pray behind a religious or irreligious man except behind habitual drunkard, or cursed man, or one disobedient to parents, or an innovator or a fugitive slave.

(5) Don't utter Takbir till row is arranged straight and look to right and left. The Prophet said: A Muezzin should wait between Azan and Aqamat for so long as an eater eats or a man passes calls of nature. So he prohibited to retain urine and stool. He ordered to finish dinners for peace of mind before Isha prayer.

(6) An Imam shall raise his voice at the time of Takbir Tahrima and other Takbirs as well but a follower will utter it in a low voice. The Imam has got three duties at the time of Quran reading in prayer. (1) He should recite the opening Dua and Auzobillah in silent voice and recite loudly the Fateha and Suras in congregational prayer of Fajr, Isha and Maghrib. One should do it even at the time when he prays alone. When he recites Ameen with voice, the followers will recite it loudly.

SECTION – V
Merits of Juma Prayer

Know, O dear readers, that Juma day is a holy day God honoured Islam therewith and gave glory to the Muslims. God says: When there is Azan for prayer on the Juma day, run towards remembrance of God and give up buy and sale. The Prophet said: God has made compulsory on you on this day of mine and in this place of mine. The Prophet said: If a man loses three Jumas without any excuse, God puts a seal on his mind. In another narration: He throws Islam on his back. The Prophet said: Gabriel came to me with a clean mirror in his hand and said: This is Juma . God has made it obligatory on you, so that it may be a festival for you and after you for your followers. I said: What good there is for us in it? He said: You have got an auspicious time it If a man seeks anything to God at this time, God has promised that He will give it to him. If he is deprived of that, many additional things are given to him in that connection. If any man wants to save himself from any evil on that day, God saves him from a greater calamity or a like calamity which has been decreed on him. Juma day is the best day to us and we shall call it on the Resurrection Day as the day of grace. I asked him: What object is there in calling it as the day of grace? He said: Your God has made a valley in Paradise made of white musk When the Juma day comes, God descends on His Throne in Illyyin and sheds His lustre and they look on towards His august face. The Prophet said: The sun rose for the first time an the best Juma day and Hazrat Adam was created on that day. He entered Paradise first on that day and he was thrown into this world on that day and his penance was accepted on that day. He died on this day and Resurrection will take place on this day. This day is a day of blessing to God. The heavens and angels have been given names on this day. There is a Hadis that God will release six lacs of men from Hell on this day. The Prophet said: When the Juma day is safe, all the days remain safe. He said: If a man dies on the Juma day or night, the rewards of one martyrdom are written for him and the punishment of grave is forgiven.

Conditions of Juma Prayer

Ten rules should be observed on the Juma day, (1) It is better to prepare for the Juma day from Thursday. After Asr of Thursday, turn attention to invocation, seeking forgiveness and Tasbih as the merits of this time are equal to those of the auspicious unknown time of Friday. (2) Make your clothes clean on this day, use scent and keep your mind free from anxieties so that you may rise up with a free mind on Friday morning. Try to fast on this day as there is a great merit in it. Pass Thursday night by reading the Quran and praying. The Prophet said: God shows mercy on the man who rises in the morning and awakes others, takes bath and causes bath of others. (3) Take bath in the morning of Friday. The Prophet said: It is obligatory on every mature man to take bath on Friday. He said: Let one who attends Juma take bath. He said: Let one male or female who attends Juma Prayer take bath.

(4) If is commendable to take recourse to beauty in this day, to take fine dress, to be pure and to use scent. Regarding purity, cleanse your teeth, cut your hairs, clip your moustache and do everything necessary for purity. Hazrat Ibn Mas'ud said, If a man manicures nails on the Jumma day, God takes out disease therefrom and gives him cure therein. Regarding dress, wear white dress as it is dear to God. To use turban is commendable. The

Prophet said: God and His angels bless those who wear turban on the Juma day.

(5) It is commendable to go to the congregational mosque in the morning. The Prophet said: He who goes to Juma in the early part gets reward of the sacrifice of a camel and he who goes at the second time gets the reward of the sacrifice of a cow and he who goes at the third time gets the reward of the sacrifice of a goat and he who goes at the fourth time gets the reward of the sacrifice of a cock. He who goes at the fifth stages gets the reward of the charity of an egg. When the Imam gets up for khutba, record is folded up and pen is lifted up. The angels gather together near the pulpit and hear the Zikr of God. The Prophet said: There are three things. If the people had known what good there is therein, they would have come to search it like a camel- Azan, first row and going to the congregational mosque at dawn. In the first century, the path way became full of men from early hours up to dawn. The Prophet used to come out with light and the mosque became filled up with men like the day of 'Id. It became obsolete afterwards. It is said that the innovation of giving up the practice of going to the mosque at dawn first entered into Islam. It is a matter of regret that the Jews and the Christians go to their synagogues and churches at dawn on Saturday and Sunday respectively and the world people go to markets for buy and sale at dawn but those who seek the next world cannot go to mosque at dawn.

(6) **Ranks** of entering a mosque. Nobody should go to the front row of the mosque crossing the necks of men. The Prophet said: On the Resurrection Day such a person will be made a bridge and the people would tread over him. Once when the Prophet was reciting khutba, he noticed that a man was advancing towards the front row after crossing over the necks of men. After finishing prayer, the Prophet called him and said: O such a person what prevented you to pray Juma with me today? He said: O Prophet of God, I prayed with you. The Prophet said: Have I not found you to cross over the necks of men? He hinted by this that his action has become void. In another narration, the Prophet said to him: What prevented you to pray with me? He said: O Prophet of God, have you not seen me? The Prophet said: I have seen you coming late

and giving trouble to the people present. In other words you have delayed to come at dawn and have given trouble to those present.

(7) Don't go to the mosque by the front of a praying man, keep wall or pillar or stick in front when praying so that the people may not pass by your front. The Prophet said: His waiting for 40 years is better than his going by the front of men. The Prophet said: It is better for any man to be powdered to earth to be blown off by air like refuges than to cross the front of a praying man.

(8) Try to take seat in the first row. There is in Hadis: If a man takes bath and tells another to take bath, if a man rises early and makes another awake early and goes near the Imam and hears, the sins which he has committed between two Jumas -and additional three days become expiation for him.

(9) Prayer should be stopped at the time when the Imam gets upon the pulpit. The Prophet said: If a man says to another at the time when the Imam delivers address 'Be silent,' he holds useless talk. The Juma of one who holds useless talk is not performed.

(10) Follow the Imam in Juma When the Juma is finished, recite before talk the chapters 'Alham do Lillah' seven times, 'Ikhlas' seven times, 'Falaq' seven times and `Nas' seven times. A certain sage said: He who does this remains safe up to the next Juma from the devil.

Good Deeds of Juma Day

(1) Be present at the assembly of learning at dawn or after prayer. There is a Hadis that to remain present in an assembly of learning is better than optional prayer of one thousand rak'ats.

(2) To meditate well for the auspicious moment. There is in a well known Hadis: There is a time on Juma day in which a Muslim is granted what he seeks. There is in another Hadis: He who prays does not lose it. There is difference of opinion about this auspicious moment. Some say it is at the time of sunrise. Some say it is after noon, some say it is at the time of Azan. Some say it is when the Imam gets upon his pulpit and begins his address. Some say it is at

the last time of Asr prayer. Some say it spreads for the day like the Blessed night. So one who seeks it should remain in meditation throughout the day. Some say it is intermingled with every time of Juma day. This is the correct view. This is supported by the following Hadis: There is a day among your days when your Lord gives out breath. Be prepared for that day. This is Juma day among the days.

(3) It is commendable to recite Darud this day on the Prophet. The Prophet said: If a man sends Darud to me eighty times on Juma day, God forgives his minor faults for eighty years. He was asked: O (Prophet of God, what is Darud upon you? He said: Say: O God, bless Muhammad, Thy servant, Thy Prophet and Thy Apostle, the illiterate Prophet.

(4) Recite the Quran more in this day specially chapter Qahaf. The Prophet said: If a man recites the chapter Qahaf on the Juma day or night, he is given such light which is visible from Mecca and his sins are forgiven up to the next

Juma and the merits of three days in addition are given to him and seventy thousand angels bless him till dawn. He is saved from diseases, pains of stomach, pleurisy, tuberculosis and the trials of Dajjal.

(5) It is commendable to recite Darud at the time of entering mosque and not to sit till one prays four rak'ats reciting therein Ikhlas fifty times in each rak'at. The Prophet said: He who prays such, will not die till he is shown his place in paradise.

(6) It is commendable to give charities on Juma day. The merits are increased manifold.

(7) Keep yourself engaged in divine service for the whole Juma day after giving up worldly duties.

SECTION – VI
Prayers other than Obligatory Prayers

There are three kinds of other prayers-Sunnat, Mustahab (commendable) and Nafl (optional). Sunnat prayer is such prayer which the Prophet observed for all times, such as the prayers after obligatory prayers. Mustabab prayer is such prayer of which the excellence has been described by Hadis and which the Prophet did not observe always. Nafl prayer is such prayer which does not fall within the first two categories. What a man prays willingly for pleasure of God other than the above prayers is optional.

Sunnat Prayer. There are eight Sunnat prayers among which five are said along with five times of prayer and three in addition-forenoon prayer, Tahajjud prayer and prayer between Maghrib and Isha.

(1) Two rak'at sunnat before Fajr prayer. The Prophet said: Two rak'ats of Sunnat prayer before Fajr is better than the world and what is in it.

(2) Six rak'ats of Sunnat prayers of Zuhr' four rak'ats before it and two after it. The Prophet said: He who prays four rak'ats after declining of the sun and makes Ruk'u and prostration well and recites the Quran well, seventy thousand angels pray for him and seek forgiveness for him up to night. The Prophet said: If a man prays 12 rak'ats daily besides the obligatory prayers, a building will be built for him in Paradise-two rak'ats before Fajr, 4 rak'ats before Zuhr and two rak'ats before Asr and two rak'ats after Maghrib.

(3) Four rak'ats before Asr. The Prophet said: O God have mercy on the man who prays four rak'ats before Asr.

(4) Two rak'ats after maghrib.

(5) Four rak'ats after Isha. Hazrat Ayesha reported that the Prophet used to go to bed after praying 4 rak'ats after Isha.

Many learned men said after collecting all traditions that there are seventeen rak'ats of Sunnat prayers-two rak'ats before Fajr, four rak'ats before Zuhr and two rak'ats after it, four rak'ats before Asr, two rak'ats after Maghrib and three rak'ats after Isha.

(6) **Vitr prayer.** Hazrat Anas said: The Prophet used to pray three rak'ats of Vitr after Isha reciting therein 'Sabbehesme Rubbikal

Ala' in the first rak'at, Kaferun in the second rak'at and Ikhlas in the third rak'at.

(7) **Forenoon prayer.** It is up to eight rak'ats Hazrat Ayesha said that the Prophet used to pray four rak'ats in the forenoon and sometimes increased it.

(8) **Prayer between Maghrib and Isha.** The Prophet said: There are six rak'at prayers between Maghrib and Isha of which the merits are great. The Prophet said that this prayer is included within the prayer of Awwabin.

Optional Prayers in Weekly Days

Sunday. The Prophet said: If a man prays four rak'ats on Sunday and recites in each rak'at the opening chapter and Amanar Rasul, innumerable merits are written for him like the number of Christian males and females. The Prophet said: Proclaim the unity of God by many prayers on Sunday as God is one and there is no partner for him.

Monday. The Prophet said: If a man prays two rak'ats in the early part of Monday reciting Fateha once in each rak'at, Ayatul Kursi once, Ikhlas once, Falaq once, Nas once and then after salam Istighfar twelve times and Darud twelve times, God forgives all his sins. The Prophet said: If a man prays 12 rak'ats on Monday and recites in each rak'at Sura Fateha and Ayatul kursi and when he finishes prayer recites Ikhlas 12 times and Istighfar 12 times, he will be said on the Resurrection Day: O son of so and so, rise up and take rewards from God. The first reward that will be rewarded to him is one thousand dresses, one crown on his head and he will be said' Enter Paradise. One lac angels will greet him and each angel will have one present and they will accompany him and they will carry him to one thousand palaces of light.

Tuesday. The Prophet said: If a man prays ten rak'ats in the early part of Tuesday with Fateha and Ayatul Kursi and Ikhlas three times in each rak'at, his faults will not be written for seventy days.

If he dies on the last day, he dies a martyr and his sins for seventy years will be forgiven.

Wednesday. The Prophet said: If a man prays 12 rak'ats after rising on Wednesday and recites in each rak'at Fateha and Ayatul Kursi once and Ikhlas three times, Falaq and Nas each three times, a proclaimer will proclaim near the Throne: O servant of God, your actions have been accepted and your future sins forgiven. Punishment of the Resurrection Day will be lifted up from you and you will be given the actions of a Prophet on that day.

Thursday. The Prophet said: If a man recites between Zuhr and Asr two rak'ats with Fateha and Ayatul Kursi in the first rak'at one hundred times, Fateha and Ikhlas in the second rak'at one hundred times and Darud one hundred times, God will reward him with fasting of Rajab, Shaban and Ramadan, the rewards of one Haj and innumerable virtues will be written for him.

Friday. The Prophet said: There is a prayer on the. Juma day. When the sun rises up to one bow's distance or more and if a believing man makes full ablution and prays two rak'ats with faith and hoping for reward, God writes for him two hundred virtues and effaces from him two hundred sins. If a man prays four rak'ats, God will open for him in Paradise 800 doors and forgive all his sins. If a man prays 12 rak'ats, 1200 merits will be written for him and 1200 sins will effaced from him and there will be for him 1200 doors in Paradise. The Prophet said: If a man on Juma day enters the mosque and prays four rak'ats after Juma prayer with Fateha 50 times and Ikhlas 50 times in each rak'at, he will not die till he sees his place in paradise or it is shown to him.

Saturday. The Prophet said: If a man prays four rak'ats on Saturday with Fateha once and Ikhlas three times and then Ayatul Kursi in each rak'at, God will write for him for every ward one Haj and one Umrah and one year's fasting and prayer for each word and he will reside with the Prophets and martyrs under the Throne of God.

Optional Prayers in Weekly Nights

Sunday night. The Prophet said: If a man prays 20 rak'ats in the night of Sunday with Fatiha and Ikhlas 50 times, Falaq .and Nas once in each rak'at and recites Istighfar one hundred times and recites Istighfar for himself and his parents and Darud one hundred times and takes refuge to God by releasing himself from his own strength and then says: I bear witness that there is no deity but God and I bear witness that Adam is the chosen one of God and His natural creation, that Abraham is His friend, Moses is Kalimulla, Jesus is the Spirit of God and Muhammad is the friend of God, he will get merits as innumerable as the persons who made calumny against God before and who did not make calumny and on the Resurrection Day be will be raised along with the believers and it will be the duty of God to admit him in Paradise along with the Prophets.

Monday night. The Prophet said: If a man prays 4 rak'ats in the night of Monday with Fatiha and Ikhlas ten times in the first rak'at, Fatiha and Ikhlas twenty times in the second rak'at, Fatiha and Ikhlas thirty times in the third rak'at and Fatiha and Ikhlas forty times in the fourth rak'at and then returns salam and afterwards recites Ikhlas 75 times and seeks Istighfar for himself and his parents 75 times and then prays for his needs to God, He accepts his invocation.

Tuesday night. The Prophet said: He who prays two rak'ats therein with chapters Fatiha and Ikhlas 15 times, Falaq l5 times, Nas 15 times, Ayatul Kursi 11 times, Istighfar 15 times, will get ample rewards. The Prophet said: He who prays in Tuesday night two rak'ats with Fatiha in each rak'at followed by chapter Ikhlas seven times, God will release him from Hell and it will be for him on the Resurrection Day guide and proof.

Wednesday night. The Prophet said: He who prays two rak'ats in Wednesday night with Fatiha and Falaq ten times in the first rak'at and Fatiha and Nas ten times in the second rak'at and then after finishing it reads Istighfar ten times and then Darud ten times, seventy thousand angels come down for him from every heaven and write for him rewards up to the Resurrection Day.

Thursday night. The Prophet said: He who prays two rak'ats between Maghrib and Isha with Fatiha and Ayatul kursi five times. Falaq five times, Nas five times and after prayer Istighfar 15 times and bestows them for his parents, obeys his duties towards his parents although he was disobedient to them before God gives him what He gives to the siddiqs and martyrs.

Friday night. The Prophet said: He who prays 12 rak'ats between Maghrib and Isha with Fatiha and Ikhlas 11 times, prayed as it were for 12 years for the nights and fasted for the days. The Prophet said: Send many Daruds on Juma day and night.

Saturday night. The Prophet said: He who prays 12 rak'ats between Maghrib and Isha, a mansion is built for him in Paradise, he gets rewards of charity to each male and female, gets release from the Jews and it becomes the duty of God to forgive him.

Optional Annual Prayers

Such prayers are four-(1) Prayers of two 'Ids or festivals, (2) Tarawih prayers, (3) Prayer in Rajab, and (4) Prayer in Shaban.

(1) **Prayer of two 'Ids.** They are Sunnat Muaqqadah and there are several duties in them. Take bath in the morning of 'Id day, take dresses and use scents. Go by one way and return by another. The Prophet used to observe it. He used to order the servants, slaves and women to come out for prayers on these days. It is better to pray 'Id prayers in open fields except Mecca and Baitul Muqdis. The time runs from sunrise to sun decline at noon. The time for animal sacrifice on Idul Azha runs from after the prayer to the end of the 13th day of Zilhaj. 'Id charity is to be given before prayer.

The form of prayer runs as follows. The Imam will pray two rak'ats with six Takbirs in addition, three in the first rak'st and three in the second. The Imam will then deliver sermon and then make Munajat.

(2) **Tarawih Prayer.** It consists of twenty rak'ats. It may be said also in congregation. The Holy Prophet sometimes prayed it alone

and sometimes in congregation. He said: I fear this prayer may be imposed on you as a compulsory duty. It was Hazrat Umar who directed the Muslims to observe it in congregation. The Prophet said: As it is more meritorious to observe compulsory prayer in mosque than in houses, so it is more meritorious to observe optional prayers in houses than in mosques. The Prophet said: The merits of one rak'at prayer in this mosque of mine is one thousand times greater than observing it in other mosques and the merits of one rak'at of prayer in the mosque of the Ka'ba is better than one thousand times than observing it in my mosque. The prayer of one who prays in a comer of his house and knows nobody than God is better than all these prayers. It is better however to pray Tarawih in congregation as Hazrat Umar did it.

(3) **Prayer in Rajab.** The Prophet said: One who fasts five days in Rajab, prays twelve rak'ats between Maghrib and Isha with a unit of two rak'ats (with certain-formalities as prescribed), his invocation is accepted.

(4) **Prayer in Shaban.** It is observed in the night of the 15th Shaban. There are one hundred rak'ats of prayer with a unit of two rak'ats. The earlier sages used to observe this prayer.

Fourth Kind of Optional Prayers

These prayers are connected with causes and there are nine in number (1) prayer of solar and (2) lunar eclipses, (3) prayer for rain, (4) funeral prayer, (5) prayer for entering into mosque, (6) prayer of ablution, (7) two rak'ats between Azan and Aqamat, (8) two rak'ats at the time of coming out of house for journey and 'two rak'ats at the time of entry into house after journey, and (9) prayer for seeking good called Istakharah prayer.

(1) **Prayer for solar and lunar eclipse.** The Prophet said: Solar and lunar eclipses are two signs out of the signs of God. They do not occur for birth or death of anybody. When you see it, turn towards the remembrance of God and prayer. He said it when his son Ibrahim died and people ascribed it to the above cause.

(2) **Prayer for rain.** The Prophet used to observe this prayer

coming out in the open field when there was drought ,and want of rain for a continued long time. This should be preceded by fast •three days and then on the fourth day prayer be said in the open field in congregation for rain with the greatest humility of spirit and earnestness of mind and then invocation should be made in the following manner: O God, Thou hast commanded us to invoke Thee and Thou hast promised us to accept it. We have indeed invoked. Thee as Thou halt commanded us. So accept our invocation as Thou halt promised us. O God, shower blessing on us with Thy forgiveness and accept our invocation by sending us rain and giving us ample provision.

(3) **Funeral Prayer.** This prayer is Farze Kefaya or binding on community as a whole. It is optional only for one who is exempted owing to the presence of some members of the community in the prayer. The Prophet said: If forty Muslims who do not set up partnership with God attend the funeral prayer of a Muslim, God accepts their intercession for him. Follow the bier after prayer up to the grave and recite the following after entering in the graveyard: Peace be on you, O the inmates of these houses of the believers and Muslims. May God show mercy on those who have gone before and who have come later We shall reach you if God wills. Then standing by the side of the grave of the person just buried, recite the following: O God, Thy servant has returned to Thee. Be kind to him and show him mercy. O God, remove the earth from his two sides and open the doors of heaven for his soul and accept it with good acceptance. O God, if be is a virtuous man, increase his virtues manifold and if he is a sinner, forgive him.

(4) **Prayer after entry into mosque. It** is two rak'ats or more and prayer after ablution is also two rak'ats. The Prophet said: I saw Bilal in Paradise and asked him: For what action have you entered Paradise before me? He said: I know nothing except the fact that I prayed two rak'ats after every ablution.

At the time of coming out of the house and entering it after journey, pray two rak'ats. The Prophet said: Pray two rak'ats when you go out of your house so that you may be saved from the harms of going out. The Prophet said: When any special work is not begun with the name of God, it goes without blessing.

(5) Istakhara Prayer. This prayer is said before an action is undertaken to know whether it will be good or bad. It is of two rak'ats with Chapter Kaferun in the first rak'at and chapter Ikhlas in the second and at the end with the following invocation: O God, I wish to know its good or bad with the help of Thy knowledge and I pray for strength from Thee and pray for Thy abundant mercy, as Thou knowest and I don't know and Thou knowest the unseen. O God, if Thou knowest that this affair will be for my worldly or next worldly good and for the result of my affairs sooner or latter, give strength to me, give me blessing therein and then make it easy for me. If Thou knowest that this affair of mine will be bad for me for my world, next world and the result of my affairs sooner or later, turn me from it and it from me. Thou art powerful over all things. The Prophet said: If any man among you proposes to do a thing, let him pray two rak'ats, name the project and invoke Him with the above invocation.

(6) Prayer for necessity. If a matter becomes necessary for his religion or for his world, let him pray twelve rak'ats for fulfillment of his necessity with Ayatul kursi and Ikhlas in each rak'at and at the end of the prayer of two rak'ats, let him invoke as prescribed.

(7) Prayer for Tasbih. It is also called Dua Masurah. The Prophet said to Hazrat Abbas: Shall I not make gift to you? Shall I not show kindness to you? Shall I not love you with such a thing which, if you do will be a cause for God to forgive your past and future sins, old and new sins, open and secret evils? Pray four rak'ats (as prescribed).

ZAKAT

God placed Zakat next to prayer and it is the second pillar of Islam out of five pillars. God says: Keep up prayer and pay Zakat. The Prophet said: Islam is founded on five pillars (1) there is no deity but God and Muhammad is His servant and messenger, and to bear witness to this formula, (2) to keep up prayers. (3) to pay Zakat, (4) to fast, and (5) to make pilgrimage. The punishment of those who do not pay Zakat has been mentioned in this verse: 'Give tidings of grievous punishment to those who hoard up gold and silver and do not spend in the way of God.' To spend means here to pay the compulsory duty of Zakat. Ahnaf-b-Qais said: We were with a party of the Quraish. Hazrat Abu Zarr, while passing by that way said: Give tidings to those who hoard up wealth that such firm impressions will be put on their backs which will come out after piercing their sides, that such firm impressions will be put on their forehead that it will come out of their forehead.

Abu Zarr said: I came to the Prophet who was then seated in the shade of the Ka'ba. He said to me: By the Lord of the Ka'ba, they are undone. I asked: Who are they? He said: Those who increase their wealth and not those who spend in His way, in their fronts, in their backs, in their right sides, in their left sides, but their numbers are few. Those who have got camels, cattle, sheep and goats and who do not pay their Zakat will meet with these animals in huge forms on the Resurrection Day. They will attack them with their horns and will tread upon them by their hoofs. If one party, finishes another party will come. This will continue till the people are brought for judgment. This punishment has been described by Sahihs Bukhari and Muslim. So the details of Zakat should be learnt.

SECTION – 1

Different Kinds of Zakat

There are six subject matters of Zakat—(1) Zakat of animals, (2) Zakat of crops, (3) Zakat of gold and silver, (4) Zakat of the commodities of business, (5) Zakat of mines, and (6) Zakat of 'Idul Fitr.

(1) *Zakat of Animals*

It is compulsory on a free Muslim whether major or minor, sane or insane. There are five conditions of Zakat which is obligatory in case of animals. (a) They are to be grazed in the grazing fields. (b) They should not be domestic animals. (c) They must be in possession for full one year. (d) One must have full ownership on them. (e) One must be the owner of Nisab or fixed number of these animals.

(A) Among animals, Zakat is to be paid for camels, cattle, sheep and goats but not for other animals like horses, asses, mules, deers and young ones of goats. (B) There is no Zakat of domestic animals which do not graze purely in fields. (C) Animals must be in possession for full one year. The Prophet said: Zakat is not due on any property unless in possession for full one year. If any animal is sold within one year, there is no Zakat for it. (D) One must have full ownership and full power of sale of the animal. There is no Zakat of animals given in pawn or mortgage, those which are lost or snatched by force. If the debts of a man be such that all his properties are not sufficient to clear them, there is no Zakat due on him as he is not a solvent man. A solvent man is one who has got surplus wealth after necessary expenses. (E) One must possess required number of animals. The minimum number of camels is, five, of cattle thirty, of goats and sheep forty. Camels, Zakat ,is one she-goat or he-goat of full two years for every five camels

above four. In case of 25 camels one she camel or one he-camel of full one year. In case of 36 camels, one she-camel of 2 years, of 46 camels one she-camel of three years and so on. Cattle. In case of 30 cattle, one calf of one year, of 40 cattle one calf of two years, of 60 cattle two calves of one year. Sheep and goats. In case of 40 sheep or goats, one she goat of one year, of 120, two she-goats and so on.

(2) *Zakat of Crops*

If anybody has got twenty maunds of rice, wheat, maize, pulse, dates or such food stuffs by which a man can maintain his livelihood, Zakat of one-tenth of the crop is compulsory on him. No Zakat is due for less than 23 maunds. There is no Zakat of fruits and cotton. If fields are watered by artificial means by taking water from canals, tanks, drains then one twentieth is due on crops.

(3) *Zakat of Gold and Silver*

Zakat of Silver is one-fortieth of pure silver if not less than 52 tolas and gold not less than 7 tolas. This is the nisab fixed for which Zakat is due. This proportion will continue in case of the value of gold and silver or of things made of them if they are in possession for full one year. For ornaments of gold and silver which are for use, there is no Zakat according to Imam Abu Hanifa. Zakat is due on money on loan after the loan is paid.

(4) *Zakat on Merchandise*

Zakat on merchandise is like that of gold and silver. One year should have elapsed from the date of their purchase and if it reaches nisab. This applies also in case of exchange of goods. Zakat is also payable on profits of commodities along with the commodities at the end of a year.

(5) *Zakat on Mines and Buried Treasures*

If gold and silver of the non-Muslims are found buried, Zakat is soon due at the rate of one-fifth. There is no condition of possession of one year or of nisab. This is just like booty gained in war. There is no Zakat of the things taken from mines except gold and silver. Their Zakat is of one-fortieth after clearance and after it reaches Nisab and completion of one year.

(6) *Zakat of 'Idol Fitr*

This charity is compulsory on every Muslim who has got food in excess of one day and one night of 'Id at the rate of 2½ seers of principal food stuffs or one sa'a per head. This is payable on behalf of all the members of the family and near relatives and parents who are maintained by him. The Prophet said: Give the charity of Fitr of all the persons you maintain.

SECTION – II
Payment of Zakat and its Conditions

Zakat is to be paid having a look to the following five things. (1) Intend to pay Zakat at the time when it falls due and fix properties and things for payment of Zakat. The guardian of for help. (5) Zakat is to be paid to eight classes of persons as described in the Quran and will be discussed in section 8.

Some Subtle Rules of Zakat

There are some subtle points for a payer of Zakat and for one who travels in the path of the next world.

(1) *The Meaning and Object of Zakat*

Zakat is the purification of properties. There are three reasons for its being a pillar of Islam. (a) The first reason is to appreciate the two words of Kalema Shahadat, to take Tauhid firmly and to witness the unity of God. Promise reaches perfection when a unitarian has got no object of love except One, as love does not admit a partner. There is little benefit in uttering Kalima Shahadat by tongue only and the trial is in giving up of other objects of love except God. To the people, wealth and properties are objects of love as they are the instruments of earthly pleasures and getting love from others. Those who claim the love of God are tried and their objects of love are snatched away from them. For this reason God says: God purchased from the believers their lives and properties in exchange of paradise for them. This was said with regard to Jihad. Sacrifice of properties is easier than sacrifice of life which has been also mentioned here to gain the love of God. From this angle of view, men can be divided in to three classes.

(1) The first class of men recognise Tauhid as true, fulfil their promise and spend their properties in the way of God. They do not hoard wealth. They do not deny that Zakat is not compulsory on them. Rather they say: For us, it is compulsory to spend all our properties. For this reason, Hazrat Abu Bakr brought all his properties to the Prophet when he called for charities in the way of God. Hazrat Umar brought half of his property. The Prophet said to Hazrat Umar: What have you left for your family? He said: Half of my wealth. He asked Hazrat Abu Bakr: What have you left for your family? He said: God and His Prophet. The Prophet said: The difference between you is in your replies.

(2) The second class of men are lower in rank. They spend their wealth at the time of necessity. The object in hoarding is not to enjoy pleasure but to spend in proportion to necessity and to spend their excess wealth in good deeds. They don't reduce the amount of Zakat. Many Tabeyins like Nakhyi, Shubi, Ata and others held that there are additional duties on wealth besides Zakat. The sage Shubi was asked: Is there any additional duty on wealth besides Zakat? He said: Yes, did you not hear the verse of God: Being prompted by divine love they spend wealth for their near relatives, orphans, the poor and the travellers. This is supported by the following verse: They spend out of what I have provided them with. God says: Spend out of what I have provided you. This means that whenever you will find a man in want, it is the duty of the rich to remove his want. This is an additional charity besides Zakat. The correct opinion according to theology is that whenever expense is necessary, to spend is Farde Kefayah as it is not legal to cause harm to the Muslims.

(3) The third class are those persons who rest contented by payment of only Zakat. They do not pay more or less. This is the lowest rank and the general people adopt this course as they are naturally miser, attached to riches and their love for the next world is weak. God says: If they beg of you and press for it, you become miser. There is a wide gulf of difference between those who

sacrifice their lives and properties for God and those who are defamed for miserliness.

(b) **The second cause** is to be pure from miserliness as it is one of the causes of destruction. The Prophet said: There are three destructive guilts-to obey miserliness, to follow low desires and self-conceit. God says: Those who are saved from miserliness have got salvation. In this way, Zakat is the cause of purification of properties.

(c) **The third cause** is to express gratefulness for the gifts of God as God's gifts on His servants are unbounded. The gratefulness for the gifts of body by doing divine services and the gratefulness for the gifts of wealth by expense of wealth are expressed. How unfortunate is he who sees no means of livelihood of a poor man and still does not give him charity in spite of his begging and who rather expresses gratefulness that God saved him from wants.

(2) *Second Subtle Point*

It is to look to the times and the rules of payment of Zakat. The religious men pay Zakat before it becomes compulsory. They transcend the limit of time. There is chance of falling into sin if Zakat is paid late and not in time. Willingness to do good deed comes from angels and it should be considered a cause of fortune. The heart of a believer is within the two fingers of the Merciful and there is no delay in its change. The devil enjoins on doing evil deeds and shows fear of poverty. Zakat should be paid in the month of Muharram, the first month of Hijra and one of the pure months or it should be paid in the month of Ramadan as the Prophet paid most of his charities in this month and there is the excellence of the Blessed Night in this month and in the month of pilgrimage. The last ten days of Ramadan month and the first ten days of the month of Zil- Hijj are days of excellence.

(3) *Third Subtle Point*

It is to pay Zakat in secret. It removes show and greed for fame. The Prophet said: The best charity is in secret charity of a poor man to a man in want. A certain learned man said: There are three matters in the secret wealth of good works, one of them is secret charity. The Prophet said: If a man acts secretly, God writes it secretly as secrecy is not maintained if it is disclosed. There is a well-known Hadis about show in open charity. The Prophet said: God will give shade to seven persons on the day when there will be no shade except the shade of God, one who gives charity in such a manner that his left hand does not know what his right hand has given in charity. There is in another Hadis: Secret charity appeases the wrath of God says: And if you give charity sincerely, it is also better for you. In secret charity, one can be safe from the danger of show. The Prophet said: If a man wants fame by incurring the pleasure of men, or rebukes after charity, or discloses his charity and thereby seeks name and fame, and or gives charity among the people for show, God will not accept his charity. A secret charity is free from the above faults. Many learned men said that the giver should not even know the person who takes charity. Some of them handed it over to the blind.

(4) *Fourth Subtle Point*

It is good to give charity openly in a place where the people are encouraged to give charity by seeing it. God say: Spend what I have given you secretly and openly. Care should be taken in open charity about show, rebuke after charity and not to break the secrets of a poor man as most of the beggars do not wish that anybody should see them as beggars.

(5) *Fifth Subtle Point*

It is not to destroy charity by rebuke and giving trouble after charity. God says: Don't make your charity void by 'Mann' that is giving trouble. There are differences of opinion for the meaning of Mann. Some say that its meaning is to remind charity to the receiver and that 'Aza' means to disclose it. Sufiyan was asked: What is Mann? He replied: To remind it repeatedly and to discuss about it. Some say that its meaning is to take boast for giving him charity and 'Aza' means to drive him away and to rebuke him by words. The Prophet said: God does not accept the charity of one who does 'Mann' Ghazzali explains it thus. Mann has got root and branches and it is expressed in tongue and limbs. The root of 'Mann' is to think oneself as the benefactor of one who receives charity. Rather the receiver should consider that he has shown kindness to the giver by accepting his charity, because he purifies the giver and gives him release from Hell fire. The charity of the giver is to request the receiver. The Prophet said: Charity falls on the hand of God before it falls in the hand of a beggar. Now it appears that the giver places his charity first to God and then the beggar receives it from God. 'Mann' comes in when the giver understands that he has done some benefit to the receiver of charity. So the meaning of 'Mann' is to discuss about charity, so disclose it and to hope to get from the receiver gratefulness, prayer, service, honour and to wish that he should be followed in his actions. These are the secret meanings of 'Mann'.

'Aza' means to rebuke, to use harsh word and to humiliate the receiver of charity. Its secret meaning is unwillingness to withdraw hand from wealth, to think to give charity as troublesome. Secondly, it means that the giver thinks himself superior to the receiver and thinks him inferior for his wants. Unwillingness to give charity is sign of foolishness, because who is more foolish than one who is reluctant to spend one dirham in lieu of one thousand dirhams in the next world? It appears from this that the object of charity and expense is to get the pleasure of God and to get merits in the next world. The pious men among the rich will go to Paradise five hundred years after the pious poor men. For this reason, the Prophet said: By the Lord of the Ka'ba, they are undone. Abu Zarr asked: Who are undone? He said: 'Those who have got much wealth.' Then how can the poor be held in contempt?

God keeps the rich only for the poor, because the poor earn their livelihood by their industry, increase their provisions and preserve them with difficulties. The rich give charity according to the requirements of the poor and guard the excess wealth. So think that the rich are servants for the livelihood of the poor. These are the conditions of charity and Zakat. This is like God-fear in prayer.

The following Hadis establishes it. The Prophet said: There is no prayer for a man except what he understands therefrom. He said: God does not accept the charity of one who gives trouble to the receiver. God says: Don't make your charity void by mentioning it and by giving trouble.

(6) *Sixth Subtle Point*

Think charity as little, because if it is considered great, it grows self-praise which destroys an action. God says: When your great number pleased you, it came of no use to you. Some say that when one considers a religious action little, it becomes great to God, and when a sin is considered great, it becomes little to God. Some say that any good deed does not become perfect without three things- to think it little, to do it soon and to keep it secret. If a man spends money in the construction of a mosque, it is possible for him to think it great, but there is no 'Mann' or 'Aza' in it. It may be called self-pleasure or self-praise. Its medicine is mixture of knowledge and action. Knowledge comes in the fact that he will not get the highest rank as he has not gifted his entire wealth in charity and so he should be ashamed, for his wealth belongs to God and He gives it to whomsoever He pleases along with Taufiq to spend it in charity. Regarding action, charity should be given after being ashamed as you were miser in not giving the entire property given to you by God.

(7) *Seventh Subtle Point*

Give in charity that is best, pure and the most lawful thing as God is pure and does not accept but pure wealth. The Prophet said: 'Good news to the man who earns wealth without committing sin and spends therefrom.' If he does not spend out of his best properties, it is impertinent on his part as he reserved the best thing for his family members and left the worst thing for God. If he gives bad things to his guest for eating, he becomes surely displeased with him. A wise man should not place others above himself. He will leave no property except what he gives in charity. What he eats finishes and what he enjoys of his property becomes a past thing. God says: 'O those who believe, spend of the good things you earn and what I grow for you out of the earth and don't intend therefrom impure things.' Don't take it without dislike and shame. So don't love to give to God impure and bad things. There is in Hadis: One dirham gains over one lac dirhams. Its cause is that a man gives one dirham in charity with pleasure of mind after taking it out from mostly his lawful earnings and another man gives charity of one lac dirhams from his unlawful earnings. God says: They keep for God what they do not like. Their tongue spread this falsehood and that this is good for them. There is no doubt that there is Hell-fire for them.

(8) *Eighth Subtle Point*

Search for Zakat such man that if he is paid Zakat, it becomes pure. The eight classes of men have been mentioned in the Quran for Zakat. It should be paid to those of them who have got these six qualities. (1) God-fear. Seek such God-fearing men who have renunciated the world and adopted the business of the next world. The Prophet said: 'Don't eat the food of anybody except that of the God-fearing men and do not feed anybody except the God-fearing men. The reason is that such men help religion. The Prophet said: Give your food to the God-fearing people and show kindness to the believers. In other words, entertain one with your food whom you love for the sake of God. Some learned men did not give food except to the poor people of 'Suffa'. They were asked: It would have been better if your charity would have been given to all poor men. They said: No, the thoughts of these people are for only about God. When they are hungry, sensation is generated in their hearts. Once a pious man was about to give up his business and he was going to be a pauper. Hazrat Junaid came to know of it and gave him some capital and said: Use it as your capital and don't give up your business as it is not an unprofitable concern for a man like you. The man used to carry on the business of vegetables and did not take price when he sold them to the poor.

(2) The second quality is education as it helps knowledge. The most honourable divine service is to remain busy in the acquisition of learning with a good and sincere intention. The sage Ibnul

Mubarak used to show kindness to the learned. He was asked; It would have been better it you have given charity to all. He said: I don't know whether after prophethood the rank of any men other than that the learned is superior.

(3) **The third quality is truthfulness.** Give charity to such a person who is truthful and sincere and has got knowledge of God-fear and Tauhid. His Tauhid is this that when he accepts charity, he praises God, expresses gratefulness and understands that all the gifts come from God and not from any intermediary, Luqman advised his son: Between you and God, don't consider anybody as the giver of gifts and the gifts of another on you as loan. He who expresses gratefulness to others except to God has not recognised his benefactor and all the people are powerless except through His help. Had not God compelled the giver, he would not have given charity and God instilled in to his mind that the well-being of his temporal and spiritual world lies in his charity. When this belief becomes strong, his wealth becomes strong.

It is said that the Prophet sent a man with charity to be given to a poor man and he said: Remember what he says. The poor man accepted it and said : Praise be to God who does not forget one who remembers Him and does not destroy one who expresses gratefulness to Him. Then he said: O God, You have not forgotten the man (himself) and don't allow him to forget You. The man informed the Prophet of his invocation and he said being satisfied: I knew that he would say this. The Prophet said to a man: Make repentance. He said: I repent to God without a partner and not to Muhammad. The Prophet said: He has recognised the right of One to whom it is due. When the verse dealing with the purity of Hazrat Ayesha was revealed, Hazrat Abu Bakr said: O Ayesha, kiss the head of the Prophet. Hazrat Ayesha said: By God. I shall not do it and I shall not praise God also for this. The Prophet said: O Abu Bakr, give up Ayesha. In another narration, Hazrat Ayesha said to Hazrat Abu Bakr: Praise be to God and for you and for your friend. The Prophet did not deny it though the verse declaring the purity of Ayesha was revealed to the Prophet. It is the fault of the unbelievers to see other things besides God. God says: When God is remembered, the hearts of those who have not brought faith in the next world become sad. He who does not purify his heart from the idea of an intermediary is not free from secret shirk.

(4) The fourth quality is to conceal wants. Zakat and charity should be paid to those who try to conceal their wants from the eyes of men and do not complain of their wants. They are honourable men. The Prophets have gone away but their honour remains. They did not live in comfort. God says regarding these people: The fools think that they are not in want on account of their refraining from begging. You will know them by their signs. They do not press the people for begging. Seek such people in every locality and give them charity.

(5) The fifth quality is to have a big family with no earning. Give charity to such a person who has got a big family or who is diseased, or is confined to the corner of house on account of any other reason. God says with regard to these people: Those poor men who are confined in the way of God and cannot move in the world. In other words, they are confined in the way of God for members of his family or for scanty means or for correction of soul or those who cannot roam on account of their defects in hands and feet are entitled to receive charity. The Prophet used to give charity according to the number of the members of a family.

(6) Another quality is near relationship, as charity to a near relative brings reward of keeping the tie of blood connection or relationship. Hazrat Ali said: To give one dirham to my brother is dearer to me than to give twenty dirhams to a stranger. To give him twenty dirhams in charity and to keep blood connection with him is dearer to me than the charity of 200 dirhams to a stranger. To give him one hundred dirhams is dearer to me than to set free a slave.

The above are the qualities which should be sought in giving charity to a person. It will increase rewards.

SECTION – III
Fitness for Receiving Zakat

Know, O dear readers, that there is no Zakat for anybody except a Muslim who must not belong to the Hashemite dynasty. Out of eight qualities, one quality is necessary for a receiver of Zakat. It cannot be paid to an unbeliever, slave, Hashemite, boy or an insane man except through his representative. The descriptions of the eight classes of people who can receive Zakat are given below.

(1) **The Poor.** A poor man is one who has got no wealth and properties and who has got no ability to earn. If he has got one day's food and wearing cloth he is not a poor man but a miskin or destitute. A poor man does not go out of poverty if he has got habit of begging as begging is not a source of livelihood. If he has got power and strength to earn his livelihood, he goes out of poverty. If he is a technician but has got no instrument or money to purchase it, he can be helped with Zakat. The Prophet said: To seek lawful earning is compulsory after compulsory duties. There is mention in it of earning livelihood by industry and trouble. Hazrat Umar said: A doubtful earning is better than begging. If a man is maintained by his parents, he cannot be called poor.

(2) **Miskin or destitute.** A man is called Miskin or destitute whose expense is greater than his income. He may be owner of one thousand dirhams but still he is a destitute under the above circumstances. (3) **Collectors of Zakat.** Out of the earnings of Zakat, collectors of Zakat may be paid. Writer, one who takes measure and one who copies registers are included within these staffs. They cannot be paid in excess of their requirements. (4) **Those who are inclined to Islam.** They are non Muslim leaders whose hearts are inclined to the .religion of Islam. The people follow them and therefore if they are inclined to Islam, there is possibility of their coming to Islam.

(5) **Slaves by agreement.** There may be agreement between a master and a slave that if the slave can pay a certain sum to the master, lie can get freedom. This money can legally be paid out of Zakat fund. (6) **Debtors.** Zakat may be paid to clear off debts of

a person who has got no means to clear them or who has property which is not sufficient to clear them. If a man runs into debts for having committed sinful acts, Zakat cannot be paid to him unless he repents. (7) **Wars in the way of God.** Those soldiers who get no salary from the state Treasury are entitled to get Zakat even if they are rich. (8) **Travellers.** One who goes abroad with good intention from his country may get Zakat if he requires money for his travels. No proof of these wants is necessary. They may be relied on their verbal words.

Duties of Zakat Receiver. A Zakat receiver should look to five matters. (1) He should know that God made Zakat compulsory so that his thought is concentrated on one object. God says: I created jinn and man with no other object except that they should worship Me. So divine service should be the centre of thought of men. He gives wealth to men that it may remove their wants and they may get opportunity of doing divine service. If God loves a man among the rich, He saves him from the world as a physician saves his patient. The poor man should know that Zakat is a gift from God to him realised from the rich, so that he may find time for divine service. (2) Be grateful to the Zakat payer, pray for him and praise him. The rich man should not feel satisfied as he is only an intermediary to help the poor with the gift of God. The Prophet said: He who is not grateful to men is not grateful to God. God Himself praises man for his good actions though He is the Creator of actions and deeds. He said: How good is the servant, he is turning to God (38: 30). Zakat receiver should invoke for the payer thus: May God purify your heart and include you among the pious. May He purify your actions like the actions of the good and may He include your soul among the souls of the martyrs. The Prophet 'said: If a man does good to you, do good to him. If you cannot do it, pray for him so that he may understand that you have done him return good. It is the duty of the giver to think charity as little and the duty of the receiver to think it great. (3) Don't accept charity if it is not from lawful wealth. God says: If a man fears God, He will find out a way for him and provide him from a source which is beyond his conception. (4) Give up the charity from earnings of doubtful nature and take up to your necessity. Don't take it until you know for certain whether you can legally accept it or not. If you are a Zakat collector, do not accept in excess of your remuneration. If you are a traveller, don't accept in excess of what is necessary for your journey. If you are a needy man, you may accept what is sufficient for your provision for a year at most. ,This is the last limit. The Prophet sometimes stored up provisions for his family members for a year. If it is for one day, it is near God-fear. Until he possesses nisab, he may accept it. The Prophet said: He who begs in spite of his being rich will appear on the Resurrection Day with his face with scratches and wounds. He was asked: What is the limit of a rich man? He said: 50 dirhams or gold of equivalent value. It is equivalent to a provision for one year.

SECTION – IV
Optional Charity and its Excellence

The Prophet said: 'Give charity of even a date as appeases hunger and wipes out sins just as water extinguish fire. He said: Save yourself from Hell-fire even by giving charity half a date, if you cannot do it, even by uttering a good word. The Prophet said: If a Muslim gives charity from lawful earning (God does not accept but lawful thing), Go accepts it with His right hand and maintains it. God maintain it till it rises up to the mountain Uhud just as one of you raises up his child. The Prophet said to Abu Darda: When you cook curry, increase its soup and present something of it justly to your neighbour having a look to his family members. The Prophet said: If a man gives charity in a good manner, God gives blessing in the property left by him. He said: Each man will remain under the shade of his charity till God finishes His judgment of the people. He said: Charity appeases the wrath of God. He who gives charity from his abundant wealth is not better in rewards than one who takes it at the time of his need.

The Prophet was once asked: Which charity is best? He said: Your charity at the time when you are sound, when you do not wish to spend, when you hope to live long or when you fear hunger. Don't make delay in giving charity lest you may say when you will be dying: I give this thing to such person and this thing to such person. One day, the Prophet said: Give charity. One man said: 1 have got a dinar. He said, spend it for you. He said: I have got another dinar. He said: Spend it for your wife. He said: I have got another dinar. He said: Spend it for your children. He said: I have got another dinar. He said: Spend it for your servant. He said: I have got another dinar. He said: Your look is best for it. The Prophet said: Zakat is not lawful for the family members of Muhammad. It is the impurity of the people. He said: Return the rebuke of a beggar by giving food even to the measure of the head of a bird. The Prophet said: He will not get salvation who refuses a beggar who speaks the truth. Jesus Christ said: Angels do not enter the house of a man for seven days who turns out a beggar from his door disappointed. Our Prophet did not entrust two duties to anybody-to collect his water of ablution for his prayer at night and to give charity to the poor. The Prophet said: He who is driven away by you not even with two dates is not a destitute but a destitute is he who refrains from begging. If you wish, read this verse: They do not come to man begging. The Prophet said: A Muslim who gives a cloth to another Muslim is in protection of God till the cloth remains upon his body.

Wise sayings. Hazrat Urwah-b-Zubair narrated that some time Hazrat Ayesha gave charity of 50,000 dirhams though her shirt was stitched. God says: They give food out of His love to the destitute, orphans and captives. Mujahed explained this verse by saying that they did it out of eagerness. Hazrat Umar said: O God, give riches to the good among us, that they may do benefit to the needy. Caliph Umar-b-Abdul Aziz said: Prayer will take you to half of the royal path, fast will take you to the royal door and charity will take you to the king himself. Ibn Abi Zaidan said: Charity shuts up 70 doors of evils. The excellence of secret charity is seventy times more than that of open charity and secret charity destroys seventy evils. Hazrat ibn Mas'ud said that a man did divine service for seventy years. Then he committed a grievous sin for which his entire good deeds were rendered void. Then he passed by a poor man and gave a bread to him for which God forgave him and returned him the rewards of the divine services for seventy years.

Luqman advised his son: When you commit a sin give charity. Hazrat lhya-b-Mu'az said: I don't know whether a seed except a seed of charity is heavier than a mountain. Caliph Abdul Aziz said: Paradise has got -three secret treasures—to conceal disease, to conceal charity and to conceal troubles and difficulties. The saint Nakhyi said: When a thing is given in charity for God, I don't like that it should have any defect. Hazrat Obaid-b-Umair said: On the Resurection Day, a man will get hungry not being hungry, thirsty not being thirsty and naked without being naked, God will give food to one who gives food for the sake of God. He will give water to drink to one who gives water to drink for the sake of God. He will give cloth to one who gives cloth for the sake of God. Hazrat Hasan Basri said: If God willed, all would have been rich and nobody would have been poor among you, but He wishes to try you by one another.

Benefits of Secret Charity

(1) It protects the secrecy of the receiver of charity. In open charity, his manliness is curbed and his want is exposed. The secret charity gives no encouragement to begging. (2) The receiver remains safe from the tongues of the people. Many a time, receiver is hated by the people in case of open acceptance of charity. The sage Abu Ayub said: I gave up putting on new cloth for fear of creating hatred in the mind of my neighbour. (3) Secret charity helps the giver to conceal his charity, as the excellence of secret charity is greater than that of open charity. To help the perfection of a good deed is also a good deed. One man gave charity to a Sufi in presence of the Prophet. He did not accept it. (4) There is no disgrace in accepting secret charity. It is not the duty of a believer to humiliate anybody. A certain learned man refused to accept charity openly as he said that it disgraces learning. (5) Secret charity removes the doubts of a co-sharer. The Prophet said: If a man is given present in presence of some men, then all become co-sharers in the present. The Prophet said: The best charity to a brother is giving his food or money.

Benefits of open charity. (1) If it is given with sincerity and honesty, one can be safe from change of condition and show.

(2) Honour is removed and humility is exposed. (3) One can remain safe from Shirk in case of open charity. It is narrated that a spiritual guide was inclined to one of his disciples more than to anybody else. This gave trouble to his other disciples. The spiritual guide intended to expose the supremacy of his favoured one and therefore he gave to each of his disciples one cock with a knife saying: You will sacrifice it so that nobody sees it. Each of them went to a distant place and sacrificed his cock except the disciple whom he loved. The other returned the cock and the knife to him without sacrificing it. The spiritual guide said to him: They have brought the cocks according to my instruction but why did you not do accordingly. He said : I have found no place where nobody could see me as God sees me in every place.

The guide then said to his other disciples: For this reason, I am inclined more to this disciple as his look is always towards God. (4) In case of open charity, the sunnat of gratefulness is expressed. God says: As for the gifts of your Lord, proclaim it. To conceal a gift is like rejecting it. If a man conceals what has been given to him by God, God rebukes him. He attaches it with miserliness. God says: Those who are misers and tell the people to be misers and conceal the gifts which God has given them. The Prophet said: If God gives a gift to a servant. He likes that it should be expressed by him. The Migrants asked the Prophet once about gratefulness: O Messenger of God, we are guests of the Ansars and we have not seen better people than them. They have divided their wealth and properties among us, we fear that they would take all rewards. The Prophet said: The gratefulness that you expressed to them for every matter and your praising them are your return good.

Now you have understood about the benefits of open charity and secret charity, you have come to know that the differences arise out of conditions of mind. So it depends on the state of your mind at the time of charity. The Prophet praised a man, because be knew that it would not injure him. He once said to a man: When any honourable man of a tribe comes to you, honour him. The Prophet once was pleased with a man when he heard of his quality and said:

There is surely a charm in oratory. The Prophet said: When anybody among you finds a good attribute in his brother, let him tell him of it, as it will give him encouragement to do good works. The Prophet said: When a believer is praised, faith increases in his mind. Sufiyan Saori said: Praise cannot injure a man who knows his mind.

Chapter 6

FASTING

Fast is one-fourth of faith, as the Prophet said: Fast is half of patience and patience is half of faith. Of all the regulations of religion, fast keeps special connection with God. The Prophet said: God says: Every good action except fast will be rewarded from ten to seven hundred folds, but fast is only for My sake and it is I who will reward him for it. God says: Those who are patient will be given rewards without measure (39 : 13). Fast is half of patience. Its reward transcends account. The excellence of fast is known from the following Hadis: The Prophet said: By One in whose hand there is my life, the fragrance of the mouth of a fasting man is dearer to God than the Fragrance of musk. God says: The fasting man gives up sexual intercourse, food and drink for My sake. So fast is kept only for My sake and it is I who will reward him for it. The Prophet said: Paradise has got a gate named Rayyan. None except a fasting man will enter Paradise by that gate. God has promised His vision as reward of fast.

The Prophet said: There are two joys for a fasting man, one joy at the time of breaking fast and another joy at the time of meeting with his Lord. The Prophet said: Everything has got a gateway. Fast is the gateway of worship. He said: When the month of Ramadan comes, the gates of Paradise are opened and the gates of Hell are shut up, the devils are put in chains and a proclaimer proclaims: O seeker of good, advance. O seeker of evil, come back. God says: Eat and drink cheerfully for what you missed in past days. In other words, eat and drink cheerfully for what you were deprived in your fasting days. The Prophet said: God will make His angels vie with an ascetic saying: O young man who has suppressed his passions for My sake and who has spent his youth for My sake, you are to Me like some of My angels.

The Prophet said about a fasting man: God says: O My angels, look to My servant, he has given up his sexual passion, his pleasures, his food and drink for My pleasure. God says: No soul knows what has been kept concealed from him pleasing to his eyes. This is the reward for what they have done. It has been said regarding the verse that this action was fast as God says: The patient will be given rewards without account (39 : 13). It appears from this that rewards will be open for the fasting men and they will not be kept for measurement as it is only for God. All worships are for God but the honour of fast is like that of the Ka'ba. Everything in the world has got a speciality . The speciality of fasting is forbearance and sacrifice, as it is the action of the mind and secret from public eye, but all other actions fall within human eyes. Nobody sees fast except God as it is a secret action with sincere patience. Secondly, it is punishment for the enemy of God as the way of the devil is sexual passion and it increases through the help of food and drink. For this reason, the Prophet said: The devil runs through human body like the circulation of blood. Curb it by hunger. For this reason, the Prophet said to Ayesha: Knock at the door of Paradise. She asked: How? The Prophet said: With hunger, specially when fast controls the devil, shuts his path and makes narrow his passage. Then its connection remains with only Good. If the enemy of God is controlled, it will be helping God.

God says: If you help God, God will help you and will make your feet firm-47 : 8. So at the beginning, a servant will make efforts and then hope for reward of God. For this reason God says: I will show certainly My path to those who strive hard for us 1 29: 69. God says: God does not change the condition of a people unless they change their own condition 113: 12 1. This change is said to be due to increase of sexual passion as it is the grazing field of the devil and a place for his movement. The devil moves in it till it is fertile. God's light is not disclosed to the person in whom he moves.

The Prophet said: If the devil had not moved in the human minds, they could have surely known the mysteries of heaven. For this reason, fast is the door of worship and its shield. When the excellence of fast is so wide, its secret and open conditions and its rules and regulations should be known and they will be discussed in three sections.

SECTION – I
Six Compulsory Duties of Fast

(1) To seek the new moon of Ramadan. If there is cloud, thirty days of Shaban must be completed. The sight of the new moon of Ramadan is based only on the evidence of one just man of intellect, while the moon of 'Eid ul Fitr is based on the evidence of two just pious Muslims. If the new moon is seen in one place and is not seen in another place and if the distance between the two places is less than about two miles, it is compulsory for the inhabitants of both the places to keep fast. If, however, the distance is more, the inhabitants of each place will decide the case separately.

(2) To make Niyyat of fasting. To make niyyat every night with firm faith is compulsory. One niyyat for full Ramadan month is not sufficient. If there is no niyyat of compulsory, it will be considered as optional fast. So niyyat should be made every night.

(3) Not to admit anything outside in the body willingly during fast. If a man eats something, drinks something and does any such act, it will break fast. If a man gets cupping, it will not spoil his fast. If water enters the belly unwillingly, it will not spoil fast.

(4) Abstinence from sexual intercourse during fast. If through mistake, a fasting man has got sexual intercourse, it will not spoil his fasting.

Atonement for Break of a Fast

There are four modes of compulsory atonement of fast if it breaks.
(1) **Making amends.** It is compulsory on every major Muslim to keep fast on other days for break of fast in Ramadan. A menstruating woman must compulsorily keep fast on other days. One need not keep Qaza fast consecutively. (2) **Kaffaraa or Atonement** is not compulsory except in case of sexual intercourse

in which case one is to set free a slave or fast for two consecutive months, failing that to feed sixty poor men with one meal. (3) **Imsak** or refraining oneself from food, drink and from sexual intercourse. If a man breaks fast carelessly but without excuse, it is compulsory on him to refrain from food, drink and sexual intercourse for the remaining portion of the day. (4) **Fidya** or expiation. If a pregnant or suckling woman does not keep fast for fear of her child, it is compulsory on her to give its compensation by giving one maund foodstuff to a poor man and she will have to fast Qaza in addition. If an old man of age is unable to keep fast, he may compensate each fast by giving food crops of one maund for each day.

Sunnats of Fast are six: (1) To eat Sehri, (2) to break fast before Maghrib prayer with dates or water, (3) not to cleanse teeth after midday, (4) to give charity, (5) to recite the Quran, and (6) to observe I' tekaf in a mosque in the last ten nights of Ramadan month. This was the habit of the Prophet of God. When the ten nights of Ramadan remained, he prepared himself for greater divine service for the remaining days of Ramadan and ordered the inmates of the house to do the same. He used to stay in the mosque without coming out of it except when pressed by necessity such as call of nature.

SECTION – II
Secrets of Fast

Know, O dear readers, that there are three classes of fast. (I) Fast of the general Muslims. It are to restrain oneself from eating and drinking and from sexual passion. This is the lowest kind of fast. (2) Fast of the few select Muslims. In this kind of fasting, besides the above things one refrains himself from sins of hand, feet, sight and other limbs of body. (3) Fast of the highest class. These people keep fast of mind. In other words, they don't think of anything else except God and the next world. They think only of the world with the intention of the next world as it is the seed ground for the future. A certain sag,: said: One sin is written for one whose efforts during the day are made only to prepare for breaking fast. This highest class of people is the Prophets and the near ones of God. This kind of fast is kept after sacrificing oneself and his thoughts fully to God. This is the meaning of the verse: Say God and then leave them sporting in their vain talks (6 : 91).

The fasting of select few pious men rests on six duties for gaining perfection. (1) To restrain eye sight from what is evil and from things which divert attention from God's remembrance. The Prophet said: Eye sight is a poisonous arrow out of the arrows of the devil. If a man gives it up, God gives him such a faith of which the taste is tasted by his mind. The Prophet said: Five things destroy fasting-falsehood, backbiting, slander, perjury and look with sexual passion. (2) To restrain the tongue from useless talk, false-speaking, backbiting, slander, abusive speech, obscenity, hypocrisy and enmity, to adopt silence and to keep the tongue busy with the remembrance of God and reciting the Quran. The sage Sufiyan Saori said: Backbiting spoils fast. Hazrat Mujahed said: Two things spoil fast, backbiting and falsehood. The Prophet said: Fast is like a shield. If a man keeps fast, let him not rebuke and dispute. If a man wants to assault or make quarrel, jet him say to him : I am fasting. There is in Hadis: Two women kept fast at the time of the Prophet. They were so much overstricken with hunger at the end of the day that their lives were about to end. They were sent to the Prophet so that he might order them to break fast. He sent a cup for them telling them that they should vomit in it what they ate. One of them vomited fresh blood and fresh flesh which filled up half of the cup. Another vomited similarly and filled up the cup. The Prophet then said: The two women fasted with !awful food but broke it with unlawful food. The two women back-bited the people and ate their flesh.

(3) To restrain the ear from hearing the evil talks because what is unlawful to utter is also unlawful to hear. For this reason, God placed the eater of unlawful food and the hearer of unlawful words on the same level. God says: The hearers of falsehood and eaters of unlawful food (5 : 46). God says: Why do not the God-fearing men and the worldly renunciated men prohibit talking sinful words and unlawful eating (5 : 68)? To remain silent at the time of

backbiting is unlawful. God says: You are then like them (9 : 138). Thus said the Prophet: The backbiter and the hearer of backbiting are equal co-sharers in sin.

(4) To save hand, feet and other organs from sins from evil deeds and to save belly from doubtful things at the time of breaking fast. There is no meaning of fasting if it is kept with lawful food and broken with unlawful food. He is like a man who destroys a town for constructing a building. It is also injurious to eat lawful food in excess and not to eat it little. He who fasts and does evil deeds is like a patient who restrains himself from eating fruits for fear of disease but who swallows poison. A sin is like eating poison. He who drinks this poison is a fool. An unlawful thing is like poison and it destroys religion and a lawful thing is like a medicine. Its little does benefit and its much spoils. The Prophet said: There are many fasting men who do not gain by fasting except hunger and thirst. On being asked the reason, he said: He refrains from eating lawful food and breaks fast by eating human flesh by backbiting. That is unlawful.

(5) To eat even lawful food so much at the time of breaking fast that it fills up the belly. A belly filled up with too much lawful food is hated more than all other reservoirs. A fasting man eats in full at the time of breaking fast what he could not eat during day time. He prepares different kinds of foods. The object of fast is to keep belly vacant in order to control passion and to increase God-fear. If the belly remains full from morning to evening, sexual passion rises high and greed and temptation reign supreme.

(6) To keep the mind of a fasting man between fear and hope, because he does not know whether his fast will be accepted or not, whether he will be near God or not. This should be the case for every divine service. Once Hasan Basri was passing by a party of men who were playing and sporting. He said:' God made this month of Ramadan for running in which the people will be running for good deeds and competing with one another. The object of fast is to anoint one with one of the divine attributes. That attribute is Samadiat meaning to be bereft of hunger and thirst and to follow the angels as far as possible, being free from passion.

The rank of a man is far more superior than that of a lower animal as he can control his passion by dint of his intellect, but his rank is lower than that of an angel as his passion is strong and he is tried by it. Angels are near God, This nearness keeps connection with attributes but not with space. The Prophet said: Fast is a trust. Let everyone of you keep that trust. When he read this verse: "God orders you to give trust to its rightful owners (4 : 61)", he placed his hands on his ears and eyes and said: Ear is a trust and eye is a trust. If it had not been a trust of fasting, the Prophet would not have said: I am fasting. In other words, I have kept my tongue as trust for saving it. How can I give it up for replying you? So it appears that for every affair there are secret and open matters.

It is now open to you to observe both secret and open matters or to observe either of them.

SECTION – III
Optional Fast and its Rules

Know O dear readers that additional fasts are sunnat if observed in the days of good and excellence. Some of these days occur every year, some every month and some every week. Those which occur every year are the days of Arafat, the days of Ashura, the first ten days of the month of Zilhaj, the first ten days of the month of Muharram and all holy months. The Prophet used to fast most in the month of Shaban. There is in one Hadis : Of all the fasts after the fast of the month of Ramadan the best fast is in the month of Muharram as it is the beginning of the year and founded on good and most dear for blessing. The Prophet said: One day's fast in the holy month is better than the fast for thirty other days. The Prophet said: if a man fasts for three days, Thursday, Friday and Saturday in the holy month, God writes for him divine service of seven hundred years in lieu of every day. There is in Hadis: When half of Shaban passes, there is no fast up to Ramadan. It is not lawful to keep fast for two or three days before Ramadan. Zil Haj, Muharram, Rajab and Shaban are the months of excellence and Zi-Qadah, Zil-Haj, Muharram and Rajab are the holy months. Zil-Haj is the best among them as there is therein the day of Haj and fixed days. There is in Hadis: Divine service for the first ten days of Zil-Haj is dearer to God than that in other months. Fast of one day during these days is equal to fast of ore year and one night's prayer is equal to the prayer of the Blessed night. They asked: Is the reward better than that of Jihad? He said: Not that of even Jihad in the way of God, but the reward is equal to that of the Jihad of a man in which his horse is wounded and he himself is martyred.

Monthly Fast. The days of month in which fast are to be kept are the first day, middle day and the last day of every month. In addition, there is the fast of Ayyam that is on the 13th, 14th and 15th of the moon.

Weekly Fast. In every week, Thursday, Friday and Monday are good. These are the days of excellence.

Annual Fast. The best way is to keep fast for one day and break it on the following day: The Prophet said: The treasures of the world were presented to me. I rejected them and said: I shall remain hungry for one day and take food on another. When I shall take food, I shall praise Thee and when I shall remain hungry I shall seek humility from Thee. The Prophet said: The best fast is that of my brother Daud. He fasted for one day and broke it on the following day. The Prophet instructed Abdullah-b-Amr to fast thus. He said: I shall be able to fast more. The Prophet said: Fast for one day and break fast on the following day. He said: I wish to keep better fast than this. Then the Prophet said: There is no better fast than this. It is reported that the Prophet did not fast any full month except Ramadan.

It has been reported that the Prophet sometimes continued to fast in such *a way* that the people thought that he won't break it and sometimes he continued to keep no fast till the people thought that he won't keep fast. He slept sometimes in such a way that the people thought that he won't arise from bed an ' sometimes he kept wakeful in such a way that the people though that he won't sleep again.

SECRETS OF PILGRIMAGE

P ilgrimage is one of the pillars of Islam, the beauty of divine service for the whole life, the end of actions, the perfection of Islam and the foundation of religion. On the day of pilgrimage God revealed the following verse: Today I have perfected your religion for you and made My gifts perfect on you and am pleased to give you Islam as a religion (5:3). The Prophet said regarding it: He who dies without making pilgrimage, dies willingly as a Jew or a Christian. So how important is that divine service without which religion does not become perfect and one becomes a Jew or a Christian or misguided one. It will, therefore, he discussed in three sections.

SECTION – I

Excellence of Pilgrimage

God says: Proclaim Haj among the people, so that they may come to you on foot or upon every camel coming from every distant place (Quran). Qatadah said: God ordered Hazrat Abraham , our Prophet and all chosen servants to Proclaim Haj among their people. Then he proclaimed: O people God created a house, make pilgrimage for it. God says: 'that they may witness benefits for them. It means trade and rewards in the next world. A certain sage said about it: By Lord of the Ka'ba, He has foigiven them. God mentions the devil as saying: I shall sit for them in your straight path. Some say that the devil will be sitting in the paths towards Mecca to prevent the people from making pilgrimage. The Prophet said: He who makes pilgrimage without doing any obscene deed and without making quarrel comes out of his sins as on the day when his mother gave birth to him. The

Prophet said: The devil does not become so much humiliated, dishonoured and disgraced as on the day of Arafat. The cause is that he sees God's blessing descending and His forgiveness of great sins. The Prophet said: There is some sins out of sins which are not forgiven except without waiting at Arafat. The Prophet said: If a man comes out of his house with the intention of making pilgrimage or Umrah, there will be written for him the rewards of one pilgrimage and one Umrah up to the Resurrection Day. He who dies at Mecca or Medina, will not be presented for account and no account will be taken from him and he will be said: Enter Paradise. The Prophet: There is no rewards except Paradise for an accepted Haj. The said: Those who make pilgrimage and Umrah are guests and neighbours of God. If they pray, it is accepted from them. If they seek forgiveness, God forgives them. If they invoke, their invocation is accepted. If they intercede, it is accepted. There, is another Hadis : He whose sin is greatest is a person who thinks at Arafat that God has not forgiven his sins. The Prophet said: 120 blessings descend everyday on this Ka'ba, sixty for those who make Tawaf, forty for those who pray and Make twenty for those who visit Ka'ba. There is in a Hadis: find much Tawaf because it is such a great thing and for which it in your book of deeds on the Resurrection Day people will envy you. For this reason, to make Tawaf at firs] before Haj and Umrah is commendable. There is in Hadis: He who makes Tawaf for a week barefooted and bare bodied will get the reward of setting free a salve. Whosoever makes Tawaf in rains for a week, his past sins are forgiven. A certain sage said: If the Arafat Day and the Juma on the same day, every person at Arafat is _forgiven and that is the best day in the world. On that day the farewell pilgrimage of the Holy Prophet took place and on that day, the verse was revealed-Today I have perfected for you your religion, bestowed My favours completely on you and chosen for you Islam as religion -5: 53.

The people of the Book said: If the verse would have been revealed upon us, we would have observed it as a day of festival. Hazrat Umar said: I bear witness that this verse was revealed on the Prophet on the day of two festivals-the day of Arafat and Juma day and he was then waiting at Arafat. The Prophet said: O

God, forgive one who has come for pilgrimage, forgive one who seeks forgiveness for a pilgrim. Hazrat Umar said: A pilgrim is forgiven and also the man for whom he seeks forgiveness in Zil-Haj, Muharram, Safar or the first part of Rabiul Awwal. It was the custom of the ancient sages that they 1 broadcast the stories of warriors, welcomed the pilgrims, kissed on their foreheads, sought blessings from them and they hastened to do these things before they would commit sins.

Excellence of Mecca and ka'ba

The Prophet said: God promised that every year six lacs people will make pilgrimage. If their number becomes less, God will fill the number by angels. The Ka'ba will be presented on the Resurrection Day, adorned with ornaments like a newly wedded bride and those who made pilgrimage will be busy in covering it with cloth. The Ka'ba will proceed towards Paradise till it enters it and they will also enter paradise. There is in Hadis: The Black Stone is a jewel out of the jewels of Paradise. It will be raised up on the Resurrection Day. It will have two eyes and one tongue with which it will speak. It will bear witness for everyone who kissed it and testified its truth. The Prophet used to kiss it much. It was narrated that Hazrat Umar once made prostration over it. He was then making Tawaf riding and he placed his staff in his hand on it and kissed one end of it. He said at once after kissing it: I know certainly that you are a mere piece of stone and you can not do any benefit or harm. Had I not seen the Prophet kissing you, I would never have kissed you. Then he wept and raised his voice high. Then he said to Hazrat Ali behind him: O Abul Hasan, take advice and I intercede, your prayer will be accepted. Hazrat Ali said: O Commander of the Faithful, it has got benefits and harms. He asked: In what way? He said: When God took promise from the descendants of Adam, He wrote a scroll on them and impressed it on this stone. It will bear witness for those who fulfilled their promise and against the infidels for infidelity. Hasan Basri said: One day's fast therein is equal to one lac fast and charity of one Dirham is equal to that of one lac dirhams. Thus its reward increases to one lac. There is in a Hadis: One Umrah during Ramadan is like pilgrimage with me. He said: I shall be the first man who will burst out of his grave. Then the inhabitants of Jannatul Baqi will resurrect with me, then the Meccans and then the people between the two Harams (Mecca and Medina). There is in Hadis that when Adam performed all rites of pilgrimage, the angels saw him and said: O Adam, your Haj has been accepted. We built the Ka'ba two thousand years before you. There is in Hadis that God looks to the inmates of the world every night. He looks first to the inhabitants of Mecca and out of them first to the inhabitants of the Ka'ba, He forgives one whom He sees making Tawaf and forgives one whom he sees standing towards the Ka'ba and forgives one whom He sees praying in the Ka'ba. A friend of God said: The sun does not set in unless an Abdal makes Tawaf of the Ka'ba and it does not set in unless a friend of God makes its Tawaf. When this sort of Tawaf will end, it will be the cause of being lifted away from the world. Then the people will see in the morning that it has been lifted away and they will find no sign therein. Then after it, nobody will make its pilgrimage for seven years. The Anti-Christ will appear and Jesus Christ will come down and will kill Anti-Christ. Then the Resurrection will come near. There is in Hadis: Before its lifting, the Ka'ba will be circumambulated always. The Ka'ba was twice destroyed and it will be lifted up at the third time. The Prophet said: God says: When I will wish to destroy the world, I will begin it first with My house and will destroy it first. Then immediately after it the world will be destroyed.

Excellence of Habitation at Mecca

The God-fearing men disliked to live at Mecca for three reasons-
(1) Fear of being equal to Ka'ba, as to be equal from the point of honour is harmful. When the pilgrims finished pilgrimage, Hazrat Umar assembled them and said: O inhabitants of Yemen, go to Yemen, O inhabitants of Iraq, go to Iraq. He said: I fear lest he people inhabit too much in the Ka'ba. (2) Eagerness for visiting it again owing to separation, as God made the Ka'ba as a refuge of the people and a safe place. (3) Not to live at Mecca for fear of sins and guilts and it is better than honouring the place. Hazrat Ibn

Masud said: There is no such city except Mecca wherein the people will be punished for niyyat before actions. Then he read this verse: If a man wishes therein to do excessive oppression, he will be given grievous punishment. This is only for the Ka'ba. Hazrat Ibn Abbas said: To store up food stuff at Mecca is said to be excessive oppression within the precincts of the Ka'ba. He said: To commit seventy sins at Ruqia is better to me than to commit a sin at Mecca. Ruqia is a place between Mecca and Tayef. Some people feared so much that they even responded not to their calls of nature in the sacred enclosure. It is better to live at Mecca if any body does not commit any sin. When the Prophet returned to Mecca, he turned his face towards the Ka'ba and said: 'You are the best place to me among the places of God and you are the dearest city to me among the cities of God. Had I not been rejected by you, I would never come out of it ?' Why should it not be, as look towards the Ka'ba is worship and if a good deed is done there, it brings abundant rewards.

Excellence of Medina

There is no such better place as Medina after Mecca. The rewards increase much if a good deed is done at Medina. The Prophet said: One prayer in my mosque brings rewards one thousand times more than the prayer in other mosques except the mosque of Mecca. This is true in case of all good deeds done here. After Medina, there is the place of Baitul Maqdis wherein a prayer brings rewards five hundred times more than that in other mosques. This is the case with all other good deeds. The Prophet said: If one prayer in the mosque of Medina is equal to ten thousand prayers, one prayer in Baitul Muqdis is equal to one thousand prayers and one prayer in the mosque of Mecca is equal to one lac prayers. The Prophet said: If a man bears hardships of Medina, I shall be his intercessor on the Resurrection Day. The Prophet said: If a man dies at Medina, let him do it because if a man dies at Medina, I shall be his intercessor on the Resurrection Day. After these three places, all places are equal except the frontiers of Islam, as guarding the frontiers of Islam is necessary from the enemies and their excellence is great. For this reason, the

Prophet said: Don't tie your camel except in three mosques, the mosque of the Ka'ba, the mosque of mine and the mosque of Baitul Muqdis. The Prophet said: I had prohibited you before to visit graves, but now I say: Visit graves, bat don't say 'Hazran' (I gave up.) The Prophet said: All places belong to God and all are servants of God. Live in the place you like and praise God. There is in Hadis: If a man gets blessings in a thing, he should stick to it. If a man gets a source of income, he should not change it, till that source of income is changed.

Duties of Haj

Two things are necessary (for the health of Haj-Time and Islam. There are five conditions of Haj which are obligatory (1) to be a Muslim, (2) to be a free man, (3) to be intelligent and able, (4) to be major, and (5) to make Haj in time. One must be of sound health and the route must be safe and sound. He must have sufficient money to go and to be back from journey and for the maintenance of the family in the mean time. If a man is unable to make pilgrimage on account of his physical illness or bodily infirmity from which he has got no hope of recovery, he must send his representative with expense to make pilgrimage on his behalf. If a man dies before making pilgrimage in spite of his solvency, there will be grievous punishment for him. Hazrat Sayeed-b-Jubair, Ibrahim Nakhyi, Mujahed and Taus said: If we knew that a certain man died without making Haj, we did not say funeral prayer for him. Hazrat Ibn Abbas said: If a man dies without Haj and without paying Zakat, he will pray for return to the world. Then he read this verse: O my Lord, send me again that I may do good deeds which I left undone.

Five compulsory duties of Haj—To don Ihram, to make Tawaf, to make Sayee, to wait at Arafat and then to shave hairs. These are also compulsory in Umrah except waiting at Arafat.

Six wajeb of Haj. (1) To don Ihram at the appointed place, (2) to throw pebbles at Mina, (3) to wait at Arafat till sunset, (4) to spend the night at Muzdalafah, (5) to stay at Mina, and (6) to make Tawaf of the Ka'ba at the time of farewell.

Modes of Haj. Haj can be performed in three modes-(1) Ifrad, (2) Qeran, and (3) Tamattu. (1) The mode of making pilgrimage by Ifrad is the best. Ifrad is a kind of pilgrimage in which Ihram is donned with the sole Intention of Haj and not Umrah and Ihram is remained after the necessary duties are performed . Then Ihram is put on for Umrah . (2) In the Qeran Haj, Ihram is put on for both Haj and Umrah at the same time. (3) In Tamattu Haj , first Ihram is put on for Haj before it actually takes place. Ihram is put on at the fixed place and then the pilgrim comes to Mecca and removes it. Just before Haj, he again puts on Ihram and removes it after Haj and thereafter makes Tawaf. When there is no Ihram, everything can be enjoyed even sexual intercourse with wife. There are some conditions in Tamatattu Haj-(1) not to be included within the people of Ka'ba, (2) to make Umrah before Haj, (3) to make Umrah in the months o f pilgrimage, (4) not to go to a distance for donning Ihram for Haj, (5) to make Haj and Umrah by the same person. It is compulsory for such a pilgrim to sacrifice a goat. If he cannot do it, he will fast before sacrifice for three days separately or consecutively and when he returns home, he will fast seven days in the same manner.

Prohibited Things in Haj and Umrah

(1) During Haj and Umrah, it is prohibited to put on shirt, trouser, sock, turban. A wearing apparel without stitch and sandal may be used. One should not cover his head as head is included within Ihram. A woman can wear stitched cloth but her face will remain uncovered. (2) He shall not use scents of any kind. (3) He shall not shave the hairs of head and not manicure nails. (4) He shall not have sexual intercourse before the end of Ihram. (5) It is unlawful to kiss, embrace or to marry or get married during Ihram. (6) It is unlawful to sacrifice game of land except game of sea.

SECTION – II

Eight Duties of Haj from First to Last

There are eight duties when one comes out of his house till he dons Ihram. (1) He shall make Tauba, pay compensation to the oppressed and clear off his debts and give expenses of maintenance for his family members till his return. He shall return the trusts entrusted to him and take legally earned money sufficient for his journey expenses till his return along with the additional sum for the poor, the destitute and the weak. He shall spend something in charity before he starts.

(2) He shall seek a religious companion. He will seek your good and help you. He will remind you if you forget. Take farewell from relatives, friends and neighbours and seek their blessings and give your blessings to them by saying: I am entrusting to God your religion and your trust and the end of your actions. The Prophet used to pray for the man who wished to perform Haj: May God keep you in His protection. May He give you provision of God-fear. May He forgive your sins, and may He keep your face towards good wherever you are.

(3) Pray two rak'ats of prayer before starting from home with Fatiha and Sura Kaferun in the first rak'at and Sura Ikhlas in the second rak'at. When you finish your prayer, raise your two hands and seek blessings with this Dua: O God, you are my friend in this journey, you are my successor for my properties, children and friends, save me and them from all calamities. O God, I seek from you in this journey virtues, God-fear and actions pleasing to you. O God, make the world narrow for me, make my journey easy and give me provision of health of body, religion and safety of properties and take us for pilgrimage of your House and for visiting the grave of your Prophet Muhammad (P.H). O God, I seek refuge to you from the troubles of journey, from change of conditions and from the evil looks of the family members and friends. O God, give us and them the blessings of your nearness, Don't deprive us and them of your blessing and don't change your kindness on us and on them.

(4) When you will come near the door of your house say: In the name of God, I rely on God, there is no power and might except in God. O Lord, I seek refuge to Thee that I may not be misguided, that I may not misguide any body, that I may not slip or that I may not cause anybody to slip, that I may not be oppressed or that I may not oppress anybody, that nobody may ascribe ignorance to

me, nor I may ascribe ignorance to anybody. I seek refuge to Thee from all these matters.

(5) When you get on board of your conveyance, say: In the name of God and with God, God is greatest. I rely on God, the Great, the Mighty. There is no power and no might except in God. Whatever God wills comes into being. God has made this conveyance subservient to us. We shall have to return to our Lord. When you sit on the conveyance, recite seven times: All praise is due to God who showed me path for it. We would not have found guidance if God did not show us guidance. O God, Thou art our carrier on backs and Thou art our helper in all our affairs.

(6) Most of your journey should be at night. The Prophet said: You should (travel at night, as the earth becomes narrow at night and not at day. Sleep little during the night that you maybe helper in journey. When you reach a high place, say: O God, Lord of seven heavens and that which casts shade, Lord of seven earths and that which reduces it, Lord of the devils and those whom they misguide, Lord of air and on what it blows upon, Lord of sea and what it blows upon, I seek good of the inhabitants of this place, I seek refuge to Thee from their evils. When you land at any place, pray two rak'ats.

(7) You should not travel during day time, Don't walk alone and don't go out of your company and keep a watch at the time of your sleep at night. Spread out your hands if you sleep at the early part of night. If you sleep by the later part of night, place your head on the palm of your hand. Thus the Prophet used to sleep in his journey in order to guard against the loss of a prayer. The loss of a prayer is more severe than the loss of a pilgrimage.

(8). When you get on a high place on the way, recite Takbir thrice and then recite: O God, Thy honour is above all honours, Thine is all praise and all glory. When you get down, recite Tasbih.

Duties from Miqat to the Entry into Mecca

(1) Take bath with the intention of donning Ihram, comb your hairs and head, manicure your nails, clip your moustache and do -

everything as described in the chapter on purity and cleanliness. (2) Put on two pieces of unsewn Ihram cloth. White cloth is dearest to God. Use scent **on** body and cloth. (3) Take journey if your walk on foot. Now make niyyat of either Ifrad, Qeran or Tamattu Haj and say Talbiyah-present to Thee, O God, present to Thee, there is no partner for Thee, all praise and gifts are for Thee, there is no partner for Thee. (4) When you enter into Ihram, recite the following: O God, I make niyyat for pilgrimage. O God, make it easy for me, help me in fulfilling its duties, accept it from me. There are other invocations also. (5) It is commendable to recite Talbiah in a loud voice at the time of ascending, descending, riding on conveyance. It is as follows: O God, I am present to Thee, I am present to Thee. There is no partner for Thee. All praise, gifts and lordship are for Thee. Thou hast got no partner. Whenever anything astonished the Prophet, he used to say: Labbaik, the life of the next world is true life.

Duties After Entry into Mecca till Tawaf

(1) Take bath to enter Mecca. When you enter the first boundary of Harem outside Mecca, then recite: O God, this is Thy sacred sanctuary, Thy safe place. So save my blood, my hairs and my body from Hell. Save me from Thy chastisement on the day Thou wilt resurrect Thy servants and include me in the company of Thy friends and those subservient to Thee.

(2) Enter Mecca by the high place of Mecca, come out of it by its low place. (3) When you enter Mecca and come near the Ka'ba, recite the following: There is no deity but God. God is greatest. O God, Thou art Peace, from Thee peace, and Thine abode is the abode of peace. Blessed art Thou, O possessor of glory and honour. O God, this is Thy house. Thou hast made it sacred and honourable. So increase its honour, respect and awe. O God, open for me the doors of Thy mercy and admit me in Thy Paradise and give me refuge from the accursed devil.

(4) When you enter the Ka'ba, enter it through the door of Banu Shaibah and recite: In the name of God, with God, from God towards God, in the way of God and upon the religion of the

Apostle of God. When you will come near the Ka'ba, recite: O God, accept my repentance, forgive my faults, reduce my burden. All praise is due to God who has taken me to His sacred House, who has made it the refuge of men and their safe place and a guide to the universe. O God, I am Thy servant. This is Thy city, this is Thy sanctuary and this is Thy house. I am present to Thee. I beseech Thy mercy and I inform Thee of the invocation of one afflicted. I seek Thy forgiveness and Thy pleasure.

(5) Then touch the Black Stone by your right hand, kiss it and recite: O God, I have fulfilled Thy trust and my promise. Bear witness of my fulfillment.

Fourth duty-Tawaf (Circumambulation). Observe seven rules in Tawaf:

(1) Observe the conditions of prayer in Tawaf. In other words, be pure from all sorts of uncleanliness and cover your private parts. Tawaf is like prayer except that conversation is allowed therein. (2) It shall be done with Ihram dress as prescribed. (3) Then wait at the Black Stone which is the preliminary point of circling the Ka'ba. (4) Recite at the start of Tawaf: In the name of God, God is greatest. O God, I begin this circling after putting faith in Thee, testifying to the truth of Thy Book, fulfilling promise with Thee and following the ways of Thy Apostle Muhammad (peace be on him). (5) After crossing the Black Stone, recite when you reach the door of Ka'ba: O God, this House is Thine, this sanctuary is Thine, this safe place is Thine and this place is the place of refuge from Hell to Thee. (6) Thus there are recitations at every point round the Ka'ba as prescribed and you will go round the Ka'ba seven times.

(7) After finishing Tawaf, pray two rak'ats at Muqame Ibrahim following the Prophet and make invocations. The Prophet said: He who makes Tawaf of the Ka'ba seven times and then prays two rak'ats will get the rewards of setting free a slave.

Fifth Duty-Sa'yl (Running between Safa and Marwa)

After finishing Tawaf, take to running between the two hillocks-Safa and Merwa seven times and recite the following before doing it: There is no deity but He. There is no partner for Him. His is the kingdom and His is all praise. He giveth life and taketh life and He is eternal without death. All good is in His hands and He is powerful over all things.

There is no deity but God. He is single. He has proved true to His promise, helped his servant and honoured His army and routed the enemies. There is no deity but God, be sincere to Him in worship though the polytheists dislike it. Then at the beginning of running, recite: O Lord, forgive and show mercy and pardon what Thou knowest. Thou art majestic and honourable. O God, our Lord, give us good in this world and good in the hereafter and save us from Hell.

Sixth Duty-Waiting at Arafat

The waiting time at Arafat is from noon of the 9th Zil-Haj to the early dawn of the 10th Zil-Haj. After reaching Mina, recite the following: O God, this is Mina, bestow grace on me as Thou hast bestowed grace here on Thy friends and those who were obedient to Thee. Reaching at Arafat, fix your tent and wait there with a great penitent mind and recite invocations and supplications as much as possible and seek forgiveness and mercy of God.

Seventh Duty-Other Institutions of Haj

At sunrise the next day, start from Arafat and reach Mazdalafah and recite the following: O God, this is Mazdalafah, people of different tongues have gathered here seeking different necessary things from Thee. Make me one of those who have sought from Thee and Thou hast granted them. Then pray Maghrib and Isha together with one Azan and two Aqamats. Stay here for one night as it is included within the institution of Haj. Next day, start for Mina and reach the place of stone-throwing and throw seven stones there as prescribed. Then sacrifice an animal and then shave your head. Then return to Mecca and make Tawaf of the Ka'ba. Then return to Mina again.

Eighth and Ninth Duties-Umrah, Tawaf of Farewell

He who intends to make Umrah before or after Haj, let him take bath, put on Ihram dress and wear Ihram from its appointed place. When you enter Mecca, go round the Ka'ba seven times recitings the prescribed invocations and run between Safa and Merwa. Then it ends with the shaving of head. After finishing all rites of Haj and Umrah, make Tawaf of the Ka'ba seven times before you start for home and seek forgiveness from God and express gratefulness for getting opportunity of making Haj and Umrah.

Tenth Duty-Visit to Medina

The Prophet said: Whosoever visits my grave after my death has met me as it were during my lifetime. He also said: He who does not visit me in spite of having means oppresses me. He also said: Whosoever does not come to me except with the object of visiting me, it is the duty of God that I become his intercessor. He also said: He who wishes to visit Medina, should send much blessings upon the Prophet on his way to Medina. When the walls and trees of Medina fall to his eyes, he will recite: O God, this is the sanctuary of Thy Apostle. So make it a shield for saving me from Hell and a safe place from punishment and bad account. When you enter Medina, recite the following: In the name of God and upon the religion of Apostle of God. O Lord, enter me a true entry and take me out a true taking out and send for me from Thee a strong helper. Then pray two rak'ats after entering the mosque and then wait near the grave of the Holy Prophet and send profuse Darud and blessings on him as prescribed. The Prophet said: The place between my grave and pulpit is one of the gardens of paradise and my pulpit is upon my fountain.

Then visit Jannatul Baqi, the place of burials of the martyrs and of Hadrat Osman, Hasan, Zainal Abedin, Imam Baqi, Imam Jafar Sadiq , Hazrat Fatema. Then observe prayer, at the Qubba mosque as the Prophet said: He who comes out of his house and comes to the mosque of Qubba and says prayer there, the rewards of an Umrah are written for him. The Prophet said: He who can die at Medina should do it, as I shall be an intercessor for one who dies at Medina. Then visit the grave of the Prophet when leaving Medina.

SECTION – III
Ten Secret Things of Haj

(1) **The money for expense will be lawful.** Hands will be free from trades and commerce and all thoughts will be centered round one God and the mind will rest satisfied with the Zikr of God and its signs. There is in Hadis: In the later days, the people will go far Haj but their object will be four. The rulers will go to increase their power, the rich for trade and commerce, the poor for begging and the learned for name and fame. These things can be earned but if Haj is performed with these objects, no reward is acquired for Haj. It will go out of the limit of Haj, specially when one goes as a representative for Haj. The Prophet said: God will admit three persons in paradise for one Haj-one who makes death-instruction for doing Haj, one who follows this custom and one who performs it on behalf of his brother. God gives the world on account of religion but He does not give religion on account of the world. The Prophet said: He who makes Jihad in the way of God is like the mother of Moses. She took remuneration for suckling her son. To receive remuneration for Haj by representation is like the receipt of remuneration of the mother of Moses and there is no fault in it, but it will not be legal to perform Haj as an agent with the object of getting remuneration, rather to accept remuneration with the object of performing Haj is legal as the mother of Moses did.

(2) **Don't help the enemies of God by keeping the properties in trust.** Some chiefs of Mecca and some Sardars of Arabia remain busy in keeping the people away from the path of Haj. To entrust them with properties is to help oppression. Try to save yourselves from their hands and if you are unable, it is better to return home than to help oppressors. This is an innovation.

(3) **Take sufficient money and provision** with you so that you may not feel difficulty for charity. Take the middle course for expenditure. Save yourself from taking delicious food and drink.

There is no misuse in excessive charity. There is no good in excessive expense and there is no excessive expense in good things. A certain wise man said: To give provisions in the path of Haj is considered as expense in the way of God. Hazrat Ibn Umar said: To have good provision in journey is honour. He used to say: The best is the pilgrimage in which sincere intention is perfect, expense is most pure and sure faith is best. The Prophet said: There is no reward for an accepted Haj except paradise. The Prophet was asked: O Apostle of God, what is an accepted Haj? He said: The pilgrimage in which good words are uttered and food is given.

(4) Give up indecent actions, evil actions, quarrels and disputes. This is the injunction of the Quran. Indecent actions mean indecent and useless talks including such talks with females, talks of intercourse with them as they increase desire of intercourse. All things which give encouragement to do prohibited things are also prohibited. Evil actions mean such actions which take away from the religion of God. Quarrels and disputes give rise to hatred and envy. Sufyan said: He who talks indecent words destroys his Haj. Quarrel is opposed to good words and the Prophet termed good words as good deeds of Haj. Don't inflict trouble on anybody and adopt good conduct. As journey discloses the character and conduct of a man, it is therefore named Safar.

(5) It is better to preform Haj by walking on foot. Abdullah-b-Abbas instructed his sons at the time of his death: O my children, perform Haj by walking on foot, as for each step of such a pilgrim there is written 700 rewards out of the rewards of Hazam. He was questioned: What are the rewards of Hazam? He said: One good deed brings one lac rewards. It is better to walk from Mecca to Arafat and from Arafat to

Mina. A perfect Haj is one in which niyat is made when one comes out of his house for Ihram and to walk on foot. God says: Make Haj and umrah perfect for God. Hazrat Umar, Ali and Ibn Mas'ud explained His verse in the above way.

(6) Don't ride without keeping the balance of burden behind and keep the things separate if possible. This gives relief to the camel.

The Prophet made pilgrimage riding on conveyance and even he made Tawaf riding, so that the people might follow him on his action. The Prophet said: Learn your institutions from me.

(7) Keep your countenance un-smooth, hairs dishevelled, body laden with dust, indifferent to pride and attachment for the world, as the Prophet enjoined his followers to remain then without beauty and with dishevelled hairs. The Prophet said: A pilgrim is dressed dishevelled and his body is dust laden. God says: Look to the visitors of My house. They have come to Me with hairs dishevelled and with body dust-laden from every distant part of hills. God says: Then perform the institutions of Haj. This means to shave hairs, to clip moustaches and to manicure nails. Hazrat Umar sent instructions to his generals: Put on old clothes and habituate yourselves to bear hardships.

(8) Show kindness to the riding animals and don't take anything on them beyond their strength. Sleeping over their backs gives them trouble and gives a sense of heaviness to them. The friends of God did not sleep on the backs of animals. The Prophet said: Don't make the backs of your animals seats, and to descend from their backs morning and evening is commendable as it gives rest to the animals. Abu Darda said to his camel at the time of his death: O camel, don't dispute with me near your Lord, as I did not burden you with load beyond your strength. Once a man said to the sage Ibnul Mubarak: I am giving this letter of mine to you. You will take it to the destination. He said: I will ask the owner of the camel about it, as I took hire of this camel. Thus he feared to carry it on account of God-fear and piety.

(9) Seek nearness of God by sacrificing an animal. Try to sacrifice an animal which is strong and stout.. If sacrifice is compulsory, don't eat its meat and if optional, you may eat its meat. God says: 'Whosoever honours the signs of God'. This is explained by saying to sacrifice stout and strong animal. The ancient people did not press for price of three things-animals of pilgrimage, setting free of slaves and animals of sacrifice, as the best of three things is that which is best in price and most valuable to the seller. The object is not the increase in meat but to purify from the guilt of miserliness and to adorn it for God with honour as its flesh and blood will not

reach God but He will accept from you God-fear. The Prophet was asked: How is Haj accepted? He said: By Say 'A'z and Sa'z. To proclaim Talbiah loudly is called A'z and to sacrifice a camel is called Sa'z. The Prophet said: Nothing is dearer to God on the day of sacrifice out of the actions of men then the sacrifice of an animal. It will come on the Resurrection Day with its hoofs and horns and its blood falls in a place near God before it falls on the ground. So purify your soul by sacrifice. There is in Hadis: There is reward for every hair of the sacrificed animal and for every drop of blood and it will be weighed near God. So give good news. The Prophet said: Sacrifice a good animal, as it will be your carrier on the Resurrection Day.

(10) To spend with a cheerful mind. Bear with pleasure sacrifice of the loss that is caused in the matter of properties or the occurrence of any calamity, because it is a proof of the acceptance of Haj. The troubles and calamities on the way to pilgrimage is like expense in the way of God and the expense of a dirham at that time is equal to the expense of seven hundred dirhams. That is the reward of bearing hardships in the way of Jihad. Nothing is spoiled near God of any trouble which is foreborn and every loss which is sustained. It is said that if one gives up sins and bad company and takes up good company and gives up assembly of useless talks and takes to the assemblies of Zikr, they are the signs of acceptance of Haj.

Significance of Internal Actions of Haj

Knowledge. The first thing of Haj is to know everything in connection with Haj. Know, O dear readers, that you will not be able to reach God tat you can control your passions and low desires, restrain yourself from all enjoyments and pleasures, make short your necessities and work only for the sake of God. For this reason, the friends of God of yore used to live far away from the localities of men and lived in lonely places in caves of mountains and hills, so that their love for God might be deep. God says about them in the Quran: Because there are hermits and those who renounced the world among them and they are proud. When they began to live contrary to it and gave up loneliness for divine service and mixed with the people to fulfil their low desires, God sent the Apostle Muhammad (P.H.) to reawaken the paths of the next world and to call them to the ways of the Prophets. On being questioned by the religious people about the life of a hermit, the Prophet said: God gave us in lieu thereof Jihad and Takbir in very elevated place (Haj). The Prophet said: God gave this gift for this people and made Haj as their monkery, honoured the ancient House as His House, fixed it as the object of desire of the people, made its surrounding places pure to show honour to the House, made Arafat an opening space as the precincts of His House and honoured the place by ; prohibiting hunting and cutting of trees therein. He made it as the Darbar of the greatest Emperor. Every visitor comes to the Darbar from ever distant and inaccessible place, dishevelled in hairs and laden with dust and in the most humble spirit. He knows that no house can encompass God and no town can cover Him and yet he does it to make his divine service and his allegiance and obedience perfect. For this reason throwing of stones at Mina, running between Safa and Merwa and other institutions do not come within understanding or seem good. But by these acts, full servitude is expressed. The object of the payment of Zakat is understood. The object of fasting to restrain sexual passion and low desires is understood. The object of prayer is also understood. But no satisfactory reason is ostensibly found in the throwing of stones, running between Safa and Merwa, nor they come within understanding. It is, however, true that true servitude is a separate thing and to serve God means that one should conduct himself according to the order of God, whether it contains any meaning or not. The object of obeying orders is nothing but to serve God. It is an act of wisdom to obey God in places where intellect cannot enter and which it cannot comprehend. Servitude to God is expressed fully when you understand a thing or not. For this reason, the Prophet said regarding Haj: I consider Haj thus a veritable truth, servitude in reality and slavery of the highest order. He did not say this with regard to prayer and other divine services. So the institutions which cannot be understood by intellect are the perfect divine services for making the heart pure because to act contrary to nature and to return from habits is the real servitude and slavery.

Desire for Haj. The Ka'ba is the House of God. The meaning of coming to it is to see God there. He who desires to visit the Ka'ba in the world should have his object not to be deprived of it. His object should be his look to the countenance of God in His permanent abode. This earthly eye has got no power to have a glimpse of the Divine light, nor can it bear the brilliance of His light. The light of eye in the next world will be permanent and will be free from the causes of destruction and change and then it will be fit for glimpse of the Lord. But one can be fit to earn it by visiting His House. So desire to meet Him will lead you to the causes of visit without doubt.

Firm determination of Making Haj

Know, O dear readers, that you will intend to be separate from your home and family by the help of your firm determination and turn your face towards visiting the House after giving up comforts and pleasures of home life. Know in your mind the honour of the Ka'ba and the exalted rank of its Owner. Make your firm determination only for God, keep distant from name and fame and make your intention sincere and pure.

To cut off tie in Hay. It means to pay compensation to oppressed and to make sincere repentance to God from all sins. Every oppression has got a compensation and every compensation is due to somebody. Don't hope to return home and make wasiat to your children in writing and think of this journey as the journey for the next world.

Provisions of journey. Seek provision from your lawful earnings and think that your good deeds are the provisions of your next world and these will go with you after your death. **Regarding conveyance.** Be grateful to God that you have got a conveyance to carry you and your loads. Remember that you are visiting a funeral prayer in the journey towards the next world. The affairs of Haj are like journey to the next world. **Ihram cloth.** When you put it on, remember the coffin cloth with which you will be clothed. As you wear two unsewn pieces of cloth to go near the House of God and change your habit of putting on fine clothes, so you will not be able to meet with God after your death unless you take clothes contrary to the clothes of this world. As there is no stitching of cotton cloth for burial, so there is no stitching of Ihram cloth.

Starting from Home. When you come out of your home, know that you are going on a journey to God after separating your family and friends. Think then in your mind-what is your object, to whom are you going, to meet whom do you hope? You are going to meet the greatest Emperor and for that you have surrendered and you have responded to it. Bring this consolation in mind that if you visit the Ka'ba, you may get glimpse of its Owner. This is your last object and it will help you towards that object. Hope in mind to reach the Ka'ba and that your Haj may be accepted. Don't depend on your good deeds and believe firmly in the mercy of God. If you cannot reach the Ka'ba and die on the way, it will help to meet Him being He guest as God says: If a man goes out of his house and makes emigration to God and His Apostle and then death overtakes him, his reward is upon God- 4 : 100. When you reach the Miqat or the fixed place for Ihram, remember all the great events when you will leave the world up to the Resurrection Day. When you remember the danger of crossing the way, remember then the questions of Munkar and Naqir. If you see the ferocious beasts on the way, remember the biting of snakes in graves.

Talbiyah at Miqat. Know that Talbiah means to respond to the call of God. Remember Him between hope and fear and depend on the mercy of God. Imam Sufian Saori said that Imam Zainal Abedin son of Hazrat Hussain made pilgrimage. When he donned Ihram, his face became changed and he had no strength to say Labbaik. He was asked: Why are you not uttering Labbaik? He said: I fear lest I may be said: You have no Labbaik and fortune. When he uttered Labbaik, he suddenly fell in swoon and remained long in that condition. As a result, he could not wait at Arafat. Abu Sulaiman Darani did not utter Labbaik even after walking a mile. Then he fell down senseless. When he recovered from his swoon, he said: O Ahmad, woe to you, I fear lest I may be said: There is no Labbaik and fortune for you. Remember at the time when you utter Labbaik the condition of the people on the day of congregation.

Entry into Mecca. Remember at the time when you enter Mecca that you have reached safely in the sacred place of God and hope from God that you will be safe from punishment on account of your entry into Mecca. When you look at the Ka'ba, remember its glory and hope to meet its Owner. Tawaf of Ka'ba is like prayer. Remember then that your Tawaf is like the Tawaf of the near angels who are going found the Throne. Don't think that the object of your Tawaf is the Tawaf of your body round the House but its object is the Tawaf of your mind with the remembrance of God. Know that an honourable Tawaf is the Tawaf of mind before God. The Ka'ba is the outward darbar of a king. He

who is not seen by external eye appears there. Soul is a thing of the spiritual world as body is of the material world. God is in the unseen world. This visible world, leads to the world unseen. This is for those for whom God opened this door. Think that the Ka'ba is the exact prototype of the Baitul Mamur in heaven. The angels make Tawaf of Baitul Mamur and the people, of the Ka'ba.

Kissing. When you kiss the Black Stone, think that it is a sign of allegiance and kiss His hand. Be firm in your will that you are fulfilling your promise. The Prophet said: The Black Stone is the right hand of God in the world. As a man handshakes with his brother, so God also handshakes with the people by means of the Black Stone.

Say between **Safa and** Merwa. Say between these two hillocks in expectation of getting His glimpse is just as a man goes forward and backward in getting a glimpse of his emperor. Think that Safa is the scale of good deeds and Merwa of bad deeds. By running between these two hillocks, think which of the scales becomes heavy. To wait in Arafat. After seeing the vast concourse of a people of different climes and tongues, you will remember the case of the great congregation on the Resurrection Day that each people will gather there with their respective Prophet and each people will expect intercession of their Prophet and remain busy to know whether his intercession was accepted or not. When you will remember this, keep your mind engaged in the remembrance of God. **Throwing of stones.** Obey God's command by throwing stones and show sincerely and honestly your servitude to God even though it does not come to your - understanding, because blind obedience of a slave to his master gains the love of the master. Then intend to follow the deeds of Abraham who drove away the evil by throwing stones at him when the latter wanted to misguide him and not to sacrifice his dearest son Ismail in obedience to God's command. The meaning of Haj is to obey God's commands without argument and without exercising intellect.

Sacrifice of animal. Sacrifice in a mass scale brings people near God. For this reason, the animal for sacrifice should be stout and strong. Hope that in lieu of every limb of the sacrificed animal. God will save your every limb from Hell-fire. The more it is stout and strong, the more you will be free from Hell-fire.

Visiting Medina. When your sight will fall on the wall of the city of Medina, remember that God selected this city for His Prophet and took him there. This is the place of the promulgation of God's compulsory ordinance and the ways of the Prophet. He fought with the enemies here and preached Islam up to his death. God established the religion through the successors of the Prophet. Then think of the footsteps of the Prophet in the city and take steps with care and honour. The Prophet said: God will present before me many people, They will say: O Muhammad, O Muhammad, I will say; O Lord, they are my companions. He will say: You don't know what evil deeds they have done after you? I will say: Then be off from me. If you have not followed the Prophet, you will be far away from him; still you will hope for the mercy of God. When you will reach the mosque, remember that God selected the place for the Prophet and the earliest Muslims. Enter it in fear and hope. When Owais Qarni entered the mosque of Medina and began to wait at the door, he said: This is the grave of the Holy Prophet. At once he fell in swoon. When he regained his senses, he said: Take me out of this. I have got no taste in the place where the Prophet has been buried.

Meeting with the Prophet. Meet with him as if he is alive and that you are standing before him. Don't go very near his grave as you would not have gone to him if he were alive. Don't touch his grave and don't kiss it and know that God knows your mind, your standing and your salutation. The Prophet said: God appointed an angel in his grave. Whosoever sends salam to him out of his followers he will take it to *hint*. This has been said with regard to that person who will not be present before his grave. How will it be in case of that man who left his home and family and relatives and journeyed in difficult places and hills and came to visit the Prophet? The Prophet said: If a man sends one Darud on me, God will send ten Daruds on him. Then come to the pulpit of the Apostle of God and think of his standing thereon and his sermons to his followers. When it will be finished, think whether your Haj has been accepted or not as he does not accept Haj of one who does not love Him.

RECITATION OF THE QURAN

All praise is due to God who showers blessings on His servants by sending revealed books and Prophets. This Quran does not contain any false stories of yore or future. It is a revelation from the Most High, the Almighty. Therein is food for reflection for those who are thoughtful and there are true stories of former nations. By its help, walk on straight path becomes easy as the commands and prohibitions are expressed there in clear terms and the lawful and unlawful things made clear. It is a light and therein there is sun for the disease of mind. God destroyed those who opposed it. God misguides one who seeks knowledge other than that of the Quran. It is a firm rope of God, clear light and firmest tie. There is everything in it, small and great. There is no end of its miracle. It is ever fresh and new to the reciters. It is a guide for the past and future. The jinn heard it and warned their classes. They said: We heard a wonderful Quran. It is a guide. We believed in it and did not set up anything with our Lord. Those who advised according to it told truth. Those who held it firm, found guidance. Those who acted up to it got salvation. God says: I have revealed it and I will certainly preserve it. The modes of preserving the Quran are: committing it to memory, writing it on papers, to recite it always , to read it in prayer, to explain it and comment on it. It will be discussed in four sections.

SECTION – I

Excellence of the Quran

The Prophet said: If a man thinks that what has been given to others is better then he considered little the dearest thing of God. He said: Prophets, angels, or anybody else cannot be better intercessors in rank than the Quran. He said: If the Quran is kept within skin, burning fire will not go near it, nor touch it. The Prophet said: Recitation of the Quran is the best divine service of my followers. He said: God recited chapter Taha and Yasin one thousand years before creation. When the angels heard them, they said: How fortunate are they on whom they will be revealed. How fortunate are those who commit them to memory. How fortunate are the tongues which broadcast them. The Prophet said: The best of you is he who learns the Quran and teaches it. He said: God says: If a man cannot pray or invoke Me on account of his being engaged in reciting the Quran, I will give him better rewards than those who express gratefulness. He said: Two persons will stand in the mountain of musk on the Resurrection Day. They will have not fear and will render no accounts, even they will be free from the wants of men-(1) he who recites the Quran for pleasure of God, (2) he who becomes the leader of the people who remain satisfied with him. The Prophet said: A reciter of the Quran belongs to the family of God and is His sincere servant. He said: Rust falls on heart as it falls on iron. The Prophet was asked: O Messenger of God, how can the rust be removed? He said: By reciting the Quran and by remembering death. The Prophet said: God hears the recitation of the Quran more attentively than the master of a singing girl.

Wise sayings. Hazrat Abu Omarah Baheli said: Recite the Quran. This hanging book will not deceive you. God will not punish one who commits it to memory. Hazrat Ibn Mas'ud said: When you wish to acquire knowledge, select the Quran as it is the embodiment of the knowledge of the previous and future generations. He said quoting the - saying of the Prophet: You will get ten rewards in lieu of each word of it. Beware, I am not saying that 'Alef, Lam and Mim' is a word but Alef is a word, Lam is a word and Mim is a word. He said: Let nobody among you ask anything about himself except the Quran. If he loves the Quran and remains satisfied with it, he loves God and His Prophet and if he disrespects the Quran, he disrespects God and His Prophet. Hazrat Amr-b-'A'as said: Every verse of the Quran is a door of Paradise and a light in your House. He said: He who recites the Quran opens as it were the door of Prophethood by his two sides, but no revelation will come to him. Hazrat Abu Hurairah said: The provision of the inmates of a house in which the Quran is recited increases, their good becomes more, angels remain present there and the devil goes out of it. The provision of the inmates of a house in which the Quran is not recited becomes straitened, their welfare diminishes, angels go out of it and the devil comes in. Imam Ahmad-b-Hanbal said: I saw God in dream and asked him: O God, for what thing one can come near to Thee! He said: O Ahmad, by means of my Kalam, the Quran. I asked Him: O Lord, by means of its understanding or not? He said: Yes, whether you understand its meaning or not. Fuzail-b-Ayaz said: One who commits the Quran by heart is the bearer of the standard of Islam He should not hold useless talks with those who hold such talks. He should not forget the Quran as others do. Imam Sufian Saori said: When a man recites the Quran, an angel kisses on his forehead.% Amr-b-Maimun said: If a man reads one hundred verses of the Quran after morning prayer, God will give him rewards of the actions of the inhabitants of the world. Once Khalid-b-Uqbah came to the Prophet and said: Read out to me the Quran. He read out to him: God enjoins you to do justice and good. He said to the Prophet Recite again. He read it again and then said : By God, therein is sweetness, heightness, its lower portion has got bases, its upper has got fruits and it is not the word of a man. Hazrat Hasan Basri said: By God, there is no greater wealth than the Quran and there is no want after the Quran. Fuzail said: If a man recites the last portion of chapter Hashr and dies on that day, the seal of martyrdom is imprinted on him. If he reads it in the evening and dies in that night, the seal of martyrdom is imprinted on him. Hazrat Ali said: Three things increase the power of memory and remove scum-toothstick, fast and recitation of the Quran.

Punishment for Heedless Recitation

Hazrat Anas said: There are some men who recite the Quran, but it curses them. Abu Sulaiman Darani said: The angels of Hell will arrest those who commit the Quran to memory but become disobedient to God. Hazrat Ibn Mas'ud said: Those who committed the Quran to memory should get acquainted with the night when the people remain asleep and should be sorry when the people commit sins and make enjoyments during day time. They will weep when the people will laugh, they will remain silent when the people hold useless talks. The Prophet said: Recite- the Quran till it prohibits you to do evil deeds. If it does not prohibit you, it will not be considered as your recitation. The Prophet said: He who knows the unlawful things of the Quran as lawful does not believe in the Quran. Hazrat Ibn Mas'ud said: The Quran was revealed to you for doing actions. So translate your recitation into action. There are men among you who recite the Quran from first to last and do not omit a single word therefrom but they don't of translate it into action. There is in the Torah; God said: O My servant, are you not ashamed of Me? I f a letter from your friend comes to you in your journey, you at once come to a side of the road and read with an attentive mind every word and sentence of it and you do not omit anything from it. But I sent My Book to you and I am seeing with what attentive mind you are reading it and how you have followed its commands and prohibitions. But you have turned your face from it. O My servant, have you considered it more mean than your friend's letter? I am present to you. I am speaking with you but you have turned your mind from Me. **Have I become** more mean to you than your friend?

SECTION – II
External Rules Reciting the Quran

There are ten external rules for the recitation of the Quran.

(1) After ablution, face the Ka'ba without showing pride in sitting with head downwards just like the sitting of a student before his teacher. The best way of Quran reading is in prayer standing in a mosque. God says: They remember God standing, sitting and lying on their sides and ponder over the creation of the heaven and earth. In this verse, every condition has been said in order o excellence-first standing, then sitting and then lying state. Hazr: Ali said: If a man recites a portion of the Quran in prayer standin

one hundred rewards are written for him for every word. If a man recites a portion of the Quran sitting in prayer, fifty rewards are written for him for every word. If a man reads the Quran outside the prayer with ablution, twenty-five rewards are written for him for every word. If a man reads the Quran without ablution, ten rewards are written for him for every word. Hazrat Abu Zarr Ghaffari said: To make much prostration at day time and to pray long at night are better.

(2) **The quantity of Quran** reciting. There are different rules for the readers about the quantity of the recitations of the Quran. Some finish the whole Quran in a day and night, some twice, some thrice and some once in a month. The best way is what the Prophet said in this Hadis: He who finishes the Quran within less time than three days cannot gain the knowledge of the rules of religion as fast reading cannot clearly be recited. Hazrat Ayesha said of a man who recited the Quran hastily: This man neither recites the Quran, nor remains silent. The Prophet ordered Abdullah-b-Amr to finish the Quran once a week. Some of the companions followed this rule. They were Hazrat Osman, Zaid-b-Sabet, Ibn Mas'ud, Ubai-i-Ka'b and others. So there are several modes of finishing the Quran. (1) once in a day and a night, (2) once in a month, (3) once in a week with seven equal portions a day.

The Quran was first free from I'rab or dots above and below. Hazrat Hasan Basri said: There is no harm in giving I'rab to the Quran. It is commendable to read the Quran slowly. The object of the Quran reading is to ponder and there are fixed places therein for slow-reading. The Prophet explained every sentence separately. Hazrat Ibn Abbas said: I prefer to read chapter Baqarah and chapter Imran slowly and to ponder about them than to read them hurriedly.

Weeping at the time of recitation of the Quran is also commendable, as the Prophet said: Recite the Quran and weep. If you cannot weep, assume weeping attitude. The Prophet said: He who does not read the Quran with sweet tone is not of us. Saleh Marbi said: I recited the Quran in dream before the Prophet. He said: O Saleh, where is your weeping in reciting the Quran? Hazrat lbn Abbas said: When you read the verse of prostration, don't prostrate soon till you weep. If the eyes of any one of you do not shed tears, let him weep by his heart. The mode of weeping by force is to bring sorrows to the mind. He who can bring sorrows to the mind can also bring weeping. The Prophet said: The Quran has been revealed for sorrow. When you read it, be in a sorrowful mode The mode of bringing sorrow is to ponder over the words of warnings and punishments in the Quran. Fulfil your duty to every verse. If you read the verse of prostration, prostrate. If you hear the verse from another, make prostration but do it not without ablution. There are fourteen prostrations in the Quran. Prostration is perfect when Takbir is recited therein.

God says: Fall down in prostration and glorify the praise of your Lord. There are conditions of prostration like the conditions of prayer-to cover private parts, to face the Ka'ba, to have the body and cloth pure. Recite Takbir for prostration, then fall in prostration, then raise up your head with Takbir and then return salam. A follower will follow the leader in prostration without reciting the Quran.

When you begin to recite the Quran, recite, seek refuge to God from accursed devil. Then recite chapter Nas and Fateha. When you finish the Quran, say: O God show mercy on me for the Quran, make it for me a guide, a light, a leader and a mercy. O God, remind me what I have forgotten therefrom, teach me what I do not know therefrom and give me provision of reading it day and night and make it a proof for me, O Lord of the universe.

To Recite the Quran with sound. Recite the Quran with such sound as you may hear it. The meaning of reciting is that you will hear yourself what is recited. Read it with such sound in prayer as you yourself may hear it. If you do not hear it, your prayer will not be valid. The Prophet said: As secret charity brings more reward than open charity, so secret Quran reading brings more reward than open Quran reading with sound. In another narration: Reading the Quran with sound is like open charity and silent Quran reading is like secret charity. There is in Hadis that the reward of a secret deed is seventy times more than that of an open deed. The Prophet said: What gives consolation is good provision and secret Zikr is the best Zikr.

There is in Hadis: Don't recite the Quran with loud voice in between sunset and night prayers. The Prophet heard one party of his companions reciting the Quran with loud voice in night prayer and considered it right. The Prophet said: If any of you stands to pray Isha (night prayer), let him read his Quran openly, as the angels and the inmates of the house hear Quran reading and pray for him in lieu of his prayer. The Prophet saw his three companions in different conditions. When passing by Abu Bakr, he heard him reading silently and asked him about it. He said: He with whom I speak hears it. While passing by Hazrat Umar, he heard him reciting the Quran with loud voice. He asked him about it and he said: I am waking up the heedless and the sleeping men and driving the devil. The Prophet passed by Bilal and found him reading some verses silently and some with sound. On being asked, he said: I am mixing good verses with good verses. The Prophet said: Each one of you has done well. In other words, he who fears show should read it silently. Open reading awakens the mind and centers the thoughts to one thing. It is better to recite the Quran by seeing it as to look to the Quran is also worship.

To read the Quran with sweet voice and slowly is sunnat. The Prophet said: God did not order sweet voice for anything except for the Quran. He said: He who does not read the Quran with sweet voice is not of us. It is narrated that the Prophet was waiting one night for Ayesha as she was late in coming. The Prophet asked her: Who prevented you from coming? She said: O Prophet of God, I was hearing the Quran reading of a man. I never heard such a sweet voice. The Prophet came to him and heard his recitation for a long time and said: The name of this man is Salem, the slave of Abu Hurairah. All praise is due to God who created such a man among my followers. One night, the Prophet heard the Quran reading of Hazrat Ibn Mas'ud with Hazrat Abu Bakr and Umar and there they remained for long time. Then the Prophet said: If anybody wishes the Quran to be read with sweet voice and slowly, let him hear the Quran-reading of Ibn Umar Abdullah.

The Prophet said to lbn Masud: Read out the Quran to me. He said: O Prophet of God, I am reading, it has been revealed to you. The Prophet said: I wish to hear it from you. When he was reading the Quran before him, the eyes of the Prophet began to shed tears. The Prophet said after hearing the Quran-reading of Abu Musa: This voice has been given to him from the sweet voice of David. Hazrat Abu Musa said on hearing it: O Prophet of God, if I had known that you would hear it, I would have read with sweeter voice. When the companions of the Prophet gathered together, they told one another to recite the Quran. Hazrat Umar once asked Abu Musa: Remember our Lord. He began to read the Quran before him. When the prayer time came, Hazrat Umar was reminded of the prayer to which he said: Are we not in the midst of prayer? There is hint in this verse of God: God's remembrance is greatest. The Prophet said: if a man hears a verse of God's Book, there will be a light for him on the Resurrection Day. There is in Hadis that ten rewards are written for him.

SECTION – III

Internal Rules of the Quran-reading

There are ten internal rules of reciting the Quran. (1) To realise the superiority and excellence of the Quran. God's word is self-existent attribute and mixed with His being and He expressed that attribute in human forms and words to mankind. When the people become unable to appreciate the attribute of God, they are able to understand it through the means of their own attributes. If the glory and excellence of the words of God, they are able to understand it through the means of their words, the heaven and earth could not stand to hear His words and all things between them would have been smashed to pieces. If God had not made Moses patient and steady, he could not have remained without falling into swoon after hearing His words as the mountain had no power to remain steady being attacked with His Brilliance. For this reason, a friend of God said: Every word of God kept in the Guarded Tablet is higher than the mountain Kaf. If all the angels try to make a word short, they are unable to do it till the guard of the Guarded Tablet lifts it up and makes it short by order of God. This is not because of the strength of its words but the Glorious God made it fit for human use dressed with words. A wise man said: We saw in case of human beings that when they wish to make their domestic animal understand something, they mix some of their words with some unexpressed words of the animal and create some language to guide its nature. It can understand it by instinct and act accordingly. Similar is the case with men. Though they are unable to understand the perfectness, dignity, beauty and solemnity of God's words, the Prophet made them understand in such a manner as man conducts his animal by a strange language . The thoughts of the Quran were stated with such words that men can understand the wisdom of the Quran, as a lower animal can understand the thoughts of men by their hints and voices. The root meaning of wisdom lies concealed in these words and voices but still it is honoured on account of its meaning. Words are the bodies of wisdom and their meaning is the soul of wisdom and voice is their life.

As human body is honoured for its internal soul, so the word of wisdom is honoured for its voice. The word of God revealed has got high rank. It is just, judge and dear witness. It orders and prohibits. There is no such strength of a void thing. As shade is unable to stand before the brilliant rays of the sun, a man is unable to stand before the words of wisdom of the Quran. As eye sight is unable to stand the scorching rays of the sun, so a man has got no power to enter into the deepest recess of wisdom. He takes so much rays of the sun as he can see and know his necessary things. In short, the word of God is like an unseen emperor in the deepest cover whose face is not visible but yet whose order is prevalent. The word of God is like the sun of which the rays are open but its constitution is secret like radiant star. By its help the paths of journey are seen. The word of God or the Quran is an invaluable treasure or an ever lasting drink of life which prevents death or it is such a medicine for a disease which leaves no ailment if it is taken.

(2) Honour the Quran containing divine words. At the time of

reciting the Quran, realise in a beautiful manner divine glory and think that what you recite is not human words. God says: None shall touch it except the pure ones. As the external papers are preserved from touch of impure hands, so its secret meaning and wisdom are shut up from the internal mind if it is not free from all impurities and not illumined by the light of honour and gravity. As the pages of the Quran cannot be touched by every body, so every tongue can not utter the words of the Quran and every heart cannot grasp its meaning. When Hazrat Ikramah son of Abu Jahl opened the Quran, he fainted and said: This is the word of my Lord. To honour His word is to honour Him and He is not honoured till His attributes and the mysteries of His creation are not ponder over, till he knows that He is the Creator of all things in heaven and earth, and that He gives them provision.

(3) To recite the Quran attentively after giving up one's own ideas. God says: O Ihya, hold fast by God's 'Book. It means that he should follow the Book with industry and perseverance. He who remains busy in an enjoyment does not think of any other thing.

(4) To think about the Quran. Thinking comes after attention. For this reason it should be read slowly as slow reading makes thinking possible. Hazrat Ali said: There is no good from the divine service in which there is no knowledge of religion. It has been said that once the Prophet read 'In the name of the Most Compassionate, the most Merciful' twenty times thinking about its meaning, Hazrat Abu Zarr said: The Prophet prayed with us one night. He recited the same verse again and again. That is this: If Thou punished them, they are merely Thy servants and if Thou forgiveth them, Thou art Forgiving, Merciful. Saeed-b-Jubair once read the following verse repeatedly standing in prayer: O the guilty, be separate today. 'Abu Sulaiman Darani said: I stood in prayer in four or five nights reciting only one verse. A certain sage of yore passed six months by reciting only the chapter Hud.

(5) To understand the Quran. Realise true and correct meaning of every verse. Therein are the descriptions of God's attributes, His wonderful creations, the stories of Prophets, the fate of the

liars and how they were destroyed and the descriptions of Paradise and Hell.

God's Attributes. God says: There is nothing to be compared to Him. He is seeing, hearing. He says that He is pure, Almighty, Guardian, Merciful, Compassionate, and Glorious. Think of the meaning and significance of these names. Behind them, there are inner meanings and none but the God gifted people can understand them. Hinting at this Hazrat Ali said: The Prophet did not inform me of any secret thing which was not disclosed to men. The real thing is that God has given some people to understand them and they remain desirous of understanding them. Hazrat Ibn Mas'ud said: He who desires to acquire the knowledge of the previous and future peoples, should seek it in the Quran.

His actions. God says He created the heaven and earth and other things. One who recites the Quran should learn from it His attributes and His glory. He who can recognise real truth sees it in everything as all things come from Him and return to Him and everything is founded on truth for Him and for His help. He who does not see it in every visible thing cannot recognise Him. He who can know Him knows that everything besides Him is void and everything except He will be meeting with destruction. If he sees his being due to the existence of God, he will see that he has come from God and with His power. If he walks in the path of servitude, he will exist and if he walks freely he will not exist. This is the root of spiritual insight. He should therefore ponder over these verses: Don't you look at what you sow? Don't you look at what you throw semen? Don't you look at the water you drink? Don't you look at the fire you enkindle? So think on these lines at the water, fire, crops and semen. Ponder over the elements with which a man is created. It is only a drop of semen. Look at its different compositions-bones, flesh, veins, head, hands, feet, liver, heart etc. Then all honourable attributes have been placed in it-power of hearing, power of seeing, wisdom, power of smell. Then it has been given attributes like anger, sexual passion, pride etc. God says: Does man not consider that I have created him from a drop of semen and he is then an open adversary?

Condition of the Prophet. I think how the Prophets were given wonderful qualities for which they were oppressed. Some of them were murdered and attributed falsehood. Think of the condition of the liars like the 'Ad, Samud, etc. Think how the rejecters of truth were punished and take advice from their fate. There is no such new or old thing which is not in the Quran. God says: If the sea were ink to describe the attributes of my Lord, it would become dry before it described the attributes of my Lord. For this reason. Hazrat Ali said: If I wish, I can load seventy camels with Tafsir of the chapter Fateha. The substance of what has been said is that care should be taken to understand and interpret the Quran.

(6) To be free from the impediments of understanding. Majority of the people do not understand the meaning of the Quran. The reason is that the devil closed the door of their hearts for which they are deprived of the secret meaning of the Quran. The Prophet said: If the devil would not have formed over the heart of men, they could have seen the mysteries of the unseen world. The real meaning of the Quran appertains to the unseen world. The thing which is outside the grasp of the five *senses* cannot be grasped except by the light of sharp insight pertaining to the unseen world. Similar is the case with the meaning of the Quran.

Four Impediments of Understanding the Quran

(1) To remain busy in extracting words from the root of words. The devil works in this matter. He keeps attached with every Quran reader to keep him away from understanding its meaning. He recites the words repeatedly and yet he understands ,that he has not pronounced it correctly and rightly. In this way, all his thoughts are centered round the pronunciation of words. How can the meaning of the Quran come to him in these circumstances?

(2) To believe the sects blindly. The Quran-reader praises the mazhabs or sects and follows the opinions he heard from others. He believes them without ascertaining the truth or otherwise of the opinion of the sects and follows them blindly. He then becomes chained with the chain of belief of the sect and does not try to remove them. His look is directed towards what he heard. A man of firm faith sees it as a share of the devil and keeps away

therefrom. Sufiyan Saori said: Sometimes learning becomes as it were a screen. He understands learning as the opinion of his sect.

(3) To commit a sin repeatedly or to be proud or to remain immersed in worldly passions. They are like dusts on a mirror and screen to radiant star of truth. It is a great screen of heart. The greater is passion and greed amassed in mind, the greater is the screen over the mind, and the lighter is the worldly burden on mind, the greater is the light of understanding. Mind is like a mirror and greed and passion are like dust on mind. For this reason the Prophet said: When my followers will consider their wealth as great, fear of Islam will disappear from their hearts. When they will give up enjoining good and forbidding evils, they will be deprived of the blessings of revelation. Fuzail explained it by saying that they will be deprived of understanding the meaning of the Quran. God made a condition of the acceptance of Tauba on under. standing and repentance. God says: This is deep insight and reminder for every penitent servant. God says: None but a repentant man remembers. God says: Only the wise remember.

(4) To accept open meaning and to believe that there is no inner meaning except external meaning of the Quran. Hazrat lbn Abbas, Mujahed and other companions said that there is provision for explaining it according to individual opinion, "If anybody explains it according to his opinion, let him seek his abode in Hell fire." This is a great obstacle. He gets understanding whom God gives it. If open meaning is accepted, then there arises difference therein.

(5) To give speciality to every verse, in others words to give speciality to every call of the Quran. If you hear commands and prohibitions of the Quran, think thus: This command has been given to me and this prohibition has been directed against me. If you hear any warning, consider that it has come about you. When you hear the stories of the Prophets and early persons, think that it is not merely a story for your information but you are asked to take lessons from it and to take what is necessary therefrom. There is surely some benefit for the Prophet and for his followers in the subject matter of the Quran. For this reason God says: 'I settle your mind therewith.' So the people should think that by describing

the stories of the Prophets, God settled the mind of the Prophet, gave him patience to bear troubles and hardships, made him firm in religion so that God's victory can be seen by him. How will you not be able to do it when the Quran was not revealed only for the Prophet alone but it is a medicine for all diseases, guide for all blessings for all and light for the whole universe. So God has directed all men to get blessings by the help of the Quran. God says: Remember the blessing of God on you all and what has been revealed to you all from the Book and wisdom with which you admonish them. God says: I have revealed upon you all such a Quran in which there are descriptions of You Don't you then mind it?

God says: I have revealed the Reminder to you that you may explain to the people what has been revealed upon them. God says: Follow the best out of what has been revealed to yore-from your Lord. This is a guide for the people, a guide and a blessing for those who believe firmly. God says: The Quran is explainer to the people, a guide for its followers and an admonisher. In these verses, all people have been addressed and not a particular man. The readers of the Quran are also among them. For this reason, their object will be as God says: This Quran has been revealed on me that I may warn you therewith and those to whom it reaches. Mohammad-b-Ka'ab said: He who reads the Quran speaks with God as it were. A certain learned man said: This Quran is an embodiment of some letters which have come to us with His promise, so that we may understand them in prayer, so that we may ponder over them in loneliness and admit them in our religious affairs and sunnat which is followed. Malek-b-Dinar said: The Quran is the fountain of a believer just as rain is the fountain of earth. God says: It is a cure and a blessing for the believers and it increases nothing but loss to the oppressors.

(8) *Mind Influenced by Reading*

As there are different verses, so different thoughts should fall in your mind. You should have change of condition and thoughts according to the meaning of each verse. So in your mind there should be feelings of sorrows, fear, hope etc. You should find forgiveness and blessings attached with some verses and a wise man tries to get it as God says: I am forgiving to one who is repentant, has got faith and does good deeds and who finds guidance. This forgiveness is based on some conditions-repentance, faith, good deeds and guidance. God says: Man is surely in loss except those who have got faith, do good deeds, advise one another with truth and for patience. He mentioned four conditions even in this verse. God says: God's blessing is near those who do good to the people. Sufiyan Saori said: By God, if a man reads the Quran in the morning and brings faith in it, his sorrows increase, his happiness decreases, his actions increase and his comforts decrease. The Prophet said once to Ibn Mas'ud: Recite the Quran to men. He said: I began to read the chapter 'Women'. When I reached this verse: How will it be when I shall bring every people with a witness and bring you as witness over them? I saw that his eyes were shedding tears. He said to me: This is sufficient now. Seeing this condition, my mind became filled up with fear.

Those were God-fearing people who used to faint when they heard some verse of the Quran and even some of them met with instantaneous death. God says: How many signs there are in the heaven and earth which pass by them but they turn their faces from them. A wise man said: Whosoever recites the Quran and does not imbue himself with that idea, God says to him: What connection have you got with My word? You have turned your face from me. The sinner who reads the Quran repeatedly, is like a man who reads the letter of the king repeatedly. Therein there is order to him for making his reign firm but he remains busy to recite it and thinks that to read the letter is sufficient. If he does not read the letter and acts contrary to the order of the king, his order is hated and he becomes an object of wrath of the king. He who acts contrary to the commands of the Quran is guilty according to this verse: They threw it behind them and took small price in lieu of it. How bad is that which they purchase.

The Prophet said: Recite the Quran till you pay attention to it and till the skin of your body is alright. Close it when this condition does not remain. God says: When God is reminded to them, their hearts become soft and when the verses are read out to them, their faith increases and they rely over their Lord. The Prophet said: The sweetest voice in reciting the Quran is that of a man who fears God when he makes its recitation. The Prophet said: The Quran is not heard from anybody so sweet as it is heard from the God-fearing men. When the Prophet expired, he left behind him twenty thousand companions out of whom only six committed the whole Quran by heart. Majority of the companions committed to memory only one or two chapters. They moved their tongue very little as the Quran reciters without action are fit to receive rebuke according to the following verse: If a man turns away from My remembrance, there is narrow provision for him and he will be raised up blind on the Resurrection Day. This verse is also applicable to him: This my verse came to you but you forgot it. You will be forgotten today in a similar manner.

(9) To raise up mind, Raise up your mind by reciting the Quran so much that you are hearing the words of God. There are three excellence in reciting the Quran. The lowest excellence is that a man should think that he recites the Quran standing before God and that He sees and hears his recitation. At this time, he should invoke and pray. Secondly your mind will bear witness at the time of reciting the Quran that God sees you and He is speaking secretly with you. You should apply your full mind to it and be careful of its understanding. Thirdly, you will see God in the recitation of the Quran and His attributes. The reciter who is outside these three things gets the rank of the heedless. Imam Jafar Sadeq said with regard to the highest rank: By God, God disclosed His light for His servants in His words but they do not see it. He once fell in swoon in prayer. When he regained his senses, he said: I was repeatedly reciting the verse of the Quran in my heart and I then heard it as it were from its Author. My body could not stand at His glory. If the mind is raised high, one can get sweetness in invocation. Hazrat Osman and Huzaifah said: If the mind becomes pure, it cannot rest satisfied only with the recitation of the Quran. The sage Sabet Bonani said : I bore hardships for 20 years and have been getting His gifts for the last 20 years. One can become fit for this verse on account of his sight of the Author

of words: Flee towards God. Another verse: Don't set up partner with God. He who does not see Him in his every action, sees some one else and he who looks to anything besides God sees towards secret Shirk. To see nobody in any action except God is sincere Tauhid.

(10) To be free from one's own strength and ability and not to see towards himself with the eye of pleasure and purity. When you read the words of praise of pious men, don't include yourself among them, but hope that God may include yourself among them. When you read the verse of the punishment of the transgressors, think that it was said about you. Hazrat Ibn Umar used to say: O God, I seek forgiveness from you for my sins and infidelity.

SECTION – IV

To Interpret the Quran According to Individual Opinion

The Prophet said: If a man explains the Quran according to his opinion, let him seek his abode in Hell. The learned men who explain it according to its literal meaning accuse the Sufis for their explanation. They explain the verse of the Quran which Ibn Abbas or other companions did not make. The spirit of the above Hadis is that the Quran should be interpreted according to the sayings and doings of the Prophet. Difference arises when it is believed that there is no meaning of the Quran except its open meaning. The meaning of the Quran is wide to the wise. Hazrat Ali said: God has given His servant the understanding of the Quran. If it is not without the Tafsirs of the early sages, what is the meaning of this understanding? The Prophet said: There are surely for the Quran open meaning, secret meaning, limits and different steps. Hazrat Ali said: 'If I wish, I can load seventy camels with Tafsir of the chapter Fateha.' What is its meaning?

Hazrat Abu Darda said: Nobody can be Faqih till he accepts the Quran in different forms. A certain learned man said: There are sixty meanings of every verse. Another learned man said: The Quran is the embodiment of 77,200 learnings as every word is a learning and it is increased four times. Every word has got its external and internal meanings and has got high, higher and highest steps. The Prophet once recited 'Bismillah' twenty times. For what purpose was it done repeatedly except for its inner meaning? Hazrat Ibn Mas'ud said: If a man desires to gain knowledge of the earlier and future peoples, he should ponder over the Quran. It is not acquired by only external Tafsirs. The Quran speaks of His glory and might which are unlimited. Therefore the explanations of the Quran are unlimited.

The Prophet said: Read the Quran and search for its unknown matters. The Prophet said to Hazrat Ali: By One who sent me with truth, my followers will be divided into seventy-three sects in matters of the fundamental principles of religion and Jamaat. Every sect will be misguided and call towards Hell. When it will occur, hold firm to the Book of God, as it contains the stories of your predecessors ant successors and decisions about what you differ ever opposes the Quran among the transgressors, God punishes him. Whosoever searches learning other than the Quran, God misguides him as the Quran is the firmest tie, open light and benefitting medicine. If anybody holds it firm, it protects him. If one follows it, it gives him salvation. There is no cutting of the miracles of the Quran and it does not become old for repeated readings. When the Prophet told Huzaifah of different sects and differences, he asked him: O Prophet of God, if I get that time, what do you order me to do? He said: Learn the Book of God and act upon it, as there is salvation in it. Hazrat Ali said: He who understands the Quran acquires all the learnings together. There is hint in this that the Quran contains all the learnings. The Quran says: He who has been given wisdom has been given abundant good. Hazrat Ibn Abbas explained this word wisdom as the knowledge of the Quran. God says: I gave Sulaiman knowledge, wisdom and learning. What has been given to him was termed as wisdom and learning. The speciality which has been given to him is learning and it has been given to him before wisdom.

Regarding the external meaning of the Quran, there are innumerable sayings of the Prophet. The Prophet said: He who interprets the Quran according to his own opinion should seek his abode in Hell. Thus he prohibited individual interpretation according to his own opinion. Hazrat Abu Bakr said: If I interpret the Quran according to my opinion, what earth will give me protection and what sky will give me shade? This prohibition has got two objects. The first object is to limit in Hadis and Tafsir, not to discover new meanings and to give up independent thinking". The second object is other than that. If its object is that a man cannot interpret the Quran except according to the standard Tafsirs, it is void for the reasons given below.

(1) One condition of interpretation is that it should rest upon the interpretation of the Prophet. It is accepted, Tafsirs of Ibn Abbas and Ibn Mas'ud cannot be accepted as they had their opinion also therein.

(2) There are different opinions regarding the interpretation of some verses among the companions. It was not possible for them to be unanimous. Everybody did not interpret it after hearing it from the Prophet. If they said anything after hearing it from the Prophet, then their own opinions are fit to be rejected. It is well known that the interpreters extracted many meanings by applying their intellect. Even they had seven interpretations of the abbreviated words at the beginning of a chapter. So how can it be said that they interpreted them by hearing everything from the Prophet?

(3) The Prophet prayed for Ibn Abbas by saying: O God, give him knowledge in theology and give him learning of interpretation. What is then the meaning of his special prayer for him if interpretation cannot come except from his saying?

(4) Those who discover meaning by their intellect know it certainly-in this verse, to discover meanings by exercise of intellect by the learned men has been spoken of. To discover open meanings is different from what is heard. The tradition regarding the interpretation of the Quran is opposed to this verse. So it appears that it is incorrect to impose condition of Tafsir only in all interpretations and it is lawful to discover the meaning of the Quran according to the limit of one's own intelligence and intellect.

There are however two reasons for the prohibition of interpreting the Quran according to one's opinion. One reason is that a man has got his own individual opinion with regard to every matter and actually he is inclined to that opinion. He also interprets the Quran according to his wish and desire to serve his own end. For this reason he thinks that his interpretation is correct and lawful. He cites the Quranic verses to support his opinion. Thus he decries his adversary and he knows that this is not real meaning. This is interpretation according to one's own misguided opinion. The Prophet said: Eat predawn meal as there is blessing in it. They interpret it as Zikr in place of the real meaning meal. The Quran says: Go to Pharaoh as he has transgressed the limit. They interpret the word 'Pharaoh' as heart.

(5) To discover the meanings of those verses which are not understandable and short without Hadis and Tafsir. He who is not expert in external meanings and discovers their meanings only by intellect commits many mistakes. He belongs to that class of men who interpret it according to their opinions. At fins, there is necessity of Hadis and Tafsir for external meanings in order to be free from mistakes and then with the advancement of knowledge meanings come out from intellect. He who claims to have internal meanings of the Quran without at first being expert in its external meanings is like a man who claims to have reached the interior of a house without first approaching its door or like a man who claims to have understood the object of a Turk without understanding his language. To learn open meanings is like learning a language. In Tafsir, there is explanation also of internal meanings. For instance, God says: I gave to the nation of Samud a she-camel as open sign but they made oppression on account of it. Here the word 'sign' is omitted. He will interpret it openly by saying that the she-camel had power of sight and was not blind. God says: On account of their infidelity, drink of calf was given to their hearts. In other words, they thought the worship of calf as dear on account of their infidelity. Here to think 'dear' has been omitted. God says: I gave you the taste of life on the taste of death. In other words: I gave you the taste of severity of punishment of life and of death. The word 'punishment' has been omitted in this verse. God says: Ask the city where we were and the mountain to which we proceeded. In other words, ask the Inhabitants of the town and the mountain.

The word 'inhabitants' have been omitted. God says: It has become heavy in heavens and earth. In other words: It has been made secret for the inhabitants of the heavens and earth. God says: You make your provision such as if you are telling lies. In other words: You express gratefulness for your provision. God" says: I have revealed it in the Blessed night. In other words, I have revealed the Quran in the Blessed night. God says: Till it became covered with screen. It means here sun. God says: Peace be on Al-Yasin. The latter word means Elias.

The word 'Qareen' has got different meanings. It means angel in this verse : His companion (angel) said: He who is near me is a rebel. It means the devil in this verse: His companion (devil) said: O our Lord, I have not misguided him. Similarly, the word "Ummat" has got different meanings in the Quran. It means a group of men in this verse: He saw a party of men to give drink of water. It means the followers of a Prophet in this verse : We belong to the followers of Muhammad (P. H.). It means the possessor of all virtues in this verse: Abraham was possessor of all virtues. It means an age in this verse: Up to a fixed age. Similar is the case with the meaning of the word 'Ruh'.

(6) To interpret the same subject gradually. God says: The month of Ramadan in which the Quran has been revealed. This verse does not disclose when it was revealed, day or night. Then the next verse says: I revealed it in a blessed night. This verse first speaks of revelation by night. Then this verse was revealed: I revealed it in the blessed night.

Then to take internal meaning of a verse, Tafsir is not sufficient. God says: You have not shot arrows when you shot arrows but God shot arrows. The external meaning of the sentence is clear, but its internal meaning is one secret as there is in the meaning of both throwing arrows and not throwing arrows which are contradictory to each other. So the knowledge of the reason of throwing is essential. The reason for which it is said that you did not throw arrow but God threw arrows is in the following verse: Fight with them. God will punish them through your hands. This lies in the deep ocean of spiritual knowledge. Firstly, know that the action of a man is tied up with his strength and that strength is tied up with the power of God. Every verse of the Quran similarly has got a secret meaning. It is clear to those whose hearts are clear of impurities of thoughts and ideas. So open Tafsirs are not sufficient for understanding the internal meaning, of verses. These internal meanings are not opposed to the external meanings. God knows best.

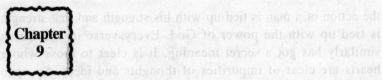

Chapter 9

ZIKR AND INVOCATIONS

God says: Remember Me, I will remember you. He ordered His servants to pray and to invoke by this verse: Invoke me, I will respond to you. So the religious, sinners, near and distant ones should pray to God for fulfillment of their desires. He says: I am near. I respond to the invocation of one who invokes Me. So there is nothing better than God's Zikr and invocations to 'Him. This will be discussed in five sections.

SECTION – I
Excellence of Zikr

God says: Remember Me, I shall remember you. The sage Sabet Bonani said: I know when my Lord remembers me. The people asked him: How do you know? He said: He remembers me when 1 remember Him. God says: Remember God too much. He says: When you return from Arafat, remember God near Masharul Haram and remember Him as God has given you guidance. God says: When you finish the institutions of Haj remember God more than you remember your parents at that time. God says: They are wise who remember God standing, sitting and lying on a side. God says: When you finish prayer, remember God standing, sitting, and lying on your sides. Hazrat Ibn Abbas said: Remember God day and night, on land and water, in journey and habitation, in solvency and want, in health and disease, openly and secretly. God says rebuking the hypocrites: They remember God very little. God says: Remember your Lord in your heart with humility and in fear silently morning and evening and be not of the heedless. God says: Zikr of God is the highest. Hazrat Ibn Abbas said: This is for two reasons. One reason is that God's remembrance of you is better than your remembrance of God. Another reason is that God's remembrance is better than all other divine services.

Hadis. The Prophet said: One engaged in the Zikr of God among the heedless is like a living tree in the midst of dry trees. He said: One busy in Zikr in the midst of the heedless is like a warrior in the way of God in the midst of those soldiers who fled away. The Prophet said: God says: I remain with a servant i ill he remembers Me and moves his lips for Me. There is no action of man except Zikr of God which can give him salvation. They asked him: O Prophet of God, not even Jihad in the way of God? He said: Not even Jihad in the way of God, except that it will give salvation only when it is cut to pieces owing to your strike by your sword and then it is again cut to pieces owing to your strike by your sword. The Prophet said: If anybody wishes to enter the garden of paradise, let him remember God much. He was asked: Which action is best? He said: Your meeting with death in the condition of your tongue being saturated with Zikr of God. The Prophet said: Saturate your tongue with the Zikr of God morning and evening, you will have no sin morning and evening. He said: God's Zikr morning and evening is better than attack with sword in the way of God and giving wealth in charity. The Prophet said: God says: When My servant remembers Me silently, I remember Him silently. When he remembers Me among the people, I remember him among a party better than them. When he comes to me half a cubit, I advance to him a cubit. When he comes to Me a cubit, I go to him two cubits. When he comes to Me on foot, I go to him hastily. The Prophet said: On the day when there will be no shade except the shade of God, God will give shade under His shade seven persons —one who remembers God sincerely and shed tears for fear of God etc. The Prophet said: Shall I not inform you of an action dearest to God, greatest to your Lord, highest in rank, better fruitful

Hadis. The Prophet said: One engaged in the Zikr of God among the heedless is like a living tree in the midst of dry trees. He said: One busy in Zikr in the midst of the heedless is like a warrior in the way of God in the midst of those soldiers who fled away. The Prophet said: God says: I remain with a servant i ill he remembers

Me and moves his lips for Me. There is no action of man except Zikr of God which can give him salvation. They asked him: O Prophet of God, not even Jihad in the way of God? He said: Not even Jihad in the way of God, except that it will give salvation only when it is cut to pieces owing to your strike by your sword and then it is again cut to pieces owing to your strike by your sword. The Prophet said: If anybody wishes to enter the garden of paradise, let him remember God much. He was asked: Which action is best? He said: Your meeting with death in the condition of your tongue being saturated with Zikr of God. The Prophet said: Saturate your tongue with the Zikr of God morning and evening, you will have no sin morning and evening. He said: God's Zikr morning and evening is better than attack with sword in the way of God and giving wealth in charity. The Prophet said: God says: When My servant remembers Me silently, I remember Him silently. When he remembers Me among the people, I remember him among a party better than them. When he comes to me half a cubit, I advance to him a cubit. When he comes to Me a cubit, I go to him two cubits. When he comes to Me on foot, I go to him hastily. The Prophet said: On the day when there will be no shade except the shade of God, God will give shade under His shade seven persons —one who remembers God sincerely and shed tears for fear of God etc. The Prophet said: Shall I not inform you of an action dearest to God, greatest to your Lord, highest in rank, better fruitful than charity of your gold and silver and your striking with sword the necks of the enemies of God and the strike on your necks? They said: O Messenger of God, what is it? He said: Constant remembrance of God. The Prophet said: God says: If a man refrains from invoking Me because of his remaining busy with my remembrance, I give him better than those who invoke Me.

Wise sayings. The sage Fuzail said: We have been informed that if a man makes God's Zikr one hour after the morning prayer and one hour after the A.N. prayer, it expiates all his sins. A wise man said: God says: If I see My Zikr prevailing in the mind of a man, I take the administration of his affairs and I become his companion, adviser and friend. Hasan Basri said: Zikr is of two kinds—(1) God's Zikr in your mind, and (2) better than this is to remember

God at the time of commission of an unlawful action. Some said that every soul will come out of the world thirsty except one which remembers God. Mu'az-b-Jabal said: The inmates of Paradise will not grieve for anything except for the time which passed without remembrance of God.

Excellence of the assembly of Zikr

The Prophet said: If a party of men are engaged in the Zikr of God, the angels surround them, mercy encompasses them and He remembers them before His near angels. The Prophet said: If a party of men makes Zikr of God for pleasure of God, a proclaimer proclaims from heaven: Your sins have been forgiven and you have been given virtues in lieu of your sins. The Prophet said: If a party of men makes no Zikr of God sitting together and send no blessing on the Prophet, they will be repentant on the Resurrection Day. Prophet David said: O my Lord, when you see me joining the heedless after giving up the assembly of Zikr of God, break my feet under their feet, as it will be a gift cast upon me. The Prophet said: An assembly of virtue of the believers expiate two thousand assemblies of sin. Hazrat Abu Hurairah said: As you see the stars, so the inmates of heaven see a house of the inmates of the world wherein God is remembered. Sufiyan-b-Aynah said: When a party of men gather together and remember God, the devil and the world become separate from them. The devil says to the world: Don't you see what they are doing?" The world says: Leave them as when they will be separate from one another, I will take them to you catching their necks. Hazrat Abu Hurairah said that he went one day into the market and said: I see you here, but the properties left by the Prophet are being distributed in the mosque. The people went to the mosque but saw no distribution of any property. They then went to Abu Hurairah and said: O Abu Hurairah, we find no distribution of property in the mosque. He asked: What then have you seen? They said: We found a party of men making Zikr of God and reciting the Quran. He said: This is the heritage of the Prophet. The Prophet said: Some angels of God roam in the world and write down additional record of deeds. If they see a party of believers making Zikr of God, they proclaim: Come with your

actions. They come with their actions and they take them towards
the heaven. God says: What action of My servants have you seen?
They say: We saw them praising Thee, glorifying Thee and
declaring Thy purity. God says: Do they see Me? They say: No.
God says: If they could have seen Me, how will it be? They Say: If
they could have seen Thee, they would have recited Thy Tasbih,
Tammid and Tamjid more. God says to them: From what thing do
they seek refuge? They say: From Hell. Gods says: Have they
seen it? They said: No. God says: If they had seen it, what would
they have done'? They say: If they had seen it, they would have
fled away more from it. God says: What do they seek? They say:
Paradise. God says: How will it be if they had seen it? They say: If
they had seen it, they would have desired it more. God says: I bear
witness before you that I have forgiven them. They say: A certain
man did not come to them with that object except for his own
personal needs. God says: They are such a party whose
companion will not be unfortunate.

Excellence of Tahlil

The Prophet said: What I said first and also my predecessor
prophets is this-there is no deity but God. He is one, there is no
partner for Him. The Prophet said: He who recites this Dua one
hundred times 'There is no deity but God, the single, there is no
partner for Him, kingdom is His and all praise is His and He is
powerful over all things', the rewards of setting free ten slaves are
written for him, one hundred rewards are written in his record of
deeds and one hundred sins are wiped out from him and he
remains safe from the machinations of the devil on that day up to
night. He who does more than this, his rewards are mot e and
nobody does more virtuous act than it. The Prophet said: He who
makes ablution and reads this Dua after looking towards heaven-'I
bear witness that there is no deity but God, He is single, there is no
partner for Him and I bear witness that Muhammad is His servant
and apostle', the doors of Paradise are opened up for him and he
enters it by whichever door he likes. The Prophet said: Those who
utter-There is no deity but God' there wili be no loneliness for
them in their grave or after their resurrection from the grave. I am

seeing them as it were when they utter it loudly, their beads are emerging from earth and they are uttering all praise is due to God who removed sorrows from us. Our Lord is Forgiving, accepter of gratefulness. The Prophet said: O Abu Hurairah, the virtues which you do will be weighed on the Resurrection Day, but the attestation of 'There is no deity but God' will not be weighed because if it is weighed in a scale and the seven heavens and seven earths and what is in them both are placed in another scale, the scale of 'There is no deity but God' will be heavier. The Prophet said: If anybody commits sin on the surface of the earth after uttering 'There is no deity but God', God will forgive him. The Prophet said: O Abu Hurairah, tell the dying man to utter —'There is no deity but God' as it destroys sins. I said: O Prophet of God, this is for the dying man. What are the rewards for a man who is alive? The Prophet said: It is destroying, it is .destroying' The Prophet said He who utters with sincere heart— 'There is no deity but God' will enter Paradise. The Prophet said: Everyone amongst you will enter Paradise except one who denies it and turns his face from God like the turning of the face of a she-camel. He was asked. O Prophet of God, who denies and turns his face from God? He said: That person who does not utter-There is no deity but God.' Utter much-There is no deity but God' before hindrance comes between you and it, as it is a word of Tauhid, word of sincerity, word of God-fear, word of purity, calling towards truth and the foundation of Paradise. God says: Is there any reward for doing (Ihsan) good except good? It is said that Ihsan of this world is-There is no deity but God' and the Ihsan of the next world is Paradise. God says: Those who do good will get good reward and still more. The Prophet said: If a man utters ten times-There is no deity but God, He is single, there is no partner for Him, the kingdom is His and praise is His and He is powerful over all things,' the reward of setting free a slave is written for him. The Prophet said: If a man utters a day two hundred times the above mentioned Dua, nobody will be able to go before him and nobody will catch him after him except one who does actions better than those of his. The Prophet said: If a man goes to the market and utters—'There is no deity but God, He is single, there is no partner for Him, His is the kingdom and His is all praise. He gives life and takes life, He is powerful over everything'- God writes for him one lac virtues, forgives one lac sins and builds for him a house in Paradise. The Prophet said: He who utters the aforesaid Dua ten times, will get the rewards of setting free four slaves belonging to the dynasty of Hazrat Ismail. The Prophet said: He who wakes up at night and utters the following Dua, is forgiven of his sins and if he prays after ablution, his prayer is accepted-There is no deity but God, He is single, there is no partner for Him, kingdom is His, praise is His, and He is powerful over all thing. Glory be to God, all praise is due to God, there is no deity but God, God is greatest, there is no might or strength except in God, the great, the mighty. O God forgive me."

SECTION – II
Tasbih, Tahmid and Other Zikrs

The Prophet said: If a man utters at the end of each prayer 'Subhan Allah' thirty-three times 'Alham do Lillah' thirty-three times and 'Allaho-Akbar' thirty-three times and then utters once "There is no deity but God. He is single, there is no partner for Him, kingdom is His, all praise is His, and He is powerful over all things" all his sins are forgiven even though they are innumerable like foams in a sea. (1) The Prophet said: If a man utters every day one hundred times 'glory be to God and all praise is his', all his sins are forgiven though they are innumerable like the foams of a sea. (2) A man came to the Prophet and said: The world has forsaken me and I have been rendered poor and I am without means. The Prophet asked him: Where do you stay? Don't you know the Dua by the blessings of which angels and men get livelihood? He said: O Prophet of God, what is that Dua?' He said: After dawn and before Fajr prayer, if you read this Dua one hundred times, the world will itself turn to you and God will create one angel from each of its words who will be engaged in reading Tasbih up to the Resurrection Day and you will get its reward: Glory be to God with all praise, Glory be to God, the great, I seek forgiveness of God.' (3) The Prophet said: When a servant utters 'Alhamdo Lillah', he fills up what is between heaven and earth. When he recites it for the second time, he fills up seven heavens and seven earths. When he utters it for the third time, God says: Pray and it will be responded to.

(4) Hazrat Refa'a Zarki said: Once we were playing behind the Prophet. When he raised his head from bow, he said: God hears one who praises Him', one man uttered from behind the Prophet: O our Lord, Thine is all praise, innumerable and pure, full of blessings therein. When the Prophet finished his prayer, he asked: Who has uttered this Dua just now? He said: O Prophet of God, I. The Prophet said: I saw more than thirty angels competing as to who of them will write rewards.

(5) The Prophet said: The following words are called everlasting good deeds: 'There is no deity but God.' Glory be to God.' 'All praise is for God'. 'Allah is greatest. 'There is no might or strength except in God'.

(6) The Prophet said: There is no such servant whose sins are not forgiven even though they are as innumerable as the foams of the sea if he utters words: There is no deity but God. God is greatest. Glory be to God. All praise is for God and There is no might or strength except in God.

(7) The Prophet said: If Zikr is recited glorifying God, and Tasbih, Tahmid and Takbir are recited, humming of voices are heard like the humming of bees round the Throne. They make Zikr along with them and nobody among you ceases to make Zikr of God.

(8) The Prophet said: I recite the following Dua and love it better than all the things upon which the sun sheds rays: Glory be to God, all praise is due to God, there is no deity but God, God is greatest.

(9) The Prophet said: To God four words are dear :Subhan-Allah, Alhamdo-Lillah, La Ilaha Illallah, Allah O Akbar. By whichever of these you begin, it will not harm you. The Prophet said: 'Subhan Allah is half of faith, Alhamdo Lillah fills up the scale. 'Subhan Allah and Allaho-Akbar fill up what is between heaven and earth. Prayer is light, charity is proof, patience is radiance and the Quran is proof for you or against you. Every man gets

up at dawn and either sells his soul and destroys it or purifies his soul and frees it.

(10) The Prophet said: Two words are easy to be uttered but heavy in scale and dear to the Merciful-'Subhan Allah Wa Behamdihi, Subhan Allah il Azim. Abu Zarr said : I asked the Prophet: Which word is dearest to God? The Prophet said: That word which God selected for His angels have recited the above formula. The Prophet said: God selected this word: Subhan Allah, Walhamdo Lillah, wa la Ilaha Illallah, wa allaho Akbar. When a man utters 'Subhan Allah' twenty rewards are written for him and twenty sins are wiped out. When he utters 'Allaho Akbar' similar rewards are written. The Prophet said: If a man utters 'Subhan Allah wa bihamdihi,' a palm tree is planted for him in paradise.

(11) Once the poor said to the Prophet: The rich take the rewards. They pray like us and fast but they get rewards for their additional properties. He said: Has not God enjoined on you charity ? Every Tasbih of yours is an act of charity, every Tahmid and Tahlil are acts of charity, every Takbir is an act of charity, every enjoining good and forbidding evil is an act of charity, the morsel of food you lift up to the mouth of your wife is an act of charity, your sexual intercourse with your wife is an act of charity. He said : O Prophet of God, does one of us coming to his wife out of passion get rewards? The Prophet said: Don't you see that if he throws his semen unto unlawful thing-will he not commit sins? He said: Yes. He said : Similarly if he throws it in lawful thing, he will get rewards. Hazrat Abu Zarr said: I asked the Prophet: The rich have already taken rewards. They do whatever divine service we do but they spend and we cannot. The Prophet said: Shall I not give you clue to such an action which if you do, you will get the rewards of the actions of those before you and you will get the rewards of those who will come after you-33 times Subhan Allah at the end of each prayer, ' Alhamdo Lillah 33 times and Allaho Akbar 34 times. The Prophet said: You shall recite Tasbih, Tahlil and Taqdis. Don't be heedless and count them with fingers. The fingers will speak on the Resurrection Day.

(12) The Prophet said: When a man utters at the time of his death.

'There is no might or strength except in God', the fire of Hell will not touch him. The Prophet said: Will not some one of you gain one thousand rewards daily? It was replied: O Prophet of God! How can it occur? He said: Utter Tasbih one hundred times, then one thousand rewards will be written for you and one thousand sins will be effaced from you. The Prophet said: O Abu Musa, shall I not inform you of a jewel of Paradise under the Throne? He said: Yes. He said: Utter, There is no might or strength except in God.

(13) The Prophet said: He who utters at dawn the following, it becomes the duty of Got to please him on the Resurrection Day: I am satisfied with God as Lord, Islam as religion, the Quran as a guide and with Muhammad as a Prophet and Apostle.

Know, O dear readers, that if you question that it is easy to utter words by tongue and there is no such difficulty in Zikr of God, then how is it that it is better than all other divine services? Know that its secrets are not understood except with the spiritual knowledge. Of all the learnings relating to worldly affairs, the most profitable and fruitful is constant Zikr with humility of spirit. If the mind is heedless at the time of Zikr with tongue it brings much less rewards. If there is no attention of mind at the time of Zikr, there is little benefit therein, but constant Zikr with attention at most times is above all other divine services. This is the end of divine services regarding actions. There is beginning and end of Zikr. There is love at its beginning and love its end. At first a pet son feels great difficulty in turning his mind towards God. If it lasts with the grace of God it begets love for the Beloved. There is no wonder in it for this habit, he makes Zikr in a lonely place far away from the bustles of the world. Thus constant Zikr begets love towards Him and so he loves more and more Zikr. Then it grows into habit. A wise man said: I have been reading the Quran for the last twenty years and getting its blessings. The blessing was not possible without love. This trouble has now grown into habit. Man is a slave of habit and his habit turns into his nature at the end. When there is eagerness for Zikr, he forgets other things except God and it exists till his death. God's Zikr will go with him in his grave and not his children and properties. For this reason the Prophet said: The Holy Spirit infused into my soul: Love what you like but you shall have to give it up at the end. In other words, sever any connection with the world and it will end with death. Don't deny that Zikr of God will go with you even after your death.

It is said how it is possible when there is the end of a man after his death? There is no end of man after his death, so there is no end of Mr. He goes from the out' side world, enters into spiritual world just as a child comes out of its mother's womb and falls into this world. The Prophet hinted at it by saying: Grave is a hole of Hell or a garden of Paradise. The Prophet said: The souls of martyrs lie in the wombs of green birds. Addressing the polytheists by names, the Prophet said: O such person, O such person, have you found true what your Lord has promised you? I have found true what my Lord has promised me. Hazrat Umar asked the Prophet: O Prophet of God, when they have become dead, how can they hear and how can they reply? She Prophet said: By One in whose hand there is my life, you do not hear my words better than they,, but they cannot reply. The Prophet said: The souls of the believers and the martyrs remain within the bellies of green birds hanging under the Throne. So the existence of Zikr cannot be refused from the hearts of the above persons. God says: Don't think those who are martyred in the way of God as dead but they are alive before their Lord and they are given provision. They remain satisfied with what God has given them and give good news to those who could not earn 'that. They get the honour of martyrdom on account of the honour of God's Zikr as their object is death in good condition and they return to God after renouncing the world. Their thoughts are for the sake of God and they become prepared for real life after giving up their children and properties.

Excellence of martyrdom. There are many traditions regarding the excellence of martyrdom, some of which have been narrated below. When Abdullah-b-Ansari was martyred at the battle of Uhud, the Prophet said to his son Jaber: O Jaber, shall I not give you good news? He said: Yes, may God give you news of good. He said: God has given your father life and kept him seated near Him and there is now no screen between him and God. God said to him: O My servant, pray to Me whatever you wish. I will give it to you. He said: O God, if Thou wisheth, send me again to the world till I am martyred for Thee and for Thy Prophet. God said: Order has gone from Me that a dead man cannot return. To be martyred in this condition is his death in good condition, because if he would not have been a martyr and lived for sometime, sweetness of the world would return to him and it would have diverted his mind from the remembrance of God. For this reason, the greatest fear of a God-fearing man is at the time of his death as mind may change at the time even if Zikr of God keeps attached to it. One dies in the condition in which he ends his life and his resurrection takes place in that condition. Thus the mind of a martyr becomes prepared only for God after all connections with the world are cut off. Hence the reward of martyrdom is greatest. Every object of desire is deity and every deity is an object of worship. When a martyr has got no object of desire except Him, he says by the tongue of condition: 'There is no deity but God'. He who utters this by his tongue but his condition does not help him, his affair is upon God and he can't be safe from harm. For this reason the Prophet gave superiority to 'There is no deity but God' to other Zikrs. Whoever likes to meet with God, He also likes to meet him and whoever does not like to meet with Him, God also does not want to meet him. This is the secret of Zikr.

Excellence of Dua and Rules

God says: When My servant asks of Me to you, say: I am near. I respond to one who calls Me when he calls Me. So invoke Me. God says: Invoke God with modesty and secretly. He does not love the transgressors as God says: Call Me, I will respond to you. Those who refrain from My remembrance out of vanity will enter Hell abased. God says: Say: God has got good names by whatever names you call Him-Allah or Rahman. The Prophet said: Munajat is divine service. Then he recited: Call Me, I will respond to you. The Prophet said: Munajat is the marrow of worship. He said: There is nothing more honourable than Munajat. The Prophet said: Let no man forget to invoke either of these three things forgiveness of his sins, hastening of good for him or preserving good for him. The Prophet said: Seek favour of God, as He loves invocation. The best worship is to wait for compulsory prayer.

Ten Rules of Invocation

(1) Choose the best time for invocation, for instance on the day of Arafat, in the month of Ramadan, on the Juma Day and the last portion of the night. God says: They seek forgiveness by the later part of the night. The Prophet said: God descends every night at its last one-third portion in the heaven of the earth and says: Who will invoke Me that I may accept his invocation? Who will seek from Me that I may accept his prayer? Who will seek forgiveness from Me that I may forgive him. Hazrat Yakub used to make prayer with his children for forgiveness in the later part of the night standing in prayer. God then said to him: I will forgive them and make them Prophets.

(2) To take advantage of honourable condition. Hazrat Abu Hurairah said: The doors of heaven are opened in Jihad in the way of God, at the time of concourse of men in rows of prayer, at the time of rain fall and at the time of Aqamat of compulsory prayer. Invoke at that time. Mujahed said: You should invoke at the end of prayer. The Prophet said: Invocation is not rejected in between Azan and Aqamat. He said: 'The invocation of a fasting man is not rejected.' The best times are the time of Sehri, purity of the mind and sincerity, the day of Arafat, the time of prostration. The Prophet said: A man becomes near God at the time of prostration. Invoke much at that time. The Prophet said: I have been prohibited to read the Quran in Ruk'u and prostration. Proclaim the glory of God in Ruk'u and take trouble of invoking in prostration, as it is the appropriate time of its acceptance.

(3) Invoke facing the Qibla and raise up your hand so high that the whiteness of the hand is visible. It is stated that the prophet waited facing the Ka'ba on the Arafat Day and kept on invoking till the sunset. The Prophet said: Your Lord is bashful and honourable. Whenever anybody raises up his hand He feels shy to return it empty handed. Hazrat Anas reported that the Prophet used to raise up hands so high that the whiteness of his hands could be seen. Once the Prophet saw a man making invocation and hinting by his two fingers. He said: One, one. He hinted to make it short. Hazrat Umar said that the Prophet extended his hands and did not

take them down until he touched his face with them. Hazrat Ibn Abbas said that whenever the Prophet invoked, he united the front portion of his hands and rubbed his face with the interior of his palms. The Prophet said: Let not the people look towards the sky at the time of invocation or close their eyes.

(4) Keep your voice between expression and silence. Hazrat Abu Musa Ash'ari said: when we came near Medina with the Prophet, He recited Takbir and the people also recited Takbir loudly. The Prophet said: O people, He whom you call is not deaf and not absent. He whom you call is between you and your necks. Hazrat Ayesha said: God says: Don't raise your voice high in prayer,' nor keep it concealed. God praised His Prophet Zakariyah when he called his Lord by silent voice.

(5) Don't use ornamental words in invocation. He who invokes should be humble. The Prophet said: Soon a people appear who will exaggerate in invocation. God says: He does not love the transgressors. This is in reference to those who use ornamental words in invocation. Pray for what is good. The Prophet said: Give up all immortal words in invocation. It is said that the learned and Abdals used not more than seven words in their invocation.

(6) Invoke with fear and hops and with humility and modesty. Humility and modesty arc dear to God. God says: They hasten in good deeds and invoke Me with hope and fear. The Prophet said: If God loves a man He tries him till he sees in him humility and modesty.

(7) Believe that your invocation will be accepted and hope therein for truth. The Prophet said: When a man invokes, let him not say: O God, give me if Thou wisheth. Be firm in invocation as there is nobody to reject it. The Prophet said: When one of you invokes, make your hope great, there is nothing great to God. The Prophet said: Invoke God and entertain a firm belief that your invocation will be accepted and know that God does not accept the invocation of a heedless man. Sufiyan Saori said: Let nobody prevent you to make invocation with what you know as God accepted the invocation of the worst being of the creation, the devil. When he

prayed: O God, give me respite up to the Resurrection Day, God said: Your prayer is accepted.

(8) Invoke firmly three times. Hazrat Ibn Mas'ud said: Whenever the Prophet invoked, he invoked thrice. Don't be hasty to see your invocation accepted as the Prophet said: The invocation of any of you is accepted if not sought hastily. Don't say, 'I invoked but it has not been accepted. When you invoke too much, as you are invoking to the Merciful. A certain wise man side; I have been invoking God for the last twenty years but He is not accepting my invocation, yet I hope, my invocation will be accepted. The Prophet said: When any of you prays to his Lord and gets sign of its acceptance, let him say: All praise is due to God under all circumstances.

(9) Begin invocation with Zikr of God. Don't invoke at the start. Hazrat Salma said: I did never see the Prophet invoking without first saying: Subhana Rabbi al Ula wal wahhab. Abu Sulaiman Daraai said: If a man wishes to invoke God for any necessity, let him begin with blessings on the Prophet and then pray and then end it with such blessing, as God accepts the invocation of those who send blessings on Prophet.

The Prophet said: When you invoke God for any necessity, begin it after blessings on me as the Merciful God fulfils one of the two honoured necessities and rejects another.

(10) Observe the internal manners and it is the root of acceptance of Tauba, means of preventing oppression, means to seek nearness to God and a near cause of acceptance of invocation. Ka'b-b-Ashab narrated that there was a great famine over the people at the time of Moses. He came out with the children of Israil for invoking for rain but it did not come. He came out for three consecutive days, but it did not come. Then God revealed to Moses: I will not accept your invocation and the invocation of your companions as there is a backbiter amongst you. Moses asked: Who is that man? We shall eject him from our company. God revealed to him: O Moses, I have prohibited you backbiting. How shall I be a backbiter? Then Moses said to the children of Israil:

Make repentance for backbiting and return to your Lord. They all repented. Then God sent down rain upon them.

The sage Sufyan Saori said: I have come to know that the children of Israil suffered famine for seven years, even they began to eat dead animals and young children. God sent revelation to their Prophet: if you come to Me walking on foot and enliven your tongues by invoking Me, I will not accept your invocations and will not show kindness at your calls till you pay compensation to those whom you have oppressed. They did so and there was rain upon them.

Malek-b-Dinar said: There was once a famine over the children of Israil. They came out several times invoking for rain. God then revealed to their Prophet: Inform them that they have come to Me with impure bodies and unlawful food in their bellies and they raised the fronts of their hands which shed unlawful blood. My wrath upon them is therefore great.

Once Hazrat Sulaiman came out invoking for rain. At that time an ant raised up its leg towards the sky and said: O God, we are Thy creation and we have got necessity of provision. Don't destroy us for the sins of others. Then Sulaiman said to the people: Go, you will get rain as a result of the invocation of others than you. Once Jesus Christ came out invoking for rain. He said to the people: Let the transgressors go out of this assembly. None but one remained with him. Jesus asked him: Have you got no sin? He said: By God, I don't know anything. One day I was praying when a woman was passing by me and I had a glance at her. When she went away, I plucked out my eyes. Jesus said to him: invoke God for acceptance. Then he invoked and there came down heavy shower of rain.

Hazrat Ata stated that when he came out one day for praying for rain, he saw a mad man near a burial ground. The mad man prayed and owing to his prayer there was profuse rain. Then the mad man recited these verses:

The ascetics and worshippers have found guidance,
For their Lord, they keep their bellies hungry,

Their eyes remain awake being pressed by love,
They spend the whole night without sleep,
In meditation and divine services of their Lord,
But people think them fools and mad.

Excellence of Darud or Blessing on Prophet

God says: God and His angels send blessings upon the Prophet. O those who believe, send blessings on him, and Salam. It has been narrated that the Prophet said being satisfied: Gabriel came to me and said: O Muhammad, are you not satisfied that if one of your followers sends one blessing upon you, I send ten blessing upon him and if he sends one salam on you. I send on him ten salams. The Prophet said: If a man sends blessings on me, the angels send blessings on him. So increase or reduce blessings on me at the time of sending it. The Prophet said: He who sends much blessings on me is best to me. He said: It is sufficient miserliness on the part of a believer that if I am mentioned to him, he does not send blessings on me. The Prophet said: Send much blessing on me on the Juma Day. He said: If a man among my followers sends one blessing on me, ten rewards are written for him and his ten sins are forgiven, He said: If a man utters after hearing Azan and Aqamat "O God, Lord of this perfect invitation and lasting prayer, send blessing on Muhammad, Thy servant and Thy Apostle and give him means, excellence and high position and intercession on the Resurrection Day", it becomes incumbent on me to intercede for him. The Prophet said: If a man glorifies me by writing books, the angels pray to God for his forgiveness till the book exists. He said: If a man sends salam on me, God sends his salam to me and I respond to his salam. He was asked: O Prophet of God, how shall we send blessings on you? He said: Say. O God, send blessings on Muhammad, Thy servant, and upon his family and wives and descendants as Thou hast sent blessings on Abraham and upon the family of Abraham. And give abundance to Muhammad, his wives and descendants as Thou hast given abundance to Abraham and the family of Abraham. Thou art the Most praised and glorified.

After the death of Prophet, Hazrat Umar began to weep and said:
" O Prophet of God, may my parents be sacrificed to you, You
used to deliver sermon to the people standing on a wood of grape.
When there were large number of people, you have taken a pulpit
to make them hear bat the wood began to tremble at your
separation. It became quiet when you placed your hand on it. At
the battle of Hunain, your followers were innumerable but they
became attached to you. May my parents be sacrificed to thee. O
Prophet of God, your excellence has reached God as God will be
obeyed if you are obeyed. God says: He who obeys the Apostle of
God, obeys God. O Apostle of God, may my parents be sacrificed
to you, your excellence has reached God. He gave you the news
of pardon before the news of sin. For that God says: God has
forgiven you for what you enjoin them.

'O Prophet of God, may my parents be sacrificed to you,. Your
excellence has reached God. He sent you as the last Prophet but
He described you before all. For that He says: When I took
covenant from you and the Prophet etc. O Prophet of God, may
my parents be sacrificed to you, your excellence has Reached
God. The dwellers of Hell will wish how good it would have been
if they bad obeyed you When they will receive punishment in
different stages of Hell, they will say: Alas, had we obeyed God
and His Apostle!

"O Apostle of God, may my parents be sacrificed to you, Moses,
son of Imran, made to flow a stream f water from a stone. Is it"
not more wonderful that water flowed down from your fingers? O
Prophet of God, may my parents be sacrificed to you, God made
the wind subservient to Sulaiman. He went one month's journey at
dawn and one month's journey at dusk. Is it not more wonderful
than the above that you travelled one night riding on a Buraq the
seven heavens and said prayer at the Ka'ba-the same very night?
O Prophet f God, may my parents be sacrificed to you, God gave
miracle to Jesus Christ, son of Mary , to make a dead man alive. Is
it not more wonderful than it that cooked mutton mixed with poison
spoke with you: Don't eat me, I have got poison mixed with me.

O Prophet of God, may my parents be sacrificed to you, Noah

prayed to God about his people: O my Lord! don't leave a single house of the unbelievers in the world. If you had prayed against us in a similar manner, we would have been destroyed. Your back was burdened, your front teeth were martyred, yet you did not invoke against them but for good and said: O God, forgive my people, as they know not what they do.

"O Prophet of God, may my parents be sacrificed to you, Noah was not followed by so many people during his long stay as you have been followed in a short time. Innumerable people believed you. O Prophet of God, may my parents be sacrificed to you, if you had not permitted people lower in rank than you to come to you, we could not have taken seat with you. If you had not married women except those of equal rank with you, we would have no connection with you. It you had not taken meal except with the people of equal rank with you, we could not get the honour of taking food with you. By God, you kept company with us, married in our families, put on Sufi dress, rode on asses and took companions behind, ate in cups of earth and licked your hands after eating".

Excellence of Istighfar or Seeking Forgiveness

God says: When they do obscene acts or oppression on their souls, they remember God and seek forgiveness for their sins. Hazrat Abdullah-b-Mas'ud said: There are two verses in the Quran. If a man recites them after committing a sin and seeks forgiveness of God, God forgives him. God says: He who does an evil or oppresses his soul and then seeks forgiveness of God, he will find Him forgiving and merciful. God says: Glorify your Lord and seek forgiveness to Him. He accepts repentance. God says: Those who seek forgiveness by the latter part of night etc. The Prophet used often to say: Thou art pure with Thy praise, Thou doth accept repentance, Thou art merciful. The Prophet said: If a man seeks forgiveness much, God gives him solace in every trouble, makes his narrow space wide and gives him provision beyond his conception. The Prophet said: I seek forgiveness of God and I make repentance to Him 72 times every day. He used to do it in spite of his past and future sins being forgiven. The Prophet said:

Consolation does not come to my mind till I seek forgiveness one hundred times a day. The Prophet said: If a man recites three times the following at the time of going to bed, God forgives his sins even though they are innumerable like the foams of the sea, or like sands in a desert, or like leaves in a tree or like the days of the world-I seek forgiveness to God the Greatest, there is no deity but He, the ever-living, the ever subsisting and I turn to him penitently.

The Prophet said: The sins of one who utters it are for given even though he flees away from Jihad. Hazrat Ayesha said: The Prophet said to me: If you are attributed any guilt of sin, seek forgiveness of God, make repentance to Him, be penitent and seek forgiveness from sin. The Prophet used to say about forgiveness: O God, forgive me of my sins, my ignorance, my extravagance and what you know of me. The Prophet said: If a man commits a sin and then prays two ra'kats of prayer with ablution and then seeks forgiveness to God, God forgives his sin. The Prophet said: When a believer commits a sin, a black spot falls on his heart. If he is repentant, returns and seeks forgiveness it is wiped out of his heart. If the sin increases, the black spot increases. At last his heart becomes enveloped with black spots. This is 'Ran' which has been spoken of by God in this verse: Never, rather rust (Ran) has fallen on their hearts ⁻for what they have done. Then the Prophet said: God created ranks in Paradise for His servants. He says: O Lord, is this rank for me? God says: This is your reward for prayer of your son. The Prophet said: O God, include me among those who receive good news when they do good deeds and seek forgiveness when they do evils. The Prophet said: When a servant commits a sin and says: O God forgive me, God says: My servant has committed a sin and he knows that his Lord will punish him and so he seeks forgiveness for it and works for My pleasure, I forgive him. The Prophet said: If a man did no viruous act during his life but he looks towards sky and says: O Lord, I have got my Lord, forgive me, God says: I have forgiven you. The Prophet said: If a man commits a sin and then understands that God is seeking him, he is forgiven though he does not seek forgiveness. The Prophet said: God says: O My servant, all are sinners except one whom I forgive. So seek forgiveness to Me, I shall forgive you. One who understands that I have got power to forgive him, I forgive without care. The Prophet said: If one says: O God, I have oppressed my soul and I have done evil, forgive me, there is none to forgive except Thee, God forgives him even though his sins are innumerable as ants. The best Dua of forgiveness is this:

O God. *Thou* art my Lord and I am Thy slave. Thou hast created me. I am upon Thy covenant as far as possible. I seek refuge to Thee from the evils Thou created. I turn to Thee with the gifts Thou hast bestowed on me. I turn to my soul with my sins. I admit my sins. So forgive my past and future sins. None can forgive sins except Thou.

Sayings of Sages

Hazrat Khaled-b-Madan said: God says: The dearest of My servants to Me are those who love one another for My sake, whose hearts keep attached to mosques, who seek forgiveness at the later part of night. I remember them when the inhabitants of the world want their punishment and turn it back from them. Hazrat Ali said: It is a wonder that one is destroyed even if he has got means of salvation. He was questioned: What is it? He said: To seek forgiveness. He also said: God forgives one in search of forgiveness even though He wishes to punish him. The sage Fuzail said: Seeking forgiveness without giving up sins is the Tauba of the transgressors. The sage Abu Abdullah said: If your sins are so innumerable as the drops of water and like the foams of sea, they will be forgiven if you invoke God with a penitent and sincere heart with the following: O God, I seek forgiveness of Thee from every sin, etc.

SECTION – III

Selected Invocations

The Prophet used to pray after morning prayer: O God, I seek mercy from Thee, such mercy with which Thou will guide my mind, unite my virtues in me, remove my dangers and difficulties, adorn my religion, protect my things in my absence, purify my actions, make my face bright, my path radiant and protect me from all evils. O God, give me true faith, such a faith after which no infidelity will last, such a mercy with which I can acquire the honour of Thy glory both in this world and in the next-up to the end.

Invocation of Hazrat Ayesha. She said: The Prophet advised me to invoke with the following: O God, I seek from Thee good, sooner or latter, known or unknown. I seek refuge to Thee from all evils I seek from Thee paradise and the actions leading to it, sooner or later, known or unknown. I seek refuge to Thee from Hell and the actions leading to it, sooner or later, known or unknown. I seek from Thee good with which Thy servant and Apostle Muhammad seeks good from Thee.

Invocation of Hazrat Abu Bakr: The Prophet instructed him to invoke with the following: O God, I pray to Thee by the help of Thy Apostle Muhammad, Thy friend Abraham, Moses with whom Thou spoke, Thy Word and Spirit Jesus Christ, the Torah of Moses, Injil of Jesus, Zabur of David and the Quran of Muhammad (peace be on all)-up to the end.

Invocation of Qabisah. The Prophet instructed Qabisah to invoke in his old age after morning prayer and to recite it thrice: Glory be to God and all praise is His. Glory be to the great God. There is no might and power except in God, the great, the mighty. The Prophet said: When you invoke therewith, you will be safe from anxieties, troubles, diseases and tuberculosis. Regarding your next world, invoke with this: O God, guide me from Thy guidance, show me favour from Thy favour, show me mercy from Thy mercy and shower on me Thy blessing.

Invocation of Prophet Abraham. O God, this is a new creation. Open it on me on account of my allegiance to Thee and end it with Thy pardon and pleasure. Give me rewards therein and accept it from me. Purify it, make it weak for me and forgive me the evils I commit in it. Thou art forgiving, merciful, magnificent and beloved.

Invocation of Prophet Jesus Christ. O God, I have risen at dawn. I am unable to remove what I dislike. I am unable to get benefit of what I like. Affairs are in Thy hand, but I rise at dawn by mortgage of my actions O God, there is none more needy than me. O God, let not my enemy be glad over me, let not my friend think bad of me. Don't give trouble in my religion, don't make my earthly anxiety great and don't entrust me to those who will not show kindness· to' me, O Ever-living, Eternal.

Invocation of Khizr. In the name of God, with the will of God, there is no might and strength except in God and what He wills. Every gift is from God what He wills. All good is in His hand what He wills. Nobody but God removes evils.

Invocation of Prophet Adam. O God, Thou knowest my secret and open matters, so accept my excuse. Thou knowest my necessities, so accept my invocation. Thou knowest what is in my mind. So forgive my sins. O God, I seek from Thee faith giving good news to my mind and true sure faith till I know that nothing may afflict me except what Thou hast recorded against me, what Thou hast allotted to me, O possessor of glory and honour.

DIVISION OF TIME FOR ACTIONS

SECTION I

Divine Service

God has made the world subservient to men not to live in its elevated places but to gather provision therefrom sufficient for their permanent abode; sufficient for rewards of their souls, so that they may save themselves from deceits and deceptions of the world. All men are travelling in this world. Their first abode is cradle and their' later abode is grave and their last abode is Paradise or Hell. The term of life is nothing but the distance of journey. Its every year is a station, every month is a furlong, every day is a mile, every breath is a step. Its religious action is a wealth and its time is the root of its wealth. Its temptations and greeds are stumbling blocks in its path, its profit is vision of God in the abode of peace and its loss is to be distant from Him and to stay in the lowest depth of Hell being tied up with chains. He who is indifferent to his breaths will be so sorry on the Resurrection Day that there will be no limit to it. That is time for the greatest dangers and dreadful questions. For that the friends of God give up the comforts and pleasures of the transient life of the world and remain engaged day and night in divine services after division of times, so that they may earn the nearness of God and life in comforts in the day of the greatest danger.

Excellence of Divine Service by Division of Time

Know, O dear readers, that there is no salvation without meeting with God. The only means to meet Him is to face death being imbued with love for Him. Love is the fruit of constant remembrance of the Beloved and to work with that end in view.

One can get acquaintance with Him if one thinks constantly of Him, His attributes, His wonderful creation and that there is no assistance of anything apart from His existence. It does not become easy if one does not give up the world except what is necessary for him. Nothing is fulfilled if time is not divided and divine services are not done according to fixed times. So divide time into several divisions. If a man spends more than half of his time for worldly pursuits, he may be inclined more towards the world. Mind feels difficulty in passing half the time in divine service. Little time is allotted to divine services. If anyone wishes to enter paradise without rendering any account, let him spend his whole time in religious actions. If any man wishes to make his scale heavy with good deeds let him spend most part of his time in doing good deeds. God says: You have got great occupations in day time. So remember your Lord at night and be engaged with undivided mind towards Him. God says: Remember your Lord morning and evening and make prostration to Him in a portion of the night and glorify Him long at night. God says: Glorify your Lord before sunrise and before sunset and glorify Him after prostration at night. God says: Praise your Lord when you stand up and read His Tasbih at the setting of the star at night. God says:

Waking at night is the firmest foot step and fruitful in invocation. God says: Glorify Him in some portions of night and some portions of day, so that you may find consolation. God says: Establish prayer at two ends of the day and a portion of night. Surely good deeds remove evils.

God says: Or that man who expresses obedience by prostrating during the whole night and saying prayed who fears the next world and hopes for the mercy of his Lord. Say: Are those who are wise equal to the ignorant ? God says: Their sides turn over their beds and they call their Lord in hope and fear. God says: They sleep very little at night and seek forgiveness at the later part of night. God says: Don't drive away those who call their Lord for His pleasure at dawn and at dusk.

The above verses make it clear to you that the easy way of getting God is to engage yourself in thoughts of God and to do all actions regularly after division of time. For this reason, the Prophet said: Those who look at the sun, moon and shade to remember God are dear to God. God says: The sun and the moon go on according to a measure. God says: Have you not looked towards your Lord how He extends the shade? If He wished, He would have made it stationary and made the sun proof therein' Then I draw it easily towards Myself. God says: I have fixed the stations of the moon. God says: It is He who made the stars for you, that they may show paths in the darkness of seas and lands. So think that movements are not only for the worldly actions but also to ascertain the measure of time by their help and to do business of the next world by dividing time. The following verse is its proof: He created the day and night alternately for one who wishes to remember Him or wishes to express gratefulness. This means that what the day makes towards loss is compensated by the night. There is no other thing between Zikr and gratefulness. God says: I have created day and night as two signs. I make the sign of day clear by removing the sign of night, so that the people may see clearly so that you may seek grace from your Lord and you may count year.

Number of Divisions of Time

There are seven divisions of day-(1) one division from early morning up to sunrise, (2) two divisions from sunrise to midday, (3) two divisions from the declining of the sun to afternoon, (4) two divisions from afternoon to sunset. Night has got five divisions-two divisions from sunset up to going to bed and three divisions from midnight to dawn. Now I shall narrate the divine service during these divisions of day and night.

(1) **First division.** This covers the period from the morning twilight up to sunrise. This is the honoured time as God say: By oath of early dawn when it gives out breath. Praising this time, God says: Say, I take refuge to the Lord of early dawn. His power has been manifested by suppression of shade at this time as God says: Then I take it to Me easily. There is hint of reciting Tasbih at this time in this verse: When there is dusk and when there is dawn, proclaim the glory and purity of God. God says: Glorify your Lord with His praise before sunrise and before

sunset. God says: Remember the name of your Lord morning and evening.

Rules of this time. After getting up from bed, remember God by saying: All praise is due to God who gave me life after He made me dead and to Him is the return. Then make ablution with cleansing teeth and pray two rak'ats of prayer in your house and then go to the mosque and pray two rak'ats of compulsory prayer. You should not miss morning and night prayers in congregation as there are good rewards therefor. The Prophet said with regard to the morning prayer: If a man goes to the mosque for prayer after ablution, one reward is written for each step he takes and one sin is forgiven. This reward is increased ten fold. When he finishes the prayer at the time of sunrise one reward is written for his every hair of his body and the reward of one accepted Haj is given to him. If he sits waiting for the forenoon prayer, one lac rewards are written for him for each rak'at. At the end of prayer, keep seated till sunrise with Zikr of God. The Prophet said: If a man keeps seated till sunrise after morning prayer and remains busy in Zikr, it is dear to me than the manumission of four slaves. Hazrat Hasan Basri said that the Prophet had said: God said: O children of Adam, make My Zikr for one hour after morning prayer and for one hour after afternoon prayer. What is acquired in between these hours will be sufficient for you. There are three kinds of recitation up to sunrise (1) Dua and Zikr, (2) Quran reading, and (3) to ponder over the creations of God.

(1) When you finish your prayer, make munajat by saying: O God, Send blessings on Muhammad and the family of Muhammad and also Salam. O God, Thou art peace, from Thee peace and to Thee peace returns. O our Lord, make us live with peace and admit us in the abode of peace. Thou art blessed, O possessor of dignity and honour. Then recite the following which the Prophet used to recite: Glory be to My lord, the Highest, the Bestower of gifts. There is no deity but God, the single, He has no partner. Kingdom is His and till praise is His. He gives life and takes it. He is ever-living, -He has no death, all good is in His hands and He is powerful over everything.

(2) **Tasbih.** It is a collection of some formulas and each formula

should be repeated from three times to one hundred times. The more you recite them, the more efficacious they re. These formulas are generally ten. (a) There is no deity but God, etc. as mentioned above. (b) Glory be to God and Il praise is due to God. There is no deity but God, God is greatest. There is no might and strength except in God the treat, the Mighty. (c) He is glorious, pure, O our Lord and ne Lord of angels and Ruh. (d) Glory be to God, the greatest and all praise is His. (e) I seek forgiveness of God, the Great, ere is no deity but He, the Ever-living, the Ever-subsisting, seek return to Him. (f) O God, there is none to reject what Thou bestoweth and none to give what Thou doth reject and man of honour can give benefit and benefit comes from Thee alone. (g) There is no deity but God, the Sovereign, he open Truth. (h) I begin in the name of God. Nothing i the world and heaven can do harm if His name is remembered and He is Hearing, Knowing, (i) O God, send blessings on Muhammad, Thy servant and Prophet and Apostle, the lettered Prophet. (j) I seek refuge to God, the Hearing the .knowing from the accursed devil. O Lord, I seek refuge from the machinations of the devil.

(3) **Quran-reading** If you wish to get the reward of Zikr, Dua and Quran reading together, read before the sunrise and .he sunset Dua which is as follows.

(1) Read each seven times-Fateha, Falaq, Nas, Ikhlas Kaferun and Ayatul Qursi, and then (2) recite seven times 'Glory to God, all praise is His, there is no deity but God and God is greatest.' (3) Then send blessings on the Prophet seven times and (4) then seek forgiveness seven times for yourself, for your parents and for the male and female believers, and (5) then utter seven times the Dua as prescribed. Don't give it up any time before sunrise and sunset.

Ibrahim Taimi saw in dream the Prophet and asked him about the Dua that Khizr had dictated to him and the Prophet said: It is true. Khizr has spoken the truth. What Khizr says is true. He knows the dwellers of the world and he is the best of Abdals. He is one of the soldiers of God in the world. If a man recites it among other rewards, God will for forgive him and will lift His anger from him and order the angel on his left side not to write his sins for one year. None observes it except one who has been made fortunate by God and none forsakes it except one who has been made unfortunate by Him.

(4) **Good thoughts.** (a) Think of your past sins and try to remove them. Remove the obstacles to good deeds and think of doing good for yourself and general Muslims. (b) think of profitable things in the spiritual world and that of the thoughts of God, open and secret. Think of the God's rewards and punishments. This pondering is the best divine service as i it contains the remembrance of God and two sincere things. (1) The first thing is the acquisition of knowledge about God as contemplation is the key to the earning of spiritual light. (2) The second thing is the increase of God's love, as love does not grow unless there is firm honour for Him in heart. Glory of God is not opened to the mind unless one is acquainted with God's attributes and His wonderful creations. The fruit of meditation is acquaintance or Ma'arfat. Honour grows from acquaintance and love grows from honour and deep attachment grows from love. There is difference between Abid and Arif The former is like one who hears about a thing and the latter is like one who sees that thing with his eyes. Arif sees God's glory with the inner light of his mind and Arif sees it with the outer light of his eyes. There is no limit to the inner light of mind, but there is limit to the external eye sight. The Prophet said: God has got seventy screens. If He had disclosed them, the brilliance of God's face would have destroyed what one could have seen. These screens are one above another and the brilliance of their lights has got degrees just like the difference of the lights of the stars, moon and sun.

(2) **The Second division** of day begins from sunrise to a little before midday. There are two duties therein. One duty is to observe Ishraq and Zoha prayers and another duty is to do all actions in connection with the people and for their good. It is better to pray Ishraq of two rak'ats just after sunrise and 4, 6, or 8 rak'ats Zoha prayer when the sun rises very high and before noon. God says: Oath of Zoha and darkness of night. Regarding the second duty, it is to visit patients, to join funeral prayer, to do good works, to be present in the assemblies of the learned and to do good to the Muslims.

(3) **The third division** of day begins just before noon and declining of the sun. There is order for prayer after every three hours. There is a prayer after sunrise. After three hours, there is the prayer of Zoha and next after three hours, there is the prayer of Zuhr and next after three hours, there is Asr prayer and next after three hours there is Maghrib prayer. In the mean time, one can do worldly business.

(4) **The Fourth division** of day begins from the declining of the sun after noon and ends after Zuhr prayer. Before Zuhr, pray four rak'ats Sunnat prayer. Make it long and this is the time of acceptance of invocation. After Zuhr prayer, pray two rak'ats Sunnat and then 2 or 4 rak'ats Nafl.

(5) **The Fifth division** of day begins from the end of Zuhr prayer till Asr or afternoon. There is a great reward for waiting for the next compulsory prayer after finishing one. This was the habit of the former sages. A certain wise man said: Three things are not dear to God. (1) to laugh without any wonderful thing (2) to eat without hunger, and (3) to sleep at day without being wakeful at night. To sleep for 8 hours during 24 hours is sufficient. Thus one-third of life is lost in sleep.

(6) **The Sixth division** of day begins from Asr prayer. Perform four rak'ats of Sunnat prayer before Azan and Aqamat and then pray *four* rak'ats of compulsory prayer. It is a most opportune time. There is no prayer after Asr.

(7) **The Seventh division** of day begins when the sun is covered with dust and snow, and is the time immediately before sunset. God says: When it is dusk and dawn, glorify Hem.

God says: Glorify Hem at the two extremes of the day. God says: Seek forgiveness for your sins and proclaim the purity of your Lord with praise at dawn and at dusk.

Five Divisions of Night

(1) **The first division** of night. When the sun sets, pray Maghreb and remain busy en Zikr between two prayers. The end of this division is up to the setting of red hue in the western sky. God has

taken oath of this time: Nay, I swear by the night fall. The excellence of prayer at this time is like that of night prayer as et is the first stage of night. God says: Glorify God en one portion of night. This is the prayer of Awwabin. The object of the following verse is this: Their sides roll en their beds. When asked about this verse the Prophet said: It is the prayer between Maghreb and Isha. Then he said: You should pray between Maghreb and Isha as et removes the sins of useless talks of day time and makes its end good. Pray two rak'at Maghreb. Then pray four long prayers and then continue prayer tell the setting of the red hues en the western horizon.

(2) **The second division of** night begins from the early time of Isha up to the sleep of the people. God says: I swear by night and what et brings (darkness). He said: Up to the darkness of the night. Pray four rak'ats before compulsory prayer and two rak'ats after et and then four rak'ats, after that 13 rak'ats and then Vitr prayer. This may be done at the earlier portion of night or later portion. The Prophet said: There is half reward en saying prayer lying than sitting.

(3) **The third division of night is in sleep.** Sleep is considered as Ibadat if certain rules are observed. The Prophet said: When a man goes to bed after making Zikr with ablution, he is rewarded as en a state of prayer tell he wakes up. An angel enters his dress. If he moves during sleep and makes. Zikr, the angel invokes for him and seeks God's forgiveness for him. The Prophet said: When a man sleeps with ablution, his soul is taken up to the Throne. This happens in all cases. How then is it regarding special persons and angels ? Secrets are disclosed to them during sleep. For this reason, the Prophet said: The divine services of the learned and their breaths are Tasbih. Hazrat Mu'az said: I sleep and then pray and what I do in my sleep, 1 think I do it in my wakeful state. This was mentioned to the Prophet who said: Mu'az has got good knowledge of religion.

There are Rules of Sleep

(1) Teeth cleansing and ablution. The Prophet said: When a man

sleeps with ablution, his soul is hung up with the Throne and his dream becomes true. If he sleeps without ablution, his soul cannot reach there and he cannot see dreams which are true.

(2) Keep tooth stick and ablution water near the head so that you may stand for prayer when awake. The Prophet used to cleanse teeth many times at night specially when he awoke from sleep. The Prophet said: If a man goes to bed with this intention that be would pray at night and his two eyes prevail upon him and he sleeps till dawn, whatever he intended is written for him and his sleep is a gift from God as it were.

(3) Sleep at night keeping a written wasiat near your head as it is no wonder to meet with death during sleep. If a man dies without wasiat, he will not be permitted to talk in grave till Resurrection Day. The dead persons will come to meet him and question him but he will not be able to talk.

(4) Sleep with sound mind after making Taubah for all sins and seek forgiveness for all Muslims. Don't pollute your mind by oppressing any man and don't be firm in committing sin after waking. The Prophet said: If a man goes to bed with the intention of doing no oppression, hatred and envy, his sins are forgiven.

(5) Don't sleep in soft bed and your bed should be of middle kind. There was nothing between the bodies of Able Suffa and earth. They used to say: Our bodies have been made of earth and shall have to return to earth.

(6) Don't sleep till it overtakes you. The sleep of Able Suffah was strong, food little and talk necessary. For this reason, it is said that they slept little at night even though it prevailed upon them. The Prophet said: Don't take too much trouble at night. Prophet was asked: A certain person prays at night. When sleep prevails over him, he keeps himself hanging with a rope. The Prophet prohibited him from that. He said: When it becomes strong, sleep. The Prophet said: Strive hard in actions as God does not inflict trouble over you until you inflict trouble on yourself. The Prophet said: He who does religious actions easily is best of you. The Prophet said: I pray and sleep, keep fast and break. This is my way. He who

does not follow my ways in not of me. The Prophet said: Don't take too much trouble for religion as it is firm. He who wishes to stick to it firmly, it will overcome him. Don't make divine service a burden on you.

(7) Sleep facing the Ka'ba. It is like keeping a dead body in grave keeping the face towards the Ka'ba.

(8) Invoke at the time of sleep and say: O Lord, I keep my side in Thy name and shall raise it up in Thy name-up to the end. Recite special verses of the Quran, such as Ayat-ul Kursi, the last portion of Sura Baqarah, Sura A'raf, Falaq and Nas and 25 times the following formula— Subhan Allah Walhamdo lillah wa la Ilaha Illallah and Allaho Akbar.

(9) Remember God at the time of sleep. Sleep is a kind of death and rising is a kind of resurrection. God says: God takes souls at the time of their death and the souls of those who do not die in their sleep. God says: He it is who causes you to die at night. As a man who is awake sees things which he does not see in sleep, so also a sleeping man sees things which his mind cannot conceive in wakeful state. Sleep is the period between life and death as Barzakh is the period between this world and the next world. Luqman asked his son: O dear son, if you doubt about death, don't sleep, As you sleep, so you will die, if you doubt about resurrection, don't be awake. As you wake up after sleep, so you will wake up after your death. Hazrat Ayesha said: When the Prophet went to bed, he used to place his head upon his right hand, think himself dead and say: O God, Lord of seven heavens and Lord of the great Throne. O our Lord and the Lord of all things and their owner.

(10) Dua after waking up. When the Prophet woke up from sleep, he used to recite the following: There is no deity but God, the Single, the Almighty, Lord of heavens and earth and what is therein, the Mighty, the Forgiving. After rising, always remember God. That is the sign of love. When you stand up after rising from sleep, recite: All praise is for God who has given us life after He has made us dead and to Him is the Resurrection.

(4) **Fourth division of night** begins from midnight and ends with the end of night except one-sixth of it remaining. At this time, a man rises to pray Tahajjud. God says: I swear by the night when it is deep. The Prophet was asked: Which time of the night is the appropriate time for acceptance of invocation? He said: Midnight. Prophet David said: O Lord, I love to do your service, but what time is most opportune? God revealed to him-O David, don't be awake in the early or later part of the night as he who does not sleep in its early part sleeps at its later part: If one keeps awake at the later part of the night, he cannot remain awake at its early part. Keep awake in its middle portion, keep alone with Me at that time and I also will remain alone with you and will raise up your necessities. The Prophet was asked: What portion of night is best? He said: The middle of the later half of night. During this time, pray two rak'ats. The Prophet used to pray at least 13 rak'ats at this time including Vitr prayer. There are prescribed invocations to be recited therein.

(5) **Fifth division of night.** The remaining portion of night is Sehri time. God says: Seek forgiveness at Sehri time. This is the time of departure of angels of night and the arrival of the angels of day. When there is dawn, there is the end of this division and the beginning of the divisions of the day. The Prophet said: If a man fasts, gives charity, visits the sick and attends funeral service every day, his sins are forgiven. In another narration, he enters Paradise. The companions did not miss a day without charity even though it be with a date or a piece of bread as the Prophet said: A man remains under the shadow of his charity till he faces judgement. The Prophet said: Save yourself from Hell by giving in charity even a portion of date. The Prophet said: If a man rises at dawn, there is the duty of charity upon every vein of his body. He has got 360 veins. Your enjoining good is an act of charity, your forbidding evil is an act of charity, your helping a weak man in bearing his load is an act of charity, your showing path to a man is an act of charity, your removing nuisance from the pathway is an act of charity. Even he named Tasbih and Tahlil as acts of charity. Then he said: Two rak'ats of prayer before noon take away all rewards.

Division of Time According to Circumstances

(1) **A worshipper** is one who has got no business except divine service. If he gives up divine service, he sits without occupation. Some of the companions used to recite Tasbih 1200 times daily, some 30,000 times, some prayed from 300 to 600 rak'ats. Others prayed at least 100 rak'ats a day and a night. Some finished the Quran once a day, some twice a day. Karrah-b-Bashrah used to make Tawaf of the Ka'ba 70 times at day time and 70 times at night. In spite of that, they finished the Quran twice every day and night. The saint Ibrahim-b. Adham said as reported from an angel that he who recites the following will not die till he sees his place in Paradise: Glory be to the Highest Judge. Glory be to the strict Law Giver. Glory be to One who effaces the night and brings the day. Glory be to One whom no affair can keep busy. Glory be to God, the Merciful, the Benign.

(2) A **learned man** is he whose learning benefits the people, such as giving legal decisions, teaching, writing religious books. His division of time is not like those of an Abid or worshipper as his reading and writing books are necessary and it requires a great deal of time. The excellence of learning and teaching proves it. The learning which we speak of and which is above divine service is that learning which creates a desire for the Hereafter, distaste of this world or such a learning which helps journey towards the next world and not that learning which helps increase of wealth and properties. He should be busy up to sunrise in Zikr and invocations and after sunrise up to noon in teaching and learning, and from noon to Asr in reading and writing books and from Asr to sunset in Hadis, Tafsir and other benefitting subjects.

(3) **Students.** The Prophet said: To be present in an assembly of Zikr is better than prayer of one thousand rak'ats, attending one thousand funerals and visiting one thousand patients. The Prophet said: When you see a garden of Paradise, roam in it. He asked: O Prophet of God, what is the garden of Paradise? He said: Assembly of Zikr. So a student should not turn away from such an assembly. When a man complained to Hasan Basri about the hardness of his heart he said to him: Attend the assemblies of Zikr.

(4) Business man. He who is required to do business for all times to maintain his family members, should do it without engaging himself in divine service for all times with this condition that he must remember God in all his dealings and not forget Him and perform compulsory divine services.

(5) An **administrator** is like a leader. Similar is the case of a judge, or a mutawalli or a person on whom the affairs of the Muslims have been entrusted. They should remember how the rightly guided Caliphs conducted themselves with heavy duties on their shoulders.

(6) Unitarian. He is one who is engaged in the meditation of God, does not love anybody except God and does not fear anybody except Him. He does not accept provision except from Him. Such a man need not observe the division of time but should keep company with God soon after the compulsory prayers with humility of mind. In other words there is lesson for him in whatever thought occurs in his mind, whatever sound falls in his ears and whatever things fall in his eyes. Such a man flees towards God as God says: So flee away to God. The support of the above version is found also in the following verse: When you put them alone and they do not worship except God, they take shelter in a cave and your Lord will provide them with space out of His mercy. There is another verse: I am going towards my Lord and He will soon guide me. This is the rank of a Siddiq.

SECTION – II

Excellence of Night Worship

The Prophet said: Sunset prayer is best to God. It has not been reduced for a traveller. It opens night prayers and ends the day Prayers. If a man prays two rak'ats after Maghrib prayer, two buildings will be built for him in Paradise. The distance of the two buildings is the path of one hundred years. In between them, there are trees which are sufficient for the inmates of the world to see after roaming. The Prophet said: If a man prays ten rak'ats of prayer between Maghrib and Isha, there will be a building for him in Paradise. Hazrat Umar asked: O Prophet of God, our buildings then would be numerous. He said: God has got much more and better. The Prophet said: If a man prays Maghrib in congregation and two rak'ats in addition without talking any worldly things in between them and reads chapter Fatiha and ten verses from the first portion of chapter Baqarah and two verses from its middle, chapter lkhlas 15 times and then makes Ruk'u and prostration and when he stands for the second rak'at and recites chapter Fatiha, Ayatul kursi and three verses of chapter Baqarah, and chapter lkhlas 15 times, his rewards will be unlimited according to a tradition.

Once Obaidullah was asked: Did the Prophet pray except the compulsory prayers? He replied: He prayed between Maghrib and Isha, that is the prayer of Awwabin. Hazrat Anas and Ibn Masu'd used to pray them always. The sage Abu Sulaiman Darani said that to pray this Awwabin prayer is better than optional fast.

Excellence of Night Prayer

Quran. God says: Your Lord knows that you stand up in prayer for two-thirds of the night. God says: Divine service at night is the firm footstep and fruitful for invocations. God says: He who says prayer standing and with prostration throughout the night and fears the next world etc. God says: Those who pass the night for their Lord prostrating and standing in prayer etc. God says: Seek help with patience and prayer.

Hadis. The Prophet said: When one of you sleeps, the devil knots three ties by his side and says to each tie: You have got a greater portion of night and so sleep. If he awakes and makes Zikr of God, one tie is loosened. If he prays, another tie is loosened. Then he rises up with pleasure or with displeasure. Mention was once made to the Prophet of a man who sleeps all the night and he said: The devil has passed urine in his ears. The Prophet said: If a man prays two rak'ats in midnight, it is better for him than the world and what it contains. Had it not been difficult for my followers, I would have made it compulsory for them. The Prophet said: There is a time at night which nobody should miss. If he prays at that time, God accepts it. This happens in all nights. Mughirah-b Shubah narrated that the Prophet used to stand so long in prayer that his feet became swollen. He was asked: What is it? God has forgiven all your past and future sins. He said: Shall I not be a grateful servant?

This shows that the additional worship is for additional rank as gratefulness brings additional rewards. God says: If you are grateful, I will give you additional rewards. The Prophet said: O Abu Hurairah, if you wish to get the mercy of God while you are alive and while you are dead in grave, get up at night and pray and seek the pleasure of God. O Abu Hurairah, pray in a corner of your house. As the dwellers of the earth see the brightness of the stars, so the inmates of heaven see the light of your house. The Prophet said: You should pray at night as it was the habit of your earlier sages. Prayer at night brings one near God, his sins are forgiven, diseases of body are cured and faults are prevented. The Prophet said: If a man prays at night though being prevailed upon by sleep, the rewards of prayers are also written for him. Sleep is an act of charity for him. The Prophet said to Abu Zarr: Don't you take luggage for your journey? He said: Yes. He said: Why don't you take properties for the Resurrection Day? O Abu Zarr, shall I not inform you what will benefit you? He said: Yes, my parents be sacrificed to thee. He said: Fast in summer for resurrection and pray two rak'ats in the darkness of night for loneliness in grave, make pilgrimage for great works and give charity to the poor.

It has been narrated that there was a man at the time of the Prophet who used to stand in prayer when the people remained asleep and recite the Quran and say: O Lord of Hell, save me from it. When it was mentioned to the Prophet, he said: Call me when he prays. He came and heard him saying that. When it was dawn, he said to him: O man, why don't you pray for Paradise? He said: O Prophet of God, I can't reach there as my actions have not reached that stage. Then Gabriel came down and said: Inform him that God has saved him from Hell and admitted him in Paradise. Gabriel said to the Prophet: How good Ibn Umar would have been if he would have prayed at night? The Prophet informed him of it. After words he used to pray at night. Hazrat Zainul

Abdin said: Once Hazrat lhya ate bread of wheat to his satisfaction and slept up to morning. God then revealed to him: O Ihya, you have considered your house better than My house, your neighbours better than My neighbours. O lhya, by My glory and honour, if you peep at the garden of paradise, your feet will be swollen to get it and your soul will proceed forward. If you look once to Hell, your fat will melt and you will shed blood after tears and you will get new skin after your old skin has melted.

The Prophet was asked: A certain man prays at night but commits theft at dawn. He said: He will not do what he does. The Prophet said: May God show mercy on him who rises up at night and prays, then wakes his wife from sleep and she also prays. If she refuses, he throws water on her face. The Prophet said: May God show mercy on the woman who rises up at night and prays and then wakes up her husband and he also prays. It he refuses, she throws water on his face. The Prophet said: If a man rises up at night and awakes his wife and both pray two rak'ats of prayers, both are regarded as remembering ones. The Prophet said: After compulsory prayer, the best prayer is prayer at night. The Prophet said: If a man sleeps in his appointed time or in any portion of it and makes divine service between Fajr and Zuhr, he worships as it were the whole night.

Wise sayings. Once Hazrat Umar fell down after reciting some verses at night and he was looked after for many days as a patient is looked after. When the people went to sleep, Ibn Mas'ud used to rise up and his voice used to be heard up to morning like the humming of bees. Sufiyan Saori ate one night with satisfaction and said: When an ass is given good grass, its actions also become good. He prayed up to dawn. Hazrat Hasan Basri said: I don't know whether it is better to spend this property in charity than to keep awake at night. He was asked: Why do the faces of those who pray Tahajjud become brighter than those of others? He said: Because they stay with the Merciful in loneliness and get light from His light.

Hazrat Fuzail said: If you cannot keep awake at night and keep fast at day time, know that you have been deprived of good and that your sins have become great. Rubi said: I spent many nights in the house of Imam Shafeyi. He used to sleep very little at night. Abu Zuairiya said: I stayed once at the house of Abu Hanifa for six months. He never kept his side on his bed for one single night. At first, he used to keep awake for half the night. While passing once by a people, he heard them say: This man keeps awake the whole night. He said: I don't do it. Afterwards he used to keep awake the whole night. The sage Malik-b-Dinar said: One night I forgot my duty and began to sleep. I found in dream a beautiful young girl with a letter in her hand saying to me: Can you read this letter? I said: Yes. She handed over to me the letter which contained:

> *What joy and hope have destroyed you!*
> *Has your mind forgotten the hope of Hurs?*
> *You will stay in paradise without death,*
> *You wilt make enjoyment then with Hurs.*
> *So rise up from sleep it is best for you,*
> *Reciting Quran in Tahajjud is better than sleep.*

Masruq once started on pilgrimage and spent the whole night in prostration. It is narrated that Wahab-b-Munabbah did not place his side on bed for thirty years. Sulaiman Taimi prayed Fajr for 40 years with the ablution of Isha.

Causes of Making Night-waking Easy

Know, O dear readers, that night waking is difficult fur many persons but it is easy for one who has got by God's mercy the secret and open conditions of night-waking. The open conditions are four-(1) Not to eat and drink much. It begets sleep and there is trouble in prayers. A certain Sufi used to advise his disciples: O congregation of disciples, don't eat much, don't eat much. If you do it, it will increase your sleep and you will repent much at the time of your death. To reduce stomach from the burden of food is good. (2) Not to make too much labour at day time, as too much labour brings too much sleep. (3) Not to give up a little sleep at day time as it is sunnat for night waking. (4) Not to commit sins at day, as it makes the heart hard and creates barrier to get mercy of God, Sufiyan Saori said: On account of one sin, I have been deprived of prayer at night for five months. He was questioned: What is that sin? He said: I said in my mind on seeing a man weeping: This he is doing for show of people.

Secret Conditions of Night-waking

(1) To keep the mind safe from hatred of the Muslims, from innovations and the sorrowful thoughts of the world. If a man is engaged in worldly pursuits, it does not become easy for him to pray at night. If he stands in prayer, thoughts of his worldly actions come in his mind.

(2) To keep fear of God strong in mind and to lessen hope. When a man thinks of the Hell and of the next world, his sleep goes away and fear comes in his mind.

(3) To know the excellence of night prayer and to hope for that.

(4) Love for God and strength of faith greatly encourage night-wakefulness, as night prayer is nothing but to hold secret talk with God. He knows the condition of mind and sees whatever faults the mind has get. Forgiveness is to be sought for these faults to God. When there is love for God, you will love loneliness without doubt and taste in munajat. This taste will give you encouragement to wake up at night. This taste should not be removed as wisdom and wise sayings testify it. The sage Fuzail-b-Ayaz said: When the sun sets in, I become glad in darkness as I can stay then with my Lord in loneliness. When it rises up, I become sorry at the advent of men to me. A certain learned man said: The pleasure which a Sufi gets in Munajat at night can be compared with that in Paradise.

Six Stages of Night—Waking

(1) To keep awake the whole night. This is the highest rank belonging only to the strong who are always engaged in divine service, those who get taste in munajat to Him. This is the food and life of their souls. For this reason, they feel easy to keep

awake for the whole night. They sleep at day time when the people remain busy in worldly deeds. This was the practice of some early sages and saints. They used to say morning prayer with the ablution of Isha prayer. Abu Taleb Makki narrated this from 40 narrators. Among them there were Sayeed-b-Musayyeb, Sufyan-b Sulaim, Fuzail-b-Ward, Wahab-b-Ward, Taus, Wahab-b-Munabbah, Rabia-b-Qasem, Hakam, Abu Sulaiman Darani, Ali-b-Bakr, Abu Abdullah, Abu Asem, Abu Zaber Salman, Malek-b-Dinar, Sulaiman Taimi, Yezid Rakkashi, Abu Hazem, Muhammed-b-Munqader and others.

(2) To keep awake for half the night. Such men were innumerable. There habit was to sleep in the first portion out of three portions of night and the last portion out of six portions of night. Their time of prayer was at midnight and that is better for it.

(3) To keep awake for one-third of the night. For this they used to sleep up to midnight and then in the one-sixth portion of the night. They liked to sleep in the later part of the night as the slumber of morning is removed by that. Hazrat Ayesha said: I did not see the Prophet but in sleep after Sehri time.

(4) To keep awake in one sixth portion of the night. It is the middle of the later part of the night and before one sixth portion of the night.

(5) To observe any time of night for prayer. Such a man keeps awake at the first part of the night till sleep prevails over him. When he wakes up, he prays. When he again feels the urge of sleep he goes to bed. Thus he gets up twice and sleeps twice during the same night. This is difficult but better. This was the habit of the Prophet, some great companions and Tabeyins. The Prophet sometimes kept awake for one third of the night, sometimes two-thirds and sometimes one-sixth. God says: your Lord knows that you stand in prayer nearly two-thirds of the night or half or one-third. Hadrat Ayesha said: The Prophet used to get up on hearing the crowing of cock. This happened in the last portion out of the six portions of the night.

(6) This is the lowest waking. To keep awake to the measurement

of four or two rak'ats of prayer or to remain busy in Zikr and invocations for one hour. For this he gets the rewards of waking up for the whole night. The Prophet said: Pray at right even though the duration of it may be about the time taken in milking a goat.

Excellence of Special Nights and Days

To do divine service in the nights which have got excellence is Sunnah. The number of these nights is fifteen. Nobody should neglect these nights as these are the seasons of good deeds and the best time for trade in religion. If a man is indifferent at the time of season, he cannot make profit. These nights are the following. Six odd nights of the last portion of Ramadan including the Blessed night, the night of 17th Ramadan in which the believers and the infidels met at Badr.

The remaining nine nights are as follows: The first night of Muharram, the night of Ashura, the first night of Rajab, the 15th night of Rajab, the 27th night of Rajab as it is the night of Prophet's ascension to heaven. The Prophet said about this night of mercy: If a men does good deeds in this night, he gets the rewards of one hundred years. He who prays 12 rak'ats in this night reading in each Rak'at chapter Fatiha and one chapter of the Quran, Tashahhud once and sends blessings on the Prophet one hundred times, invokes for himself what he wishes for him in this world and the next and gets up at dawn with fast, God accepts all his invocations. Then there is the middle night of Shaban. One is to pray one hundred rak'ats of prayer and recite ten times Ikhlas in each rakat. Then there are two nights of two Eids. The Prophet said: One who wakes up in the nights of two 'Ids, his soul will not die when all souls will die.

There are nineteen days of excellence: The day of Arafat, the day of Asdhura, the night of 27th of Rajab (If a man fasts on the day, he keeps fast as it were for sixty months and God sends Gabriel on this day with His message), the 17th day of Ramadan (the day on which the battle of Badr was fought), the 15th day of Shaban, the Juma day, two days of two Id's, ten days of Zil-Hajj and the day of Tashriq. The Prophet said: If the day of Juma is safe, all the days are safe. If the month of Ramadan is safe, the whole year is safe.